Globe Law
and Business

Good Governance in Law Firms

A Strategic Approach to Executive Decision Making and Management Structures
Second Edition

Consulting Editor **Norman K Clark**
on behalf of the International Bar Association

Consulting editor
Norman K Clark

Managing director
Sian O'Neill

Good Governance in Law Firms: A Strategic Approach to Executive Decision Making and Management Structures, Second Edition
is published by

Globe Law and Business Ltd
3 Mylor Close
Horsell
Woking
Surrey GU21 4DD
United Kingdom
Tel: +44 20 3745 4770
www.globelawandbusiness.com

Good Governance in Law Firms: A Strategic Approach to Executive Decision Making and Management Structures, Second Edition

ISBN 9781787429345
EPUB ISBN 9781787429352
Adobe PDF ISBN 9781787429369

FSC
www.fsc.org
MIX
Paper | Supporting responsible forestry
FSC® C013604

Table of contents

Introduction

Norman K Clark
Walker Clark LLC

Most lawyers around the world would agree that the nine years since the publication of the first edition of this book could be described in terms such as 'challenging' and 'disruptive'. Many of those same lawyers would also use the word 'instructive', as new insights and innovations have been incorporated into their practices. It is time, therefore, to consider the lessons that we have learned.

The traditional governance and management structures that still exist in most law firms in the world continue to be significant obstacles to running a business entity that delivers highly skilled, professional services profitably and at a reasonable cost. They can also make it more difficult to meet unanticipated challenges and crises.

Some might argue that the traditional law firm is obsolete, with its requirements that the owners play significant, time-consuming, hands-on roles in managing the business; selling the firm's services and supervising their delivery; producing the largest portion of the revenue; and – one must not forget – finding some time to practise law. The emergence in some jurisdictions of alternative business structures for law firms, along with the continuing frustrations of trying to make the traditional model work as a viable, cost-effective business structure in a modern business environment, suggest that the traditional law firm could become extinct in most parts of the world long before the end of this century – even in the unlikely event that we escape another global crisis on the scale of the COVID-19 pandemic.

Even if the traditional law firm structure disappears, the demand for legal services, and for business structures and organisations to deliver them, will continue. In the meantime, even if they might be an endangered professional species, law firms must continue to try to manage the many strategic, financial and professional challenges that they face here and now. Good law firm governance is therefore a strategic imperative for every law firm and, for some, a basic survival skill.

To describe law firm governance as a skill suggests how the authors of this book view the role of governance in the 21st century law firm. We define 'good governance' as a foundation and framework by which law firms set and achieve strategic goals, make and execute well-informed business decisions, and respond to the unprecedented challenges of accelerating changes that affect every aspect of the practice of law. Good governance encompasses not only the formal ownership and management structures of the law firm, but also the informal policies and practices by which it functions day to day. Good governance provides continuity and stability, but it can also focus attention and resources on the need for profound change. Ultimately, good governance is how the firm makes good decisions and ensures that things get done.

Consistent with this holistic view of governance, this book does not explain how to write a good partnership agreement (although it does frequently urge the reader to document certain matters in a partnership agreement or other constitutional corporate document). Instead, the authors investigate some of the most difficult but strategically important issues confronting law firm leaders today, their implications for the governance of the firm and *vice versa*. Our focus is not necessarily on the *what* but the *how* – specifically, how better structures, policies and practices can help to resolve issues that can be critical to a law firm's long-term resilience and sustainability.

In Part I, "Building an effective structure", the authors develop the principle that good governance is a strategic construct – in other words, that a law firm's strategy should drive the development of its governance structures; and that, reciprocally, the structures and practices of the governance of a law firm should facilitate, not obstruct, strategic achievement. We describe the evolution of general principles of good governance in law firms, exemplified by the International Bar Association (IBA) Law Firm Governance Initiative Best Practice Guidelines, published by a working group of the IBA in 2008. Of course, as is always the case with any set of best practices, one must never assume that 'one size fits all'. Good governance therefore is an organising framework, not an impenetrable wall, for managing the professional practice and the business of the law firm. In selecting from among the various structural options, a firm should try to strike the right balance among highly firm-specific factors. The need to integrate and manage governance structures, strategic objectives, the defining professional characteristics of the firm and business operations is leading small and medium-sized law firms to move away from the traditional approach of lawyers as amateur, part-time business managers and towards the employment of experienced managers to run the business.

Part II, "Challenges for law firm governance", begins with the "Leaders' insights on law firm governance" chapter, which includes a 'virtual roundtable' of a global group of law firm leaders and managers, in which they outline their experiences and insights and their implications for the governance of a law firm. We then investigate the decision-making processes in law firms today and the critical, but often overlooked, relationships between strengths and vulnerabilities in a firm's governance system and its ability to resolve strategic management problems.

These include the usually uncomfortable and frequently avoided issues of partner performance management; a partner compensation system that supports the firm's strategic objectives, is fair and reflects and supports the partnership culture; the management of information that the managing partner really needs to know; the adoption and implementation of cost-effective risk management policies and procedures; and succession planning and retirement from the perspective of both the firm and the older partner.

Each of these issues consumes enormous amounts of partner time and attention. Each can have a devastating effect on a law firm's financial performance, reputation or long-term sustainability if not managed well.

Finally, in Part III, "Governance tomorrow", two of our authors consider the lessons of the past and the challenges of the future, and how good governance can help law firms to prepare for and respond to them. We examine the implications of the emergence of 'alternative law firms' in the early part of this century, principally in the United Kingdom and Australia. Although this chapter has not been updated for this edition, we have included it for the excellent historical perspective it provides and, we would argue, the borderless implications for law firms and jurisdictions that are still considering structural alternatives such as multidisciplinary partnerships and public ownership of law firms.

We conclude Part III and this book with a comprehensive exposition of change leadership skills and methods as essential parts of good governance in 21st century law firms. They are critically important to lead the changes that today's law firms need to make in order to prepare for long-term success in the future. We have just begun to discern and understand some of the outlines of that future; but, as our shared experiences over the past nine years have compellingly demonstrated, we must now craft new governance structures, implement new management strategies and learn the new leadership skills that we will need not only to survive the changes and disruptions, but to thrive in the midst of them.

Strategy drives governance

Leopoldo Hernández Romano
KermaPartners
Rocío Vázquez Zavala
Modum

---

1. Introduction

A comprehensive and coherent business strategy is an essential starting point to achieve a firm's short- and long-term objectives. But it is still the case that many firms fail to develop a proper strategy, knowing only that they want to survive, grow or make more money, which is no strategy at all. And those that do have a business strategy often stumble when it comes to translating their long-term goals into a strategy that can then become any kind of reality – because they don't manage to integrate them into the structures and governance of the firm.

There are several reasons for this, including:

- difficulty in seeing where the firm should be in five to 10 years' time, due to a failure to analyse existing strengths and weaknesses, current and desired market position and immediate and longer-term competitive challenges;
- a lack of understanding of how the long-term goals and strategy connect with the firm's structure and governance, including its people, culture, leadership and all operational and decision-making processes of the business; and
- resistance to new strategic, structural and governance processes because partners will not change ingrained and negative behaviours.

Without an underlying strategy, a firm's organisational design and governance structures will become reactionary, operating as a knee-jerk response to internal and external events, with processes becoming embedded in the culture through habit and convenience rather than effectiveness. And a strategy that is not interconnected with the right structure and governance model will quickly fall by the wayside, often overridden by the individualistic whims of partners who see no personal benefit in supporting firm-wide goals.

With this in mind, this chapter explores the critical interrelationship between strategy, structure and governance. Taking in turn the three points above, we look at how strategy, structure and governance feed into one another, and how firms can effectively use their organisational design and leadership structures to bring a firm's strategic purpose to life.

As an aside, and for the purposes of this chapter, the terms 'structure' and 'governance' have a commercial, not legal, meaning, with the following definitions applying throughout:

- Strategy: A plan to move the firm from today towards a defined future state (long-term objective), identifying the competitive challenges to be tackled and how to do so in order to achieve that future state.
- Structure: How the people in the organisation are brought together and how these different groups (both lawyers and non-lawyers) interact with each other.
- Governance: The decision-making framework – that is, how decision making is distributed among these different groups of people within the organisation.

2. Strategy: vision, choices, challenges and strengths

What is the optimum structure and governance model for a modern and growing law firm? There is no single right answer to this question. The best structure and governance system depends on the firm in question and, in particular, its competitive challenges: the geographies in which it sits, the market opportunities and challenges that it faces, its inherent strengths (and weaknesses) in terms of its people, practices and service offerings; and then its vision for where it sees itself in the future. It is, in other words, dependent on each individual firm's core strategy.

Personal though the exercise might be, there are some common pointers to help break down the strategy-structure-governance process into more manageable parts. To begin with, it is worth looking at the groups into which today's law firms generally fall. Each requires a different strategic and structural approach. The five groups are:

- global firms;
- international firms with some overseas, but not global, penetration;
- top-tier national firms;
- specialised/boutique firms of varying size; and
- small and medium-sized regional and local law firms.

Each type of firm faces unique challenges and opportunities that will characterise the kind of strategy, structure and governance required to flourish in each space. But a firm will first have to decide exactly where it sees itself across the groups, both now and into the future. A national firm that wants to break into the international space, for example, will immediately have some structural and governance issues to consider arising from that long-term ambition.

And yet many firms continue to try to operate without any real knowledge of their existing market position, their ambitions for the future or the competitive challenges that they are likely to face along the way. These firms are operating without a clear picture of where they want to go. Consequently, they do not have a true plan – a strategy of how to get there – which in turn makes any kind of supportive structure or governance model impossible.

Take, for example, a firm that wants to be a top-tier national firm. What does it need to do to achieve this goal? What are the current and emerging market opportunities and competitive challenges? Can it develop a pragmatic strategy in relation to its long-term goals – which will then help to clarify the short- and medium-term steps required to meet those objectives? Only with a specific strategic direction can a firm hope to structure and govern itself in a way that ensures it stays on target.

Without that knowledge, the firm is effectively operating in a vacuum. How can a firm structure or govern itself effectively if it does not know what it is, where it wants to be in five or 10 years' time and whether its current course is taking it in the right direction to achieve that ambition?

2.1 Understanding competitive challenges

A good example of a firm operating in a vacuum is one operating the traditional 'full-service' model. For many firms, the full-service structure is no longer fit for purpose, as it presents numerous problems in today's increasingly competitive and specialist legal landscape.

Except for the very largest of legal operations, it is virtually impossible to be convincingly excellent in all areas of law. Firms may list pages of practice and sector specialisms, when the reality is that a few groups have developed and grown to dominate the rest. This can then create an imbalance that even distorts and destabilises a business if one practice is draining resources and/or is at odds with the rest of the business. In such a situation a firm might require anything from a minor adjustment to a more radical structural overhaul. But it cannot do either without understanding what kind of firm it wants to be and its strategy for the future.

Likewise, in the traditional full-service firm, it is typical to have an insular focus on lots of practice groups without a more external focus on industry sectors or clients. But that no longer works for many firms, as clients expect their law firms to demonstrate good knowledge of both their industry and their specific business. This has pushed many firms to restructure to include not only practice groups, but also sector and client groups.

This may reflect a firm's increasingly external focus, but it means little unless it is underpinned by a strategy to determine exactly which sectors and clients will build on existing strengths to deliver real value in terms of legal service delivery and help drive the firm's future profit.

In addition, sticking with the traditionally inward-facing full-service model heightens the risk that firms will overlook or misunderstand changing forces within the external market. A mid-tier firm in the current market may, for instance, notice that it is acquiring more clients. Even better, they are clients of the top-tier firms which appear to be shifting more of their work away from the leading global firms to the mid-tier. The firm in question may consider itself to be doing well; it may see itself as moving up the chain to compete more closely with the larger businesses.

However, it fails to realise that those clients are only giving their less important work to the mid-market, retaining the top-tier firms for the high-end, high-value business. And the existing clients of the mid-tier firm are beginning to do the same, passing their lower-end work to firms further down the chain. Caught in between, the mid-tier firm is in danger of losing work and clients if it fails to demonstrate greater efficiency in both capturing and retaining the right kind of business. Until the firm registers this market shift as a challenge that requires a strategic and structural response, it is in danger of losing out.

Many firms struggle to understand these kinds of competitive challenges and translate them into a proper strategy. And without a strategy that is based on market realities, a firm's structure and its decision making may be based on flawed reasoning, outdated custom or any number of misplaced ideas, such as merely a desire to grow. This is no strategy and yet many firms still seem to think it is a basis on which to build a business.

Even where firms do have a proper strategy, they are by no means out of the water. A strategy in isolation is meaningless – it needs to be tied into the organisational design, culture and management processes of the firm.

The biggest firms, for instance, benefit from large strategy departments that help to define and regularly review strategy. Where many or most firms struggle is in the implementation: managing the partners so that they behave in a way that reflects the strategy; penetrating and owning defined target markets and/or client groups; or dominating specific service lines. This is where we turn next – to the ways in which a strategy becomes a structural reality.

3. Successfully implementing strategy: structure and governance

Assuming that a firm has devised for itself a proper strategy with a good sense of where it wants to be in five or 10 years in terms of target markets and/or client groups, it then comes to the challenge of implementing that strategy through the structure, processes and governance (ie, the decision making) of the firm.

3.1 Tackling structure

With a strategy in place, the task now is to align strategy and structure to ensure that the latter serves a more strategic function – that it fits and supports the strategy and related goals.

The strategic view should begin with consideration of five organisational elements:

- Geography: Where the firm has offices and in which countries, and what kind of market penetration and strengths the firm has, and wants to have, in each location (ie, where it wants to focus resources and investment).
- Practice groups: including which practice groups are likely to evolve or devolve.
- Service lines: The services, often across departments, that the firm currently offers and may wish to deliver in the future.
- Industry sector: The choice of focus in order to gain recognition and expertise.
- Client: Types of client according to size, location, industry, etc.

Establishing the right structure will depend on a firm understanding of what kind of balance of business units or practice groups it needs to deliver the right legal services to a specific client group in a given geography that will best offer growth potential. It requires an understanding of the varying strengths (and weaknesses) that a firm might have in each of the above dimensions, as well as where it wants to focus in future. Only then can a firm structure itself in a way that will focus resources and investment into the right specific elements to generate growth. The interrelationship of strategy and structure should be obvious here.

Thinking about the five elements of structure and how to prioritise them will help a firm in one important respect: to become more externally focused as it shifts from an internal perspective based on its own offices and practice groups to a more external view, aligned to industry sectors and client needs and types. This will enable the firm to meet an important demand coming from the client side.

Attempting to manage a five-dimensional matrix structure can be problematic, however. Many professional service firms, including international law firms, have struggled to manage themselves across a fixed matrix holding too many dimensions. Attempting to do so may also fail to recognise a firm's strategic priorities – whether that be expanding in certain markets, developing project areas or creating new service lines, for example. The firm risks returning to the problem of the full-service model: attempting to be all things to all people.

The better approach is to take one of the five organisational dimensions, make it a 'home' for the lawyers and design the organisation around this base. The 'home' is the professional base camp for all the firm's reporting, management, accounting and so on. In global and international law firms, this base is likely to be the practice groups, with other dimensions such as the sector and client groups making up 'communities of common interest'. In contrast, in the Big Four global auditors, the primary unit of accountability remains the office or country. Meanwhile, the elite continental European firms tend to have a base that remains primarily linked to offices.

The point is that, using a 'home' base, a firm can more effectively translate its strategy into a meaningful matrix where communities of common interest across the other organisational dimensions enable differentiation and help to present opportunities for specialist skills building, client service, marketing and so on. As these communities increase in number and become larger, clear priorities become more and more important to ensure effectiveness and efficiency. The strategy feeds into the matrix, which in itself feeds back into the strategy, as it enables easier reviews of strategic progress and highlights where a firm's opportunities or challenges may lie.

Establishing a rational network or matrix structure allows a firm to deliver on its strategy, so, for example, enabling a firm to take on additional countries or offices in emerging markets and hiring lateral partners in growth areas. It may also help to bring together the whole organisation in a more outward-looking focus that better aligns people with the firm's strategic objectives by fostering greater organisational and cultural cohesion.

A structure alone, however – even with the best underlying strategy – will not get people to behave in an appropriate way in relation to the long-term goals – or, if necessary, to change their behaviour. This is where governance becomes critical, as the management and leadership of the firm determine the day-to-day running of the management structure and processes and, just as importantly, instil the right behaviours across the partnership to ensure that strategic goals are met through the actions of both lawyers and non-lawyers.

3.2 Strategy drives governance

If a firm has a well-aligned strategy and structure in place, it suggests that someone somewhere in the firm has been making the right decisions. So in a sense, good governance drives strategy just as much as the other way around.

But seeing through a strategy and ensuring that the supporting structure does not fall apart at the first hurdle requires a governance model that reflects the needs of the strategic vision and can see through its implementation.

In practice, this means determining which management bodies are needed to take which kind of decision; and who specifically will take responsibility for what kinds of decisions on behalf of the rest of the partnership. Role descriptions can then be created to clarify responsibilities and set clear hierarchies for different types and levels of decision making. Without such agreement, both strategy and structure may quickly flounder in the face of internal intransigence brought about by endless consultation or dispute.

Delegating decision-making authority remains a struggle for some smaller firms that may continue to operate with the idea that the whole partnership should have input on all important decisions. But as many firms have grown, they have realised that decision making by such consensus actually makes for very little decision making at all. Devising a governance structure that is fully aligned to a firm's strategy and structure has therefore become increasingly important – albeit often difficult to implement.

Governance should be structured around the decisions that need to be made, establishing governance bodies, sub-structures and reporting lines which allow good decisions to be reached effectively. Once established, this governance model also plays a critical role in ensuring that the firm sticks to its strategic plan (or takes an informed diversion), as it makes for more efficient monitoring and reviews a firm's ongoing performance.

This approach works right through the partnership and up to senior management, defining for every firm the best distribution of decision making from the managing and/or senior partner through to the management board(s), heads of practices or business units, all the way through to individual partners. Role descriptions then clearly lay out who has decision-making authority over areas such as:

- firm development – for example, mergers and acquisitions, lateral hires and the formulation and review of strategic plans;
- hiring decisions – senior/junior associates and interns; and
- client acceptance policies.

Leadership, too, plays a critical role in the governance model, providing the direction, motivation and glue to bind decision-making processes into a cohesive organisational whole. Therefore, a governance structure should include proper leadership induction and training, as well as succession planning to successfully guide partners into future leadership roles.

With good governance and leadership in place at all levels, firms can look forward to placing the final and yet critical piece in the jigsaw puzzle: the right firm-wide behaviours.

4. Strategy to structure to behavioural change

A strategic review that results in a revised management and governance structure doesn't complete the process. The combined approach then has to be geared to successfully influence internal behaviours to support a common, firm-wide way of doing business.

Organisational behaviour is induced by a firm's strategy, structure and governance. But even with the right strategy, structures and processes in place, influencing behaviour remains one of the most significant challenges facing the legal profession. That is because law firm partners still have a tendency to think of themselves first and foremost as individual lawyers who 'own' their clients, sometimes at the expense of the interests of the firm.

The aim of bringing together strategy, structure and governance is that firms can hope to get partners working together in a more structured way to achieve organisational goals. But to succeed, a firm's leadership must involve the partners from the earliest stage to ensure they fully buy into the strategic plan and the change process required to achieve it. If a firm fails to do this, partners may quickly derail the process with outright objections or just the continued practice of the wrong, individualistic behaviours. This is a prime reason why many firms fail to translate their strategy into reality.

Partners should be involved in every stage of a strategy and structural review project, albeit in various degrees along the way. This means that by the implementation phase, the partners already share in the ownership of the strategy and have bought into the short and long-term processes required to bring it to fruition. They are then more likely to delegate decision making to others, knowing that they have already agreed the direction in which the firm is heading.

4.1 Contribution management

This does not mean that the firm's management will then be free of challenges. It still has to ensure that the partners exhibit the right behaviours to support the ongoing requirements of the strategic plan. This means that the firm has to agree what kind of behaviour it wants to see and what it considers unacceptable. And it then has to integrate that into a contribution management system that recognises and rewards the right behaviours, using both financial and non-financial measures. It is no small challenge, given that the system must be designed in a way that is acceptable to partners who for the first time will have to agree to submit themselves to be appraised on a non-financial basis.

Nevertheless, more firms are moving in this direction. And for good reason: it is the contribution management system that will act as the linchpin for a firm's strategic success. It forms a critical part of the organisational structure and governance, because it is the element that enables desired behaviours that will support management and change processes, while minimising detrimental behaviours.

Ultimately, an effective contribution management structure recognises that a firm is not a mechanical operation but a social system that depends on the right behaviours of its people.

There remain numerous firms that do not have contribution management systems. Here, remuneration tends to be based on the individual financial performance of partners, or on a formula or lockstep model, with no discussion around a lawyer's broader performance. Not only does this reinforce a 'my desk, my clients' way of thinking; but by missing out an annual (or other) opportunity to have such a discussion, firms are failing to foster any kind of entrepreneurial element in the organisation. Worse, if this system is combined with weak leadership, firms end up with partners who only do what they want at the expense of the team.

There has been some debate over the criteria used to measure non-financial performance, with some arguing that it is difficult to make a contribution management model impartial, opening the doors to favouritism and flawed judgement. The argument goes that this then in turn creates internal suspicion and discord at the expense of collegiality.

But even in a pure financial system, there can be disputes over 'who' owns the turnover. What's more, disputes arising from a contribution management system can typically be addressed through a structural device: a remuneration committee entrusted by the partnership, which can oversee the way in which the measurement criteria are applied and the system managed. It is again a question of properly aligning strategy, structure and governance so that each fully supports and feeds back into the other elements. The use of such a committee also provides an apt example of the interdependence of strategy, structure and governance – strategy without structure or governance is as useless as a management and governance structure that lacks strategy.

In this chapter we have taken a journey. It is one that firms will have to embark on themselves if they are to successfully meet their strategic objectives. And it is one that takes a firm all the way from the first consideration of its long-term goals through to translating them into a strategy and subsequently into organisational design, leadership and then personal behaviour. If done correctly, the result will be firm-wide behaviour and culture that feed right back into the core strategy.

The journey is full of potential obstacles and each firm will face its own unique challenges along the way. But more and more firms are realising that this is one journey that must be taken if they are to enjoy organisational success.

This chapter is published as it appeared in the previous edition.

Fundamental elements of modern governance in law firms

Norman K Clark
Walker Clark LLC

1. The twilight of the traditional law firm?

The changes, disruptions and innovative models for service delivery in the legal services industry since the 1990s have raised the question of whether the traditional law firm structure can survive to the middle of the 21st century. Even as contemporary corporate structures – such as limited liability partnerships, limited liability companies and professional corporations – have replaced the general partnership in most jurisdictions in the world, the basic way in which most law firm partners[1] govern themselves and manage their practices, regardless of the formal structures they use, have remained largely unchanged.

As law firms have attempted to navigate the fast-changing, often tempestuous seas of the economic, public health and geopolitical crises of the first two decades of the 21st century, it has become apparent that most of them – especially small and mid-sized firms – are structurally unequipped to respond efficiently and effectively to the external and internal challenges that they face, some of which are discussed in detail elsewhere in this book. Some of these pressures are due to the so-called 'new normal'[2] in legal markets in most jurisdictions, characterised by phenomena such as:

- increased price sensitivity among clients;
- globalisation and consolidation of law firms;
- the entry of non-traditional service providers into the legal services market; and
- increased competition to recruit and retain the best legal talent.

Actually, this is not a 'new normal' in any sense of the phrase; instead, it is business reality finally catching up with the legal profession.

---

1 This chapter uses the traditional term 'partner' to describe an owner of a law firm. Except where specifically indicated to the contrary, the term 'partner' also applies to law firm owners, with titles such as 'member' or 'shareholder', in other law firm corporate structures (eg, professional corporations, limited liability partnerships or publicly traded corporations).

2 The author detests this cliché. It locks one's thinking into the paradigms of the past or factually unsupported assumptions about the present and, moreover, assumes that the 'new normal' (however it is defined) will continue. Such smug thinking could be professionally fatal to lawyers and law firms that engage in it.

A major part of the difficulty that law firms have in responding to new demands and challenges originates from the traditional structural and management paradigms that drive most law firms,[3] despite their adoption of a modern corporate structure or an 'alternative business structure' (ABS).[4]

Consider the multi-faceted role of partners in a law firm. They are expected, collectively and individually, to carry out the duties of:

- the owners of the business;
- the principal investors;
- managers of significant corporate functions;
- prominent members of the firm's marketing force;
- revenue producers;
- supervisors of other professionals;
- principal points of contact for clients; and
- ambassadors of the firm in the business and professional community.

Obviously, it is almost impossible for even the most talented and best-organised partner to do all of these things well – especially when one's partners also expect 1,500 to 1,800 billable hours of legal work, or even more.

This dilemma is compounded by a realisation that as clients' needs for and expectations of legal services become more sophisticated, and many law firms find themselves in a maelstrom of market forces that they have never experienced before, basic principles of good management and business prudence require that partners, in their various roles, dedicate more personal time, attention and intellectual energy to management issues that previously were not priorities and could be delegated to staff or ignored completely.

As one equity partner in a fast-growing firm in Latin America said: "I feel as if I am being pulled apart into pieces."

Can law firms survive; or have we entered the twilight of the law firm? Will traditional law firms as we know them disappear from most of the legal markets for significant commercial law matters and dispute resolution, to be replaced by something completely new and different? Or will they evolve into better managed, more efficient, more responsive providers of sophisticated legal services, retaining at most the external shells of the quaint 18th models upon which most law firms are still based?

This chapter does not attempt to answer these broad questions. Some of them would require the simultaneous use of a crystal ball, tarot cards, tea leaves

---

3 See Walker Clark, "Understanding Paradigms" *Walker Clark Work View*, 13 November 2017, www.walkerclark.com/worldview-blog/previous-worldview-posts/300-understanding-paradigms.html.

4 For example, ABS were introduced in England and Wales by the Legal Services Act of 2007. For a practice note outlining the major provisions, see The Law Society of England and Wales, "Alternative Business Structures", 22 July 2013, www.lawsociety.org.uk/advice/practice-notes/alternative-business-structures/. See also the exceptional discussion in the chapter "Governance for lawyers in a new era – 'alternative' law firms".

and the entrails of a chicken. Instead, it reviews the current scope and components of governance in law firms, as outlined in the International Bar Association's (IBA) IBA Law Firm Governance Initiative Best Practice Guidelines,[5] first published by a working group of the IBA in 2008. This important guidance has become even more relevant in the years since its original publication. It can serve as a useful checklist describing the modern scope and areas of priority concern for the governance of law firms. Finally, this chapter comments on three specific areas that the author has observed as dominant issues of concern while advising law firms on governance.

2. What does 'governance' mean in law firms?

One of the central points of this chapter, as well as in this book, is that the concept of governance is expanding and evolving from its traditional scope. It goes beyond formal corporate structure and, in modern professional services firms, also documents the systems and processes that relate to and support:

- consistent management practice;
- cohesive policies, guidance and processes; and
- decision-making rights and procedures.

Several points from this definition are important because they refer to substantial shortcomings in the governance of many law firms today.

2.1 Consistent management

Although most law firm partners are conscientious and care deeply about their firms, management styles in law firms frequently range from being largely *ad hoc* responses to the crisis of the day to being rigidly consistent to the point of denying obvious and compelling changes in business and professional realities.

2.2 Cohesive policies

As discussed later in this chapter with reference to the IBA Best Practice Guidelines, outdated or non-existent documentation has been a major challenge for law firms, especially fast-growing ones in emerging legal markets.

2.3 Guidance

Overworked partners frequently complain: "We always can find time to fix the latest problem, but we can never seem to make the time to ensure that will avoid the same problem in the future." Decisions are frequently reactive, rather than precedential. As a result, some law firm partnerships spend inordinate

---

5 International Bar Association, "IBA Law Firm Governance Initiative Best Practice Guidelines", 10 September 2008, www.ibanet.org/document?id=IBA-Law-Firm-Governance-Initiative-Best-Practice-Guidelines-22. The guidelines are quoted verbatim in this chapter and their numbering is as in the original document.

amounts of time pondering anew how they will decide on an issue almost identical to one that they have decided on before.

2.4 Processes

Decision-making processes are seldom documented in law firms and many law firm partners can work for many years in a law firm without knowing how basic business operations are conducted. As internal customers of these processes, they see only the results – the internal services and products that other fee earners and staff deliver to them – without any real interest in or understanding of how those processes operate.

2.5 Decision rights

The rights and prerogatives of partners sometimes inhibit efficient decision making, especially with respect to important strategic issues. 'Collegiality' is often used to justify[6] the *de facto* prerogative of any partner to veto a proposal; and this usually vaguely defined value can also inhibit the candid assessment and discussion of sensitive critically important issues in areas such as the need for significant changes or sub-standard partner performance.

To be fair, none of these observations is characteristic of all law firms today. Indeed, some firms manage the governance responsibilities in each of these areas very well; but this has not been easy. The basic demands of good governance in modern law firms, competing in the 21st century legal services market, with respect to each of these defining points and other important issues have required well-governed law firms to move from the limited traditional view of governance to a concept that envisions good governance as a central coordinating point for managing the most important issues affecting the current and future performance of the firm. It is no exaggeration to state that for some law firms, good governance has become necessary for survival. Without it, they lack the intellectual, strategic and operational structures they need in an increasingly unpredictable future.

3. Can your governance system do this?

The IBA Best Practice Guidelines, published in 2008 and updated in 2009, provide a conceptual checklist of the issues that law firm governance should consider. As the preamble points out, not every guideline is necessarily relevant to every firm, but it must nonetheless be considered:

> *These guidelines attempt to identify certain general principles and standards that may help law firms manage their practices in a way that will achieve these objectives. Some of its points may be of more relevance to larger firms, or to those with a broader element of international work. Some may fit more naturally in*

6 The phase 'cowardly excuse' often comes to mind as a more accurate description of this phenomenon.

certain cultures and less so in others. Some may need to be adapted over time to reflect changing conditions and concerns. There will be few firms (if any) that will adopt every provision. But all law firms should benefit by thinking about the extent to which each of the guidelines applies to them and could make them more effective and successful.[7]

The guidelines are organised into seven major areas, each of which should be a concern for every partner in the firm, even if some of the specific guidelines are not applicable. These seven areas are:

- the firm;
- its people;
- its organisational culture;
- its clients;
- wider engagement;
- legal and regulatory compliance; and
- transparency.

3.1 The firm

The IBA Best Practice Guidelines suggest six guidelines to describe how the firm, as an institution, should be governed:

1. *The firm should set out in writing its governance and decision-making structure.*
2. *It should have a transparent process for the selection of leaders and the appointment of managers.*
3. *It should establish an appropriate mechanism for partners to communicate with each other and with the firm's leadership/ management.*
4. *The capital structure of the firm should be described to partners in a clear way which distinguishes between different kinds of capital and explains the way in which capital can be contributed and withdrawn by partners.*
5. *The way in which the profits of the firm are distributed among the partners should be clearly described to all partners in the firm.*
6. *All those who are held out as partners should be treated as such, whatever legal and financial arrangements exist between them. Being a partner in a firm should involve the acceptance of a clearly defined role and a set of rights and responsibilities.*[8]

One of the common themes running through the guidelines is the need for documentation of these fundamental aspects of the firm. By contrast, most law firms still operate from a partnership agreement or other operating agreement that meets only the bare minimum requirements for the firm to be registered in its domicile jurisdiction. When the author's firm is engaged to advise a law firm on a merger opportunity, one of the first documents that we ask to see is the

7 IBA (n 5), p1.
8 *Ibid.*

current partnership agreement. In approximately 20% of cases, our clients cannot produce anything more than the original registration documents, frequently signed by partners who retired from the firm decades previously.

3.2 Its people

The IBA Best Practice Guidelines are most extensive with respect to the management of the firm's staff and legal talent, even more so than with respect to clients. This reflects a recognition that talent management has become a more important component of a successful law firm strategy than ever before. Nonetheless, many small and mid-sized law firms have no documented policies or guidelines and, especially with respect to lawyers, rely on *ad hoc* decision making – usually with inconsistent and arguably unfair results.

The IBA Best Practice Guidelines state as follows:

Recruitment and retention

1. *The firm should set out its recruitment policies and processes in writing so that all potential recruits (partners, associates and support staff) have access to enough information to allow them to make an informed decision about whether or not they wish to pursue recruitment discussions with the firm.*
2. *Firms should adopt recruitment and promotion policies and processes that are non-discriminatory and that are designed to encourage diversity at all levels within the firm.*
3. *When hiring new recruits (at any level) who have previously worked for another firm, the hiring firm should do what it can to ensure that the recruit does not thereby breach lawful duties owed to the previous firm.*
4. *The firm should ensure that every new recruit receives an appropriate induction which introduces him or her to the firm, its values, policies and procedures.*

Training and development

5. *The firm should offer appropriate support to those within the firm (whether or not they are lawyers) who are studying for or taking relevant professional qualifications.*
6. *It should give qualified lawyers associated with it appropriate support and encouragement to undertake relevant continuing professional education and to develop their personal and professional skills.*
7. *A firm should identify career transition points that are relevant to those within the firm and offer support to those reaching such points in their careers. A career transition point is a moment in a person's career when his or her role changes significantly. Examples in respect of lawyers include admission to the bar, admission to partnership, promotion to a management role and retirement.*
8. *A firm should encourage every person in the firm (at whatever level) to produce*

and maintain a written training and development plan which is suited to their needs and to the culture and structure of the firm.

9. *Firms should ensure that all lawyers receive appropriate supervision and are given an opportunity to undertake a suitable range of work. Lawyers should be encouraged to develop a range of skills and to undertake a variety of work.*

Performance management

10. *Firms should ensure that every person in the firm receives a clear written statement of the performance and behaviour expected of them. The role and responsibilities of each person and their duties to the firm should be clearly stated.*
11. *Firms should ensure that every person in the firm is given clear feedback in respect of performance and behaviour. Where appropriate, feedback should be gathered on a 360 degree basis including upward feedback from those supervised by the person concerned. Those giving feedback should be encouraged to express their views frankly and in appropriate cases in a confidential and non-attributable manner.*
12. *A firm should have a clear and transparent appraisal process and procedure. Appraisals should take place at least annually (for everyone, including partners) and should be properly prepared and, where appropriate, documented. The appraisal process should include a face-to-face meeting with the person being appraised and should be conducted on a confidential basis. In appropriate cases immediate oral feedback should also be encouraged in the day to day working environment.*

Remuneration and benefits

13. *Firms should adopt a remuneration and benefits policy which is designed to ensure that the firm takes a consistent approach when determining the remuneration and benefits to be received by all its people. This policy should be clearly communicated to all those within the firm.*

Dealing with problems

14. *A firm should ensure that everyone in the firm has an appropriate opportunity to complain about or comment on the work or behaviour of any other person in the firm. Complaints should be dealt with fairly and with due regard to the well-being of all concerned. Once a complaint has been investigated all those involved should be given appropriate feedback and guidance. In appropriate cases complaints should be dealt with on a confidential basis.*
15. *Firms should have a written grievance procedure. This should seek to ensure that any grievance of any person in the firm is dealt with in a fair and sympathetic manner.*
16. *Firms should adopt clear policies and procedures for communicating both*

exceptional performance and poor performance to persons in the firm (including partners). Firms should identify a member of the firm to be responsible for this.

17. *Firms should pay due regard to any personal problems experienced by anyone in the firm. In appropriate cases firms should offer help and support to those seeking to overcome such problems, provided that doing so is consistent with preserving a high performance working environment.*

Career development

18. *Firms should state clearly and openly the basis on which people are promoted to higher positions in the firm (including partnership). Selection criteria and processes should be clearly and fairly described to all interested parties (both those currently within the firm and potential recruits).*
19. *Where possible, firms should seek to allow people in the firm to undertake secondments to other parts of the firm, to other firms or to clients. Secondment opportunities should be clearly and fairly described, as should the terms of any secondment.*
20. *Firms should state clearly whether and in what circumstances flexible working is permitted. In this context flexible working includes part-time work, reduced working hours and increased holiday entitlements. Firms should also state their policies on parental leave.*
21. *Firms should recognise and support efforts by persons in the firm to balance the demands of their job with the need to have a rewarding life outside of the office environment (work/life balance).*
22. *Firms should seek to ensure that their support staff are respected and included in the firm's activities. Integration between support staff and lawyers should be an objective of every firm.*
23. *Where possible, firms should seek to maintain contact with people who have left the firm (alumni), providing them with appropriate information about the firm and fostering a continuing relationship between such persons and their former firm. In this context, firms should regard both former members and future recruits as relevant stakeholders.*[9]

Many small and mid-sized law firms do almost none of these things, dismissing them as 'only for the big firms'. However, some progressive smaller firms are making substantial investments in their people – not only to improve the quality of service offered to their clients and the efficiency of their operations, but also to be more attractive in the competition for legal talent. These initiatives are not abdicated to the human resources department, but instead are closely guided and managed by one or more partner and are a continuous concern of the entire partnership.

---

9 *Ibid*, pp2–4.

3.3 Organisational culture

There are four guidelines relating to the values of the firm and the way that they are expressed in the community:

1. *Firms should seek to define and communicate a limited number of fundamental values which underpin and inform decisions taken by the firm.*
2. *Firms should encourage their lawyers to undertake pro bono work. They should develop and communicate a policy for pro bono work undertaken by the firm and by members of the firm with its support. The policy should explain how the firm decides whether to undertake a particular piece of work on a pro bono basis, how that work is allocated and valued if it is undertaken and how the policy of the firm is affected by relevant bar requirements.*
3. *Firms should develop, communicate and encourage participation in their community service policy. In this context community service means voluntary work in or with local communities in countries where the firm operates.*
4. *Firms should develop and communicate a policy on charitable giving. This should deal with giving by the firm itself and also any support which the firm offers to charitable efforts by persons in the firm.*[10]

This is probably the weakest area of the IBA Best Practice Guidelines, because it totally misunderstands the concept of the culture of a law firm. A good argument could be made that these are not really governance concerns, but more likely effective marketing and public relations tactics. It also could be argued that, compared to other guidelines, these are relatively trivial.

3.4 Clients

The IBA Best Practice Guidelines with respect to clients have a strong risk management flavour, especially with respect to financial risks and professional responsibility:

1. *A firm should ensure that it has a clear understanding of the needs and expectations of its client before beginning any piece of chargeable work for that client. Where possible, client requirements and expectations should be recorded in writing.*
2. *A firm should adopt procedures and processes designed to ensure that every client knows the terms on which the firm is acting for that client. Terms of engagement (including billing and fee arrangements) should be recorded in writing.*
3. *It should develop a policy on dealing with conflicts of interest which has due regard to the rules and requirements of relevant Bars (as well as the laws applicable in the jurisdictions in which the firm operates). Such policies should include a mechanism by which possible conflicts of interest are to be identified and dealt with. Firms should ensure that clients know the circumstances in which the firm may cease to act for them.*

---

10 *Ibid*, p4.

4. *Billing practices should be clear and transparent. Clients and people in the firm should be able to understand how the firm decides what to bill and when to bill it. Clients should be clear about the way in which they can influence the basis on which work for them is to be billed.*
5. *Firms should adopt and implement procedures to ensure that confidential information relating to clients (and its people) is protected. In appropriate cases (and to the extent permitted in the relevant jurisdiction) such policies should also deal with the development and operation of information barriers within the firm.*
6. *Firms should encourage their clients to give feedback on work done and on the client satisfaction with the people in the firm dealt with by the client. Firms should consider developing a written complaints procedure which is available to those clients of the firm who request it. The firm should inform those involved when a client complaint is received and give them an opportunity to respond to it.*
7. *In appropriate cases firms should make arrangements for handling client money.*[11]

It could be argued that these guidelines will be more important in the second quarter of the 21st century than they were when they were published in 2008. Some of them seem obvious, merely parts of prudent client management; but in the author's experience and observations, many law firms – especially smaller ones that are otherwise well managed – are deficient in this area, with what are at best vague policies or guidelines and a "We'll cross that bridge when we come to it" predisposition.

All of these issues in fact require senior-level partner attention and oversight. Law firms with weak governance systems usually overlook these issues until problems arise and then attempt to deal with them on an *ad hoc* basis. This usually dooms these firms to make the same mistakes again and again.

3.5 Wider engagement

Although specific guidelines might not be relevant to every law firm, the IBA Best Practice Guidelines communicate the concept that a well-governed firm should be active in the life of the community it serves, as well as in promoting the general interests of the legal profession in the rule of law:

1. *Firms should seek to maintain a courteous and professional relationship with other law firms and other professional advisers and should seek to ensure that their people comply with all applicable professional rules and ethical standards.*
2. *A firm should seek to maintain a good relationship with, and give appropriate*

11 *Ibid.*

support to, every Bar to which persons in the firm belong and should encourage such persons to become active in the work of the Bar.

3. *The firm should seek to support the work of the judiciary in each of the jurisdictions it operates in and to promote the rule of law.*
4. *Firms should seek to engage with, and play an appropriate role in, the local community in each location where the firm practices.*
5. *Firms should seek to apply consistently high ethical standards in relation to all of their work and activities.*
6. *Firms should seek to play an appropriate role in relation to relevant domestic and international law reform projects and in the evolution of the legal environment.*
7. *A firm should take appropriate steps to promote the good standing and development of the legal profession. It should provide opportunities for its lawyers to participate in the activities of legal professional bodies and support those who do so.*
8. *Firms should play an active role in promoting the rule of law and access to justice.*
9. *Firms should actively promote the independence and values of the legal profession.*
10. *Firms should do all they reasonably can to promote human rights and the freedom of the individual.*[12]

One can reasonably argue that these guidelines have little to do with law firm governance;[13] but a consensus about, and documentation of, these values and supporting policies and procedures are critically important to assure that these aspirations are met consistently.

Some of these guidelines are controversial, especially in socially or politically conservative societies and law firms. They might reasonably be perceived as promoting ethnocentric political and social values, and as not really relevant to the governance of the law firm.[14] Nonetheless, each one can produce significant benefits in appropriate legal services markets in terms of improving the national and international visibility of even the smallest law firms.

3.6 Legal and regulatory compliance

There are five IBA Best Practice Guidelines that address compliance, placing responsibility squarely on the shoulders of the partners:

1. *A firm should seek to ensure that its lawyers comply with the laws and regulations applicable in the jurisdictions in which it operates and the requirements of every Bar of which its lawyers are members.*

---

12 *Ibid*, p5.
13 The author would agree with this proposition.
14 At the same time, one must acknowledge that they are consistent with traditional role of the IBA in promoting the rule of law, the independence of the judiciary and human rights.

2. *A firm should put in place appropriate processes and procedures to promote compliance with regulatory obligations imposed on the firm and its people. Firms should have particular regard to the impact of money laundering regulations so as to develop policies and procedures that comply with such regulations in a way that is properly consistent with other professional obligations.*
3. *A firm should seek to operate according to the highest professional and ethical standards. To this end, it should establish a framework, perhaps by putting in place a code of conduct, to encourage its people not only to comply with relevant laws and regulations but also to respect the concepts and principles that lie behind them. Each firm should identify a member of the firm to be responsible for this.*
4. *Firms should seek to maintain good relations with regulators and regulatory bodies in each jurisdiction they operate in.*
5. *If a firm operates in more than one jurisdiction it should seek to ensure that conflicts and inconsistencies between Bar rules or legal or regulatory requirements in each relevant jurisdiction are addressed and (where possible) resolved.*[15]

One of the most challenging weaknesses in the governance of many small and mid-sized law firms is that the structures to support compliance are undocumented or function (usually inadequately) only in response to a crisis. Hoping for good luck is not an effective risk management strategy.

3.7 Transparency

This might appear to be an empty cliché, but the three final guidelines, published under the heading of "Transparency", involve wider issues that must not be ignored:

1. *Firms should seek to put in place mechanisms that encourage frank and effective internal communication.*
2. *If firms choose to disclose financial information they should ensure that it is fairly and accurately presented.*
3. *Firms should strive to be culturally inclusive, culturally aware and integrative in their dealings with their people and with clients and the wider community.*

The first transparency guideline is much more easily stated than achieved in most law firms, but it should nonetheless be pursued because of the importance of information flow as strategic resource in a modern law firm.[16] Although the final guideline might appear to some traditional firms to be merely 'good works', it describes a marketing tactic that is becoming increasingly important in many parts of the world.

---

15 IBA (n 5), pp4–5.

16 See Lisa M Walker Johnson, *Stress and Burnout in Law Firms: Leadership Challenges and Choices* (Globe Law and Business, 2022), pp125–160 for an extensive discussion of the role of transparent communication in the internal management and organisational effectiveness of law firms.

4. High-profile issues in contemporary law firm governance

The IBA Best Practice Guidelines comprise a formidable, and perhaps to some law firms discouraging, list of major issues, most of which have been neglected in many law firms. If a law firm is serious about good governance (and therefore serious about its survival during the twilight of the law firms), where should the partners focus their attention first?

The author's consultations with clients concerning governance issues over the past 11 years highlight three high-profile issues that every partnership should consider:

- updating and documenting the decision-making processes of the partnership;
- defining the limitations on actions by partners; and
- succession planning.

4.1 Better decision making

Most law firm partnership agreements are out of date. The structures and processes that they describe for decision making – if, indeed, they describe any – might have worked well years ago, when the firm was much smaller; but those customary ways of addressing important issues probably are no longer as effective in facilitating the development and implementation of efficient yet thoroughly well-informed decisions. As one managing partner of a law firm that has grown from 45 to more than 130 lawyers in the past decade observed: "It is taking us much longer to make the same decisions that seemed to be easy 10 years ago."

Modern partnership agreements, or similar operating documents, should address decision-making issues such as the following:

- Which issues require a formal vote of the partnership and what are the voting rights of partners on those issues?
- Which issues require a super-majority vote?
- If there are multiple classes of equity partners, what are the qualifications, rights and privileges of each class?
- If the founding partners are still members of the partnership, what (if any) special rights and privileges do they have (eg, the ability to veto action approved by a majority of the other partners)?
- Which issues are delegated to a managing partner, management committee or specifically designated partners in areas such as marketing, risk management or finance; and which of the decisions and policies for those issues require ratification by the full partnership?
- What are the eligibility requirements and selection criteria for admission to the partnership?
- Does the firm have non-equity partners? If so, what are their rights and responsibilities?

- What are the procedures and voting requirements to elect a new partner?
- What are the grounds and procedures for expulsion of a partner?

4.2 Limitations of actions by partners

One of the most controversial issues in some partnerships concerns limitations on the actions of individual partners. Some firms prohibit their partners from engaging in any outside business interests. Others rely on a system of confidential disclosure of outside business interests. Firms also follow varying rules on compensation for outside activities that relate to the practice of law.

In the author's opinion, there is no set of substantive rules in this area that is inherently superior as good governance. Local business culture and custom, the nature of the firm's practice and the individual and collective values and ambitions of the partners usually drive the decisions. However, a well-governed firm ensures that these issues are addressed and that the policies resulting from these discussions are clearly documented.

Perhaps no other governance issue is more likely to spark emotional debate, and even lingering bad feelings, than this one. Nonetheless, it is important to have these difficult discussions because the destructive force of accusations of professional misconduct that can arise from misunderstandings can be much greater.

A well-governed law firm should ensure that its partnership agreement addresses issues such as the following:

- How does the partnership define the duty of fidelity that each partner owes to the firm?
- What are a partner's duties to protect the confidentiality of information concerning the governance and operation of the firm?
- To what extent may a partner pursue an external business activity and what, if any, disclosure or approval of that activity is required?
- What is a partner's duty to account to the firm for compensation from external sources for personal services involving, or related to, the practice of law, such as fees earned as a member of a board of directors, an arbitrator or an officer of any for-profit commercial enterprise?
- Under what circumstances will the partnership indemnify a partner for personal liability incurred as an officer or director of an external corporation or commercial enterprise?
- May a partner retain as his or her separate income any external compensation received from his or her personal services as an author, lecturer or teacher; or as an officer or director of a professional, charitable or other not-for-profit community organisation? What (if any) duty does the partner have to report such income to the partnership?
- What is a partner's duty to report to all other partners any investment

opportunities offered by or through clients of the firm that are not also available to the general public?

- To what extent (if at all) may a partner use or refer to his or her affiliation with the firm, or use any other brand identity of the firm, in connection with external business activities or participation in professional, civic or charitable organisations and events?
- What, if any, restrictive covenants will apply to a partner's professional activities after he or she withdraws from the partnership and ends all affiliation with the firm?

4.3 Succession planning

Almost every governance consultation that the author has conducted in the past 25 years has involved succession issues. Law firm partners are right to be concerned about succession planning. The survival of any law firm, but especially small and mid-sized ones, depends in part on the ability and willingness of its partners to plan for and manage an efficient, productive transition of ownership and leadership from the senior generation of partners to the next generation.

Passing the baton in a law firm has never been more difficult. The succession plans of most law firms are complicated by one of more of the following factors:

- Founding partners might still have too much equity in the firm to permit their partners to purchase their interest without either imposing a substantial, long-term capital expense on the remaining partners or being forced to receive less than full value for their lifetime investments. Neither option is satisfactory.
- Lawyers are tending to work longer. It is not unusual to see equity partners working actively into their 70s and early 80s. With advances in medical science, it is likely that more partners will be able to remain fully productive past age 100.[17] Many of these very senior partners are in good health and want to remain mentally active; in the words of one 70-year-old partner, "I'm having too much fun."[18] Few law firm partners want to kick out their seniors, especially if they are founding partners and – as frequently is the case – family members.
- Some older partners are financially unable to retire, especially in law firms that do not have pension schemes or in which equity partners do not build up capital accounts over the years.
- Older partners may have a variety of personal reservations about retirement, such as:

---

17 Lisa M Walker Johnson, *Until Death…or Retirement: Thinking Differently About the End of a Legal Career*, monograph presented to the 2010 Annual Conference of the IBA (Walker Clark LLC, 2010), pp1–2.

18 *Ibid*, p6.

  - fear of a loss of purpose and personal identity that one has previously derived from work;
  - a desire to 'maintain control' over one's life; and
  - the absence of a bridge to life after retirement.[19]
- Many law firms have no plans to transfer responsibilities for client relations and project management from an older partner to his or her probable successor in the client relationship. As a result, when the older partner retires, the firm must improvise strategies to retain the client, often in an *ad hoc* manner and on short notice – neither of which impresses the client.

Law firms are using innovative governance structures to plan these transitions well in advance and to manage them successfully. These should be documented in, or as an annex to, the firm's partnership agreement, because they affect the rights, responsibilities and financial obligations of the partners, both individually and collectively. The issues to be considered include the following.

(a) Presumptive and mandatory retirement ages

The partnership sets a presumptive retirement age at which it is planned that a partner will withdraw from the equity partnership and retire from the firm. The most frequently presumptive retirement age currently appears to be 65, but some 'first-generation' firms are nudging that up to 70.

When an equity partner reaches the presumptive retirement age, he or she is normally required to withdraw and retire, unless he or she requests to continue as an equity partner for an additional period of time, typically 24 months. Most firms that have this continuation option also allow the partner to request successive continuations up to a mandatory retirement age (usually 70, 75 or in some firms 80).[20]

Most firms that use presumptive retirement ages and continuation allow the partner to remain an as an equity partner, subject to the commencement of a plan to sell his or her interest over a period of years.

Most firms require a simple majority vote of the partnership to approve a continuation request, with the provision that such approval shall not be unreasonably withheld.

(b) Partner emeritus status

Some law firms allow an equity partner to withdraw from the equity

19 *Ibid*, pp3–8.

20 This 'mandatory' retirement age usually applies only to withdrawal from the equity partnership, with the opportunity to remain active, full time or part time, in an 'of counsel' or some other contracted consultant status, or with a non-equity title of 'partner emeritus', described below.

partnership but retain the title of partner emeritus – essentially a non-equity partner but with responsibilities consistent with a partner of his or her seniority and experience.

(c) *Buy-out policies and schedules*

Firms in which equity partners are required to make more than token cash payments for their shares or interest in the firm should develop a plan to begin to buy back an older partner's equity, preferably when he or she is within three to five years of the presumptive or mandatory retirement age.

5. Beyond the twilight

It is probable that many traditional law firms will lose competitive ground in the next 20 years; and many of those will eventually disappear because they can no longer govern themselves in a way that permits them to meet all of the challenges of rapidly changing legal markets with their limited financial and organisational resources.

Good governance is no longer just a matter of having a reasonably good partnership agreement (although that remains an excellent start). It has become more than figuring out how many votes each partner gets or how to carve up the profits at the end of the year. Governance in law firms has evolved from its origins in simpler times, when law firms were small and their management was much easier.

As illustrated by the IBA Best Practice Guidelines – and as discussed in other chapters in this book – good governance can be a unifying, integrating and coordinating system that allows partners to continue to carry out their responsibilities as owners of the business and leaders of the professional practice. The strength of a firm's governance system, structures and policies is a critically important strategic foundation that will enable law firms to move beyond the twilight and into sustainable long-term success, notwithstanding the great changes that will continue to sweep through the legal markets in which they compete.

Governance as an organising framework for managing the practice and the business

Tony Williams
Jomati Consultants LLP

1. Introduction

Law firms have grown in both size and complexity over the last 35 years, from firms with primarily one main office and perhaps 30 partners to firms with, in many cases, a multiplicity of offices and over 200 equity partners. Indeed, near the end of 2021, almost 60 law firms had recorded revenues of over $1 billion.[1]

It is against this context of the increased size and complexity of law firms that the governance structure of law firms must be considered. In many firms, it is no longer possible for the partners to meet together around a conference table to discuss and agree operational and strategic issues. Many of the equity partners may not know each other well or have ever met. Others may be practising in areas of law or locations where other partners have no experience. Yet lawyers still operate in a partnership model and many lawyers still aspire to equity partnership.

This chapter considers how the governance structure of law firms has developed and is continuing to develop.

2. The key drivers of a governance structure

As law firm governance structures have developed, there have been a number of key issues that lawyers have sought to protect and enhance. These can be summarised as:

- the culture of the firm;
- the involvement of the partners as both workers and owners of the firm;
- the efficient management of the firm;
- the development of the key clients of the firm;
- the continued profitability and success of the firm; and
- the firm's reputation and profile in its market.

1 ALM Global, Law.com, "The Global 200: Ranked by Gross Revenue", 21 September 2021, www.law.com/international-edition/2021/09/21/the-2021-global-200-ranked-by-gross-revenue/.

2.1 The culture of the firm

Most law firms talk of their unique culture; but whether it is genuinely unique or even capable of being clearly articulated is often a moot point. Firms may not actually live the culture they espouse (eg, by examining how their promotion and remuneration systems work to see what values and behaviours they really reward); but when cultural values are both articulated and lived, this can be a strong part of the glue that holds the firm together and motivates the partners and others in the firm. Accordingly, changing a firm's perceived culture can risk demotivating partners and causing some to leave, which can start a rapid and vicious cycle of decline that is very difficult to stop.

2.2 The involvement of partners

The traditional small partnership affords all partners a high level of involvement in operational and strategic issues. Generally, the partners know each other well and can discuss these matters at regular meetings of a manageable size. As firms grow larger, this level of involvement becomes difficult or impossible to maintain. However, many partners are reluctant to devolve all of their decision-making powers to their governance bodies.

Accordingly, firms have developed a series of replacement mechanisms, such as:

- the establishment of senior management roles;
- an elected board;
- the inclusion of clear management roles and responsibilities in the partnership agreement;
- reserved items for a partnership vote (often including new equity partners, new offices, the remuneration report, the annual accounts and budgets and the approval of a firm's strategy);
- regular reporting to the partnership by the management team; and
- regular partners' meetings.

The key here is to enable the partners to feel that they are involved in the major decisions made by the firm, but without imposing a level of paralysis due to micromanagement. Different firms at different stages of development will accept greater levels of operational and strategic leadership.

2.3 The efficient management of the firm

Law firms are now increasingly large and complex businesses, often with revenues of between $100 million and $3 billion. They therefore need to be run efficiently and be capable of responding decisively to changes in the economy and business environment. Tough decisions may need to be made, including:

- restructuring offices or practices;
- retiring or 'de-equitising' equity partners; and
- exiting certain practice areas or locations.

Given the sensitive nature of these decisions, they often cannot be discussed at length with the partners as a whole. In addition, myriad operational business decisions need to be made almost on a daily basis. Only a few partners can, of necessity, be involved in such matters, as most must focus on winning clients and doing client work.

2.4 The development of key clients

Any firm, whatever its size, must increasingly have regard to its client base. Getting, keeping and developing clients is more difficult than ever. Clients have become increasingly demanding as to both the service they receive and the price they are prepared to pay. Law firms are increasingly focusing more time and resources on their key clients: those which have a significant legal spend and are likely to instruct the firm multiple times over a sustained period. The governance structure needs to encourage the development of these clients and their use of the firm in multiple practice areas and locations.

2.5 The continued profitability and success of the firm

Paradoxically, the COVID-19 pandemic saw a major increase in law firm revenue and profitability; but there is now more market uncertainty. It is often forgotten that law firms can and do fail, such as Howrey and Dewey LeBouef in the United States and Halliwells and Cobbetts in the United Kingdom. Size, in itself, is no guarantee of a firm's sustained health. The governance structure, while being efficient, must have regard to:

- the strategic position of the firm;
- movements in the market;
- the risks being taken on by the business (including the cost of rapid expansion, the level of debt carried by the business and dependence on certain clients or industry sectors); and
- the way in which such risks can be identified and mitigated.

2.6 The firm's reputation and profile

In an increasingly competitive environment, a firm's competitive position as demonstrated by its market reputation and profile is its key (some would say only) asset. As anyone who watched the implosion in 2002 of one of the world's largest accountancy firms – Arthur Andersen, following the Enron crisis in 2001 – will realise, a reputation is very hard won, but relatively easily lost. Once the reputation is lost, the business is soon lost too. Accordingly, ensuring that all within a law firm are behaving appropriately at all times is an essential role of the governance structure; as is the ability to take rapid and decisive action when inappropriate activity is discovered.

This is a complex and at times contradictory range of issues that the governance structure will seek to address. Very few firms will claim to have achieved the optimum balance (and those that do claim this may be delusional). Even when equilibrium is achieved, events will inevitably cause an imbalance that needs to be addressed.

3. Developing the key management and financial metrics

Developing the right management financial metrics by which to run a law firm is a complex and ongoing process.

In the late 1970s and early 1980s, law firms were smaller and more generalist in nature. Partners tended to do a range of work for their clients, with relatively little regard to practice specialisms. Then a degree of practice specialisation and practice groupings started to develop. Most firms had one main office and, if they had other offices in the country or internationally, these tended to be very small. Accordingly, geography tended to be the main governing metric, with office revenues and expenses compared – although even at this stage it was relatively rare to prepare full profit and loss statements for these locations with an appropriate allocation of central overheads.

As firms grew during the 1980s, the practice groups became more established, although the boundaries between them were not always clear. Increasingly, for example, practice groups operated within the geographical structure and, due to the size of the office, the practice group became a management unit for recruitment, work allocation and the proposal of equity partner candidates. More detailed financial reports became available, primarily on a geographical basis, but possibly with financials also being prepared on a practice group basis.

In the late 1980s and 1990s, larger firms started to look at their major clients and how these relationships could be managed and developed across the firm. This led firms to consider a move to whole firm practice groups, which sought to develop and service key clients across the platform. Law firms continued to grow in size; and by the late 1990s and early 2000s, many of the larger international firms had started to move to a primarily practice group basis, with the leadership of the practice group having responsibility and accountability for the performance of the practice group firm wide. Geography was still relevant and office-based profit and loss accounts were also prepared, with the office managing partner responsible for the performance of his or her office. However, by the 2000s, it was apparent – in terms of both representation on the firm's management bodies and the level of authority and accountability – that the practice groups were often considered as more important than geography.

Law firm mergers continued and, since the financial crisis, have increased both domestically and internationally. With larger mergers, after an initial integration period, it was seen as beneficial to move to a practice group-dominated matrix, to enhance integration and cross-selling of client relationships. It was feared that a geographically dominated matrix would impede integration and perpetuate a 'them and us' culture between the constituent parts of the merged firm.

A multi-office firm effectively has four dynamics that it must consider:

- Practice group: So as to develop the firm's capability in that discipline, where relevant, across its offices in order to provide a high level of service and expertise across its locations and to develop its reputation in that area.
- Industry group: So as to develop the firm's capability in that industry across its offices, demonstrating to those in that industry its understanding of the legal and business issues that the industry is facing and developing its clients and reputation in that industry. In some cases, the industry group and practice group will be largely the same (eg, real estate), but others may draw on a multiplicity of practice groups.
- Geography: So as to develop the firm's profile and reputation in the local marketplace and deal with the necessary management and operational issues in the local office.
- Key clients: So as to protect, develop and broaden and deepen client relationships, so that the firm works for the client across practice groups and geographies and has as many effective points of relationship across the client as possible. Many major law firms now generate a clear majority of their revenue from their top 100 clients, so these are in effect the firm's crown jewels.

Law firms often feel inherently uncomfortable with the four-part matrix referred to above and therefore seek to default to one primary metric, with the others playing a related but to some extent subordinate role. In the case of most large UK firms, the default choice is the practice group. However, for other major firms in other countries, geography may still have a leading or the leading role.

The use of a management matrix can be complex and confusing. Partners and staff often feel that they want to belong to one key business unit by which their success or otherwise is judged. Furthermore, recruitment, work allocation, remuneration and promotion need to be effectively managed, which militates towards the use of one clear and dominant management unit, albeit within a more complex global structure.

Much of the development of the practice group-focused matrix has been driven by the wish to form broader and deeper relationships with a firm's key clients. This has assumed increased urgency as clients become more demanding, reducing the size of their legal panels and expecting their law firm to service more of their legal needs. Evidence also suggests that clients which use multiple practice groups and geographies are likely to produce not only higher income per client, but also a higher overall profit margin (although this is not universally the case). Offices that operate as standalone silos must compete not only with national and international firms present in their location, but also with local firms on the basis of an undifferentiated offering, but probably a higher cost base due to their larger and more sophisticated platform.

The focus on key clients is causing law firms to devote more resources to the development of their key clients and sector expertise. These are seen to be market-facing indicators of a firm's capability. The practice groups, on the other hand, tend to be an indicator of the firm's internal organisation. However, given that clients and sectors can cover multiple practice groups and geographies, it remains likely that the practice group or geography, as a workable internal structure to which most lawyers can readily relate, will remain the dominant part of the matrix for larger, multi-site law firms, although key clients and sectors are and will become an increasingly relevant feature of the matrix.

4. Governance bodies

Law firms have grappled for some time with the constitution and role of their governance body (or bodies). This reflects the tension between involving sufficient partners in governance to represent the various constituencies in the firm – including practice groups, geographies, the heavy hitters, growth areas and a diverse range of partners (eg, in terms of age, time with the firm, gender, cultural background) – and achieving efficient decision making while focusing most partners on servicing the firm's clients. It is clear that once a governance body reaches a certain size, it may cease to be effective. Too large a body may result in unfocused and unprepared discussion, with many participants reverting to a default position of considering what is in their or their constituents' best interests rather than the best interests of the firm as a whole. Conversely, a very small governance body may appear to be a cabal of the leader's friends or supporters which fails to address effectively key issues or to hold the leadership to account.

As a result, a number of major law firms have experimented with a range of governance structures, often in response to strong or weak leaders, strategic missteps (eg, failed expansion or merger discussions) or a declining market position.

Law firms are still developing in terms of governance structures, but increasingly – whatever the partnership agreement provides – many firms have moved or are moving towards *de facto* supervisory and executive governance bodies. Under this scenario, the board (which may also be called the 'partnership council', 'management committee' or 'policy committee', for example) is the body that is seen to represent the interests of the partnership as a whole and is responsible for holding the leadership team to account for their actions. It may also have a key role in the development or approval of the firm's strategy and input on key strategic issues including new offices, new practice areas and possible mergers. The other body is effectively the leadership team (which may be called the 'executive', 'executive committee', 'management committee' (confusingly, given the above) or 'operations committee'), which has primary responsibility for day-to-day operations and management and the development and implementation of strategy.

In different firms, the composition, roles and authorities will vary. In some, these will be clearly set out in the partnership agreement; in others, only one body may be mentioned in the partnership agreement and the other may have arisen out of practicality and practice. Furthermore, the roles and responsibilities ascribed by the partnership agreement may not be the same as those applied in practice.

This may reflect the development of the firm or the strength or otherwise of the firm's leadership. A very strong leader may welcome a large and diverse board, as this may mean that he or she is not effectively challenged or held to account; but conversely, he or she may welcome a small and effective board which supports and legitimises his or her actions. Much will depend on the strength and personal chemistry of the individuals involved. What is clear, however, is that an effective way of working must be achieved if the governance bodies are to facilitate effective decision making, and to ensure that the partners as a whole feel that their concerns are properly addressed and that the firm is being run in the interests of the partners, and not just in the interests of a small but powerful group of partners.

If a two-tier structure is adopted, the board usually has three key roles:

- to communicate the concerns of the partners and to ensure that the partners are treated fairly and honestly;
- to receive reports as to the actions or proposed actions of the leadership group and to hold the leadership to account for their actions (or inaction); and
- to be consulted on matters of key strategic importance such as new offices, new practices, key developments such as team hires and potential merger activity (in this chapter we are not considering law firm remuneration structures, but the operation of the remuneration system may be a major role of the board).

Such a board will typically include the chair of the firm, senior partner and/or managing partner as an *ex officio* member (usually the chair); and it may have a majority of members drawn from the partnership to reflect the range of interests among the partners. Often these members will be elected (sometimes after a nominating committee or similar process); and in many firms (but not universally), those with management roles (except the *ex officio* members) may be barred from membership of the board. To ensure that membership of the board is constantly refreshed, some firms adopt term limits for board membership (typically two consecutive three or five-year terms). This structure is akin to a corporate board of directors; but as the partners are also the shareholders (although, with alternative business structures in England and Australia, outside shareholders are possible), they have the role of ensuring that the firm is run in the best interests of its owners (ie, the partners) as a whole, while having regard to the legitimate interests of other stakeholders in the business. Some law firms have also experimented with external non-executive members of the board to bring different experiences and rigour to their deliberations.

In a two-tier model, the executive team may be somewhat more informal in structure. The chair or managing partner of the firm will usually chair the team. Other members may depend on the matrix used (see above), so will typically include the leaders of practice and/or geographical groups. Other senior professionals – such as the finance director, chief operations officer or human resources director – may also be members of the team or attend all or part of its meetings. The role of this team is primarily operational; but as firms have grown and become more diverse, these operational issues may be restricted to more significant matters that affect more than one geographical or practice area, or that are significant to the firm as a whole. The executive team may receive detailed reports from the practice group or geographical leaders and seek to hold them responsible for their group's or office's performance. Typically, the executive team will be the body that considers:

- the development of strategy;
- annual budgets and performance against budget;
- partner promotions (lateral and internal);
- new offices and practice areas; and
- strategic developments such as mergers.

Some of these may in turn need to be referred to the board for review and approval.

Over the past decade in particular, the diversity of a firm's leadership has become an increasingly important issue. Firms have felt the need to move from sometimes unfairly characterised 'male, pale and stale' leadership to a more diverse range of leaders in terms of gender, age, ethnic background, social background and so on. Indeed, increasingly, firms are taking steps to positively encourage a diverse leadership and developing measurable targets for such diversity. Given that diverse bodies should help to avoid 'groupthink' and allow for constructive debate, it is likely that this trend will continue.

5. The law firm leaders

The role of the law firm leader has also evolved over the last few decades. It has moved from a largely titular role to a key leadership and management role of major significance to the development and success of the firm. US firms traditionally work with a partner chair and a relatively strong (usually non-lawyer) chief financial officer and chief executive officer (CEO). UK firms often have a lawyer senior partner and a lawyer managing partner (although some UK firms have used non-lawyer CEOs, with mixed success). Elsewhere, the position varies depending upon the size of the firm and its stage of development.

Law firm leaders (or leadership teams) have a number of key roles, including:

- dealing with a range of partner-related issues so as to ensure the cohesiveness and success of the firm;
- being an external ambassador of the firm with the various bars, government agencies, the legal profession generally, the media, key clients and potential partner hires;
- developing and executing the strategy of the firm; and
- being responsible for the operations of the firm, from financial performance to client satisfaction, performance against peers (in reputational and financial terms), premises and information technology.

In most law firms, at least one of the leaders is elected by the partners (sometimes after the use of a nominations committee which may result in a one-candidate 'coronation'). Some firms have started to use term limits for their leadership, but this is still fairly uncommon. Where there is more than one partner with a leadership role, the roles and responsibilities of each must be clear and their working relationship strong if they are to work as an effective and cohesive leadership unit.

Given the size and complexity of many modern law firms, it has become increasingly common for the leadership roles to become full time. This has been the case for longer in the United Kingdom than in the United States, but the size and diversity of most large law firms have increasingly resulted in leadership becoming a full-time role. This introduces a number of challenges. Law firm leaders are often elected to the role due to their strengths as a lawyer and manager of major client relationships rather than their management skills (although increasingly, leaders have run practice groups or offices); so taking them out of that environment can be difficult in terms of their career after the leadership role and in terms of their legitimacy in the eyes of their fellow partners (ie, they are no longer a revenue generator but a cost centre, and they are no longer experiencing the pressures of servicing clients). Some leaders try to mitigate this by retaining some key clients, but this is fraught with difficulty in a larger firm where the leader is trying to do two high-pressure, full-time jobs. Some leaders default to maintaining a very close and strategic relationship with key clients, but involving other partners to service the work on a day-to-day basis.

In a period when in many firms, the issue of partner performance has gained greater significance, partners are increasingly required to prepare partner objectives and targets, and are held accountable (in the remuneration system and more generally) for their performance against these objectives and targets. For the leadership group – from the firm leader(s) with primarily full-time roles to the practice group and office leaders (often with part-time roles but in larger firms sometimes with full-time roles) – this is more complex. In order to demonstrate a partnership level playing field, they need to be held accountable for their actions. But the usual partner metrics will not necessarily apply to them. The metrics used for such people may include:

- performance against strategy and budget;
- the firm's performance against its peers;
- partner satisfaction with their role and communication; and
- similar matters.

The difficulty here is that in a very competitive market, the leadership may have limited direct impact on these measures. A second issue is who should judge their performance. Firms have found this a fraught and difficult process, but many good law firm leaders welcome a degree of informed and fair analysis of their performance, as they feel that it strengthens their mandate within the firm.

6. Communication

Whatever governance structure a law firm employs, one of the biggest challenges that firms face is how to achieve effective communication between the partnership and those performing leadership roles. Such communication is essential so that the management group does not become isolated from the business or seen as aloof by the partners. It is important that this communication is two way. If those in full-time leadership roles regularly meet major clients and other market participants, this can help to maintain their awareness of market trends and their credibility with the partners. However, in larger firms, the range of events that can consume a leader's time are substantial. Making time to regularly meet up with the partners (and not just the noisy ones) is difficult, but essential if partners are to remain engaged. Regular written reports and presentations can help, but may leave partners feeling talked at rather than with. Of course, this is not just an issue for partners, but for all in the firm who need to be reassured as to the firm's direction and continued success. A full review of communication strategies is beyond the scope of this chapter, but – especially in an uncertain market – effective communication is key for those with leadership responsibility.

7. Conclusion

Law firm partnerships are a relatively complex structure of individual and collective relationships. Full partner involvement in every business decision is usually not practical, but a corporate-style 'command and control' environment is also likely to be ineffective in a community of highly intelligent, motivated and questioning individuals. Finding the right balance in a law firm is a continuous process, which needs to have regard to the issues and challenges identified in this chapter.

Governance and structure: supporting the long-term success of a partnership

Michael Roch
MHPR Advisors

1. Introduction

Good governance is an important element driving the long-term competitiveness of any business. Services-led businesses, including law firms, are no exception. This chapter:

- examines what good governance means in successful law firms today;
- helps to identify the advantages and limitations of a law firm's governance structure; and
- provides pointers on how to go about evolving governance.

As an anomaly to other commercial organisations, law firms often assume that a detailed governance structure and a good partner remuneration system are the only ingredients required to make for an effective organisation. While these are without question important, they are only that – ingredients. A sound strategy, a continuous strategic planning process, a cohesive partnership culture, a good partner contribution and performance management process and sound leadership are incredibly important elements to bring any governance structure to life. All of them form a critical foundational basis for a firm to compete. But because these are more difficult to 'codify' in writing, they can cause discomfort in legal services organisations, where so much importance is placed on the written word.

Governance itself is an abstract concept with several meanings. 'Governance', as we use the term in this chapter, refers to the elements that a firm has in place to achieve effective and efficient commercial decision making. The principles outlined in this chapter apply irrespective of the firm's legal structure – they apply equally whether the firm is constituted as a partnership, a limited liability partnership or a corporation; and the word 'partner' is used to include 'shareholder', 'member' or any other equivalent of co-owner as appropriate for the firm's legal form. We also exclude from this discussion all of the regulatory requirements of 'corporate governance' that apply to a legal services entity formed as a stock exchange listed company.

This chapter is organised as follows. Section 2 provides context on how the size, type and maturity of an organisation influence governance choices. Sections 3 to 5 outline typical governance arrangements for firms at three stages of maturity:

- small firms with tightly held decision making;
- growing firms with elements of delegated authority; and
- mature firms with more complex governance structures.

Sections 6 to 10 explore myriad topics that arise irrespective of firm maturity, such as special committees, the roles of key individuals in leadership positions, non-executives and special factors to consider in the internationalising firm. Section 11 concludes the chapter with tips on effecting governance changes, including factors to benchmark governance structures.

2. Factors influencing governance choices

Choices about how to structure governance depend largely on five major influencing factors:

- partnership size;
- the complexity of the firm's organisational design;
- the degree of centralisation based on the partnership's ethos;
- the stage of development; and
- the degree of founder involvement.

2.1 Partnership size

The number of partners and equity holders is a key driver influencing the choice of governance. Thus, this parameter drives initial choices as to governance design.

For example, a small law firm (eg, with up to 12 partners) usually does not require a complex governance structure. Day-to-day decisions are made either collectively or by a single managing partner, often with a healthy dose of consultation with key partners or all partners (see section 3). Firms may have both a managing partner and a senior partner if this is convenient or if the country's legal system follows an English tradition. Again, context matters here. For example, a firm situated in a Sub-Saharan African country may be the largest in its country but have only three partners; in more mature markets a firm of 100 or more partners may be considered mid-sized, and the same could apply to a personal injury firm in the United States or the United Kingdom with, for example, two partners, 10 managers and more than 200 professional staff. Whatever the number may be, we define as 'small' law firms that have few stakeholders influencing the management of the firm.

As the organisation grows to 50 partners or more, a single management board is sufficient (see section 4), perhaps in combination with one or more special purpose committees (see section 6). As the number of partners grows, the influence of non-lawyer professionals providing commercial expertise (eg, a chief operating officer or chief financial officer) also increases, sometimes with or without formal representation on the management board.

Today's larger firms (from about 75 to 100 partners) almost always find that a dual-board structure, with a full suite of special purpose committees, provides a more effective way of making decisions (see section 7). External advisers in the form of independent directors or advisory boards are the norm in most large firms today (see section 9). As the firm internationalises, governance is influenced heavily by the degree of integration of multiple partnerships and the degree of centralisation (see section 7).

The other influencing factors described below are often related to the firm's size.

2.2 Complexity of organisational design

The second most important determinant of the appropriate governance is the complexity of the firm's organisational design and the resultant 'organisational structure', which refers to how professionals are organised (eg, teams, practices, offices, client teams, sectors).

The firm's business model and strategy play a key role here. For example, a firm offering nothing but patent prosecution services requires a simpler governance structure than a full-service commercial firm – fewer decisions on services, quality and knowledge management arise.

A broad geographical footprint often requires a more complex structure; managing five offices in different cities or countries involves different decision-making processes than managing a single office in one country. Whether the firm is generally organised around individual partners who manage their 'own' associates (eg, *Dezernate* common in German firms) or around practices where associates are pooled within teams of partners also influences governance choice.

Thus, a firm operating multiple practices, multiple partner teams and multiple offices requires a more sophisticated decision-making framework than a firm that does not. Modern firms often also form less formal partner groups around 'routes to market' or special technical topics; self-organisation of these 'communities of common interest' is to be encouraged (partners tend to deliver on what they co-create, rather than what they are told to do). However, it is worth reviewing decision-making responsibilities between these informal groups and the more formal 'lines of organisation' within the firm periodically.

2.3 Degree of centralisation based on partnership ethos

A partnership's ethos is a key determinant in how much decision-making power is, can be and should be centralised to a single decision maker or a management body. Three factors influence the degree of centralisation within a firm's governance.

The first factor has nothing to do with the partnership itself: the cultural norms of the country in which the partnership operates. In some countries, the individual is much more at the forefront than the collective; in others, the collective is more important. The importance of and interaction between groups and subgroups also depend on these cultural norms.

The second factor is the influence that this national culture has on the self-understanding of what it means to be a professional and what it means to be a partner in a professional services firm. In other words, the country's partnership tradition plays a major role in determining the degree of centralisation in a law firm. For example, professionals in the United States are much more likely to think of 'my client' as the norm. On the other hand, in traditional English partnerships, it is much more accepted that clients are assets of the partnership, and that partners are custodians of client relationships that have lasted for many partner generations. (In some cases, these relationships may well be more than 100 years old. Yet the influence of US professional services firms becoming established players in Europe has diminished this distinction).

The firm's organisational culture forms the third factor. Often, firms that refer to themselves as 'elite' value the concept of a very cohesive and tight, full partnership. This translates into a highly egalitarian organisation in which, for example, individual partner billings are not the primary determinant of a partner's position in a lockstep remuneration system. These firms tend to be more comfortable with delegated decision making, as long as partners are involved in major decisions. Firms that describe themselves as 'meritocracies' or firms with an 'eat what you kill' financial structure often require more governance – that is, decision-making rules that are defined in more detail because delegated authority to a central managing partner or management committee is less trusted.

2.4 Stage of development

The needs of an organisation change over time and the organisational structure must adapt with them. Academic research has charted the different developmental stages in the lifecycle of organisations, from start-up through expansion and development to maturity. Each stage outlives its governance approach and a new stage emerges.

Initially, firms are launched on the back of the energy, enthusiasm and legitimacy of the founders. Their initial success leads to the first crisis as partners feel excluded; a first management infrastructure develops as the business grows, passing over the baton to the next generation of leaders. With time, this focus on management can develop into excessive control, red tape and bureaucracy – innovation and entrepreneurialism are stifled. This stage, the crisis of control, leads an organisation to its next phase: decentralisation to business units that manage certain responsibilities at their business level and simultaneous delegation to effectively manage the firm.

Firms in which the founders are still heavily involved or which are essentially managed and mainly owned by one or more families present special governance challenges. Many firms in new or developing economies, such as Eastern Europe (where firms were founded after the fall of the Iron Curtain in the early 1990s), are undergoing a generational shift – transforming from founder-led entities to becoming lasting institutions that survive their original founders. It is important that the founders invest early by coaching leadership skills and giving operational and strategic projects to their most promising partners. Whether the succession strategy involves a capital buy-out also influences governance structure in various phases of transition.

Having briefly outlined the factors that influence a firm's governance structure, the next three sections explain the common elements of typical governance structures based on the firm's size and complexity, with size determined by the number of partners and complexity by the organisation's development.

3. Small firms: decision making by democracy

Governance in small firms usually takes one of three simple forms. First, in very small firms, each partner tends to operate largely independently. If a partner desires to make a major financial or commercial decision, such as the employment of a new receptionist or the renewal of an office equipment lease, he or she will typically seek the input of the other partners. Decisions occur by either consensus or majority. Majority is achieved on the basis of one partner, one vote in most cases.

Second, the firm designates one managing partner who takes on the day-to-day management of the office, usually supported by a competent all-rounder or the secretary, who doubles as the office manager. Again, major decisions are made by either consensus or majority. A formal vote is the exception; approval after input is usually reached very informally.

Third, it is not uncommon for partners to share the management burden. For example, one partner may serve as the managing partner, taking care of most practice management issues, with different partners respectively taking care of financial management, information technology, knowledge management and marketing. The partnership's reward model also influences how the management burden is shared.

Irrespective of which variant the firm prefers, clarity is needed on which decisions a partner may undertake individually and which require the involvement and input of the other partners.

In terms of governance (and ignoring the other elements that make for an effective commercial deal among partners), often a simple decision-making chart is sufficient to achieve clarity about decision-making rights and responsibilities. The level of detail of this chart will depend on how long the partners have been in business together – and how much they trust each other as partners. When we advise firms on agreeing a decision-making framework, we usually start with seven broad categories and then drill down to whatever level of detail is required to reach agreement among the partners.

The seven broad decision categories are:

- day-to-day client service and client management;
- team and practice management issues;
- financial matters and commercial commitments to others;
- composition of the partnership (promotions, laterals, leavers);
- elections (if there is a managing partner);
- strategy and business model; and
- other major decisions.

For smaller or founder-led firms, it is not unusual for the partners to have been operating for many years without a written partnership agreement. This, of course, is not ideal. More formality is usually needed when a new partner is admitted, when the firm wants to acquire another firm or when the trust among partners has broken down. In these cases, all commercial aspects of how the partnership – as a 'new' partnership – should operate in future must be decided. These include all aspects around strategy, practice management, succession planning, decision making and finances. Aspects of this 'partnership blueprint' should then be turned into a proper partnership agreement, either by the partners themselves or by external counsel specialising in partnership matters.

We cautiously present the following health warning: all too often, lawyers get lost in the detail when attempting to put together a partnership agreement for their own firm for the first time or when attempting to modify their existing agreement. The focus first should be on the big commercial issues. Many day-to-day interactions between partners cannot – and should not – be hardwired into a legal agreement.

4. Delegated decision making in a growing firm

As the firm grows, it is appropriate to relieve the managing partner of his or her management burden. Many firms establish a management board on which three to five partners serve. For the purposes of this chapter, we refer to partners who do not serve on this board or who otherwise have no formal management role as 'client partners'.

It is surprising how aggressively lawyers negotiate decision-making powers for their corporate clients, yet how often they use contorted euphemisms in the governance documentation of their own firm to avoid the perception that their firm's management board decides anything of meaning. Many firms are uncomfortable with the mere notions of management, delegated decision-making authority or power. Checks and balances abound. In the management board charter or even in the partnership agreement, delegated decision making sometimes only extends to 'monitoring', 'informing' or 'consulting with'. These are not, by themselves, tenets of effective decision making.

Where decisions purport to be delegated to a management board, three elements are required for effective decision making:

- a decision-making framework as outlined in section 3 above;
- a clear charter of the board's remit; and
- a clear understanding of roles for partners who serve in a management function, but who do not occupy formal board positions.

We consider the latter two in turn.

4.1 Decision-making framework

In section 3, we outlined seven areas of decision making. A DARCI or similar matrix creates clarity about who gets to decide what, and the decisions on which partners are entitled to consultation or vote.

The DARCI matrix works as follows: for each of the seven areas of decision making and the main decisions that are likely to come up within each area, the partners clearly indicate which partner, committee or board:

- **D**ecides (on the action to be taken);
- is **A**ccountable and **R**esponsible (does the work to prepare for the decision each step of the way);
- is **C**onsulted (has input into the decision); and
- is **I**nformed (is informed of the decision when done).

Figure 1 on the next page shows the DARCI matrix outline.

For example, to select advisers for a governance review project:

- a partner on the management committee is responsible for contacting advisers and seeking proposals;
- the firm's senior partner is consulted on the selection;
- the management committee decides; and
- all partners are informed of the management committee's decision.

The level of detail of a DARCI matrix is driven primarily by partnership size, maturity and partnership complexity (see section 2). Again, there's no need to go overboard; but the most important partnership decisions will want to be captured in this way.

Figure 1: Example DARCI matrix

	D **Decider/delegator** Holds the ultimate power. Power can be retained as the right of final approval/veto, or delegated to the A.	A **Accountable** The single person fully accountable for making the matter happen	R **Responsible** Those responsible for doing the work on the matter	C **Consulted** Those from whom input will be solicited	I **Informed** Those to be kept apprised of relevant developments
Topic 1	Partner/Committee 1				
Subtopic 1	Partner 1				
Decision 1	Partner 2				
Decision 2	Partner 3	Partner 3	Partners 4 and 5	Partnership board management committee	All partners
Decision 3	Partner 3				

Source: © 2023 MHPR Advisors, all rights reserved.

4.2 Management board charter

A management board – and indeed any partnership body – should have a brief but clear charter outlining 10 elements, as follows:

- the purpose of the management board;
- how its members are appointed or elected;
- to whom the management board is accountable (typically the equity partners of the firm), who is accountable to this body and the relationship of the management board with other partnership bodies (eg, if there is a remuneration committee, whether it serves as a sub-committee of the management board or whether it is a separate committee consisting of different partners and appointed separately by the partnership);
- the responsibilities of the board;
- the specific powers of the management board, including all decision-making rights that the management board can make on its own and any matters that remain reserved to the partners;
- the ability to delegate decision-making rights and reserved matters;
- meetings and the mechanics of decision making;
- qualifications for individuals to serve (eg, number of years as a partner, previous management roles in the firm);
- the expected commitment (full-time equivalent) of the board members; and
- the term and removal of board members.

Again, this is a management instrument, not a legal document. This means that it needs to strike the right balance between providing certainty and flexibility to allow the board to make decisions effectively and efficiently and to further the goals of the partnership as a commercial enterprise. Too much detail comes at the expense of flexibility. We have been involved in many partnership situations where the draft of a management board charter has been in circulation for a year or more because the partners argue – as lawyers – about irrelevant minutiae in order to preserve individual power, instead of concluding – as co-entrepreneurs – on basic principles that they need to develop the firm.

4.3 Partner roles

As the firm grows in both size and complexity, it is helpful to establish a more comprehensive decision-making framework that includes not only the management board, but also other management roles that will have developed for line partners not serving on the board.

It is here that the firm's organisational design and decision-making structure need to work in unison. For example, a firm that has developed – in addition to its practices or departments – sector groups comprised of partners from different departments requires the partners who lead these groups to have a clear understanding of both their rights and their responsibilities with regard to:

- the management board;
- the heads of department;
- the office managing partners; and
- the partners who are housed outside their own department or offices.

Often, partners in these sector or other groups (referred to as 'communities of common interest') are given a role without any clarity whatsoever over their decision remit. Are they permitted just to call for meetings or are they also permitted to call partners to account for not following through on commitments to the group? How do they influence decisions related to the remuneration of these partners? These and other questions often plague the growing multi-dimensional law firm.

As the firm becomes more complex, the simple decision-making framework outlined in section 3 becomes strained and good leadership skills become more important (see below); as do practical guidelines for all roles that have a title.

In our consulting work, we typically prefer to work through these practical guidelines for decision making with the practice leaders, top management and groups of partners concerned to ensure that they fit the strategic and operational needs of the growing organisation. There is neither a blueprint nor a single right answer – often, we help the partnership to choose from among a number of viable options to arrive at the best solution for the partnership.

We again refer to a DARCI-style matrix and now seek to define the roles of all partners with responsibility beyond day-to-day client work broadly around the same five elements:

- To whom are they primarily accountable?
- For what are they responsible and what specific results are to be agreed periodically with the person to whom they are accountable?
- Whom do they need to consult before making a decision?
- Whom do they need to keep informed?
- For what do they have the right – and the obligation – to make decisions on behalf of the partnership?

It is vital that this is not a one-off exercise. In a rapidly changing market, roles may appear, change and disappear, depending on the needs of the business. These roles should not become so entrenched as to become perks or items of right. The best partnerships adjust their governance and adjust their organisation periodically in accordance with market conditions, and also conduct a fundamental review of their structure every few years or when major events (eg, a merger or major acquisition) occur, to ensure that it remains fit for the firm's strategic purpose.

5. Dual boards in complex firms

To repeat, a growing firm almost invariably becomes more complex. Most large firms will operate several service lines in several offices and in several countries. Recent years have seen many mergers of large firms, with varying degrees of integration. These firms have outgrown a simple delegated structure with only one management board, pointing to a dual-board structure with sub-committees as a more effective way to reach decisions efficiently. Many global law firms also have a cascade of management bodies, including a global dual-board structure that is cascaded or duplicated regionally, with one each for the Americas, Europe, the Middle East and Africa and Asia-Pacific, for example (see section 7.)

The international partnership board is usually responsible for setting broad strategic and operational policies and direction. The partnership board is typically elected by the partners at large. In *Verein*-type firms, the number of partners who constitute the members of the *Verein* determines the number of partners that the member firm can elect to the partnership board; often, a small number of legacy firms dominate the board, with the other members' positions being pooled. Again, this differs widely from firm to firm.

The management board may be further subdivided by operational function or by region; also common is a small executive committee to further efficient and quick decision making. There are myriad variations and each international firm has chosen its own variant to suit its purposes.

In our view, it is important that the management board is appointed by the elected partnership board, the managing partner after consultation or a combination – and not by the partnership. This is to avoid congressional-style representation by individuals of 'their' constituents (usually their office or their department). In many firms, governance – decision making – is ineffective because management board members do not have the good of the firm in mind, but rather 'represent' their client or constituency, being their home crowd. Indeed, where possible, we prefer that members of the management board move offices and sit together rather than within their traditional teams, to help weld the top team together as one decision-making unit.

It is normal that the political aspects increase with firm size. Clarity on the inter-relationship between the various boards is as important here as it is in less complex organisations; the basic principles are similar to those outlined in section 4. It is paramount to keep decision rights as simple as possible, but as nuanced as necessary to manage the various dimensions of the firm. A good balance helps client partners to get on with serving clients and delivering the firm's global, regional and local strategic objectives. If in doubt, simplicity wins over complexity.

6. Special committees for the growing firm

As firms grow, it becomes appropriate to establish sub-committees of the boards (ie, the partnership board, the management board or both). Below we outline the purpose of the most common committees.

6.1 Remuneration committee

The remuneration committee remains the most common of all committees in law firms today. Its importance depends on the powers given to it by the partners. Its purpose is to apply the firm's remuneration policy and to determine partners' remuneration annually or at whatever interval has been agreed in the partnership agreement. In some firms, especially those dividing profit according to an agreed formula, the remuneration committee also arbitrates disagreements among partners about credit allocation – for example, who should be rewarded for bringing in a matter or client.

In many firms, the remuneration committee also has the task of determining the contributions (ie, performance) of individual partners during the past year(s). We distinguish between the assessment of a partner's contribution and the determination of pay on the basis of these contributions – these are two separate commercial processes. In our view, as in other commercial organisations, partners with management roles (eg, a department head, practice group chair, team leader) are in the best position to input on or even determine a partner's contributions. This is because partner-managers have the best information about a client partner's performance and can put into context the measures and metrics used to assess that partner's contribution (in our experience, measures and metrics tell only half the story about partners' contributions). At the very least, partner-managers should have significant input into the assessment of performance.

Firms take two approaches to the independence of the remuneration committee. Either it exists in parallel to the management board, with different partners, to ensure a checks-and-balances approach; or it can be a sub-committee of the partnership board (or of the management board in a single-board structure).

In our experience, having worked with countless large domestic and international law firms across the globe, it is more effective for the remuneration committee to serve as a sub-committee of the partnership board, because a remuneration committee that acts independently hinders the effective operation of the management board. For example, in the context of lateral hiring, we have seen far too many cases where an otherwise solid and strategically important candidate, having been vetted fully by the management board, has been effectively rejected by the elected remuneration committee because of political power games between it and the management board, causing the firm to lose out on a strategic opportunity.

6.2 Nominations committee

The nominations committee serves the function of vetting internal or lateral candidates for partnership. This committee is especially important in larger international firms, where partners in the home office may not know local market realities or internal candidates sufficiently well. Again, we prefer that the nominations committee serves at the discretion of the partnership board.

For remuneration and nominations committees, it is important that the appointed partners reflect the geographical and practice diversity of the firm as a whole.

6.3 Risk and audit committees and strategy committees

Increasingly, firms are adopting two additional committees.

The risk and audit committee serves a similar function to that served in commercial enterprises, focusing on conflicts, risk management and financial compliance. It is common that at least one outsider serves on this committee; in some firms, the majority of committee members are from outside the partnership.

Large international firms also appoint a strategy committee which, as the name indicates, continuously monitors and fine-tunes the firm's strategy execution. The strategy committee recommends and its members help to execute the commencement of new practices and entry into new geographical markets. Increasingly, strategic sourcing, innovation and service delivery integration ('seamless service') also fall under the remit of this committee.

6.4 A word on *ad hoc* committees

In high-growth firms, we sometimes see myriad *ad hoc* committees occupying the time of far too many partners whose time would be better spent elsewhere. In one 150-partner independent firm, more than 80% of the partnership served on a committee of some type at any one time. Often, these have sprung from the well-meaning ideas of individual partners and have then been perpetuated. Or they seek to make up for the lack of proper management support in the form of professional managers who would be likely to better serve the partnership (albeit at a cash cost that is more visible than the opportunity cost of wasted partner time). Often, we seek to assess the opportunity cost of having partners serve on these committees as a starting point for reform. This is not to say that the partners, or groups of partners, should not be consulted on topics as important as talent, diversity, finance or marketing strategy; but the balance needs to be appropriate for the ambition, size and sophistication of the partnership.

In the end, *ad hoc* committees should remain *ad hoc*: they should be established for a purpose with a sunset date, and their remit should be renewed periodically by the partnership board.

7. Governing the global or international firm

While the nuances of the governance structures of the world's global and international law firms are beyond the scope of this chapter, we highlight the basic features for completeness.

7.1 The continuum of international integration

The most significant influencing factor related to the choice of governance structure in these complex organisations is the degree of integration. Figure 2 shows our starting point to assess the degree of integration among international professional services firms.

The chart in Figure 2 should be read as a continuum – the delineation is intentionally fluid.

As a starting point, the commercial approach indicates the primary commercial aim: does the international organisation exist merely to drive referrals or is the aim an integrated, one-firm approach to markets, clients and service delivery? The more tightly integrated the firm, the more exclusive the dealings of the various member partnerships, developing into a single partnership. This in turn informs the financial deal among the member partnerships and their partners. Where partners of the member firms become partners of the international organisation as a whole, the financial structure also becomes more integrated, with the cascade of relationships being optimised for tax considerations.

In terms of decision making, the balance shifts from the local – with common global elements – to a global governance structure that accommodates local requirements and elements.

7.2 A word on the Swiss *Verein* versus integrated partnerships

A number of law firm mergers have been effected by tying individual partnerships into a common structure whereby the global aspects of the business are managed through a central entity (usually a Swiss *Verein*, a Swiss cooperative or an English private company limited by guarantee) as an alternative to a fully integrated global partnership.

This international structure is not new and has been widely used by the international accounting firm networks. Many commentators have questioned whether these types of organisations are proper integrated businesses capable of serving a global client base or whether the model is merely a 'patch' that is inferior to a fully integrated structure.

We posit that the accounting firms in particular have proven beyond doubt that the legal structure chosen is much less relevant than how these organisations operate day to day. We know of numerous *Verein*-type professional services firms that serve their clients in a seamless way; and we know as many integrated partnerships where the client experience very much differs from office to office.

Figure 2: Integration continuum for international PSFs

Degree of commercial integration	Loose					Tight
Commercial approach	Referral network	Best friends/ preferred firm programme		Formal affiliation		One firm
Exclusivity	Non-exclusive			Exclusive		
Governance/ decision making	None; membership rules only	Generally local; *ad hoc* jointly for common initiatives	Local; veto over small number of decisions affecting other party	Mostly local, some common decision making	Mostly common; local offices given autonomy over local issues	Generally common with parameters for local decision making
Financial integration	None; maybe membership dues	Generally none; *ad hoc* cost sharing for joint initiatives		Cost sharing only	Partial profit sharing	Full profit sharing (with/without local performance element)
Typical structural means	None; membership rules only	Memorandum of understanding	Bilateral/multilateral strategic alliance (contractual without global association entity)			
				Global association	Global association coupled with legacy partnerships and commercial service companies	
					Parent-subsidiary; global partnership/ parallel partnership with value partners	

Source: © 2023 MHPR Advisors, all rights reserved.

What matters much more than the legal structure is the degree of common decision making across borders.

8. Key roles of individual partners

Ideally, each partner who has a management role – that is, each partner who is vested with power to take decisions on behalf of the partnership that go beyond managing client files – should have a proper role description so that there is clarity about what he or she should and should not do. Given the ambiguity that exists in large professional partnerships – and that serves these organisations well in a rapidly changing market environment – this may be neither realistic nor necessary. And the stronger the cohesive elements of the firm's culture, the less important the formal role descriptions.

There are exceptions. These include the roles of the managing partner, the senior partner (if there is one) and key individuals in management roles – typically the department head and the office managing partner. Role descriptions for these individuals will want to follow the broad frameworks outlined above. Often, the managing partner looks after the day-to-day management of the firm, while the senior partner is the external face of the partnership; but this need not be so. As an exception to the usual tenet that the role should come first and should not be tailored to the individual, in this instance the roles should suit the individual's strengths so that he or she can best deploy them for the good of the firm.

If there is a formal senior partner role (as is the case in many UK firms), it is especially important that the senior partner and the managing partner act jointly and work out among themselves a clear understanding of who is responsible for what and what single decision-making rights each of them has. This goes beyond formal role descriptions and the words of the partnership agreement; it should be based on the individuals' strengths. We have seen many sophisticated international law firms become paralysed because the senior partner and managing partner are barely on speaking terms – a direct contributor to stagnation, partner departures, loss of opportunity and decline of market position.

9. External advisers to the board

Many larger law firms have appointed non-executive directors to their partnership board. This trend is welcome in a profession that has traditionally viewed outsiders with indifference or suspicion. These individuals can provide general commercial acumen and client-based viewpoints to inform decision making or can be subject-matter experts to address organisational weaknesses.

Some firms have appointed advisory boards consisting of individuals who are not partners of the firm. Again, this is a positive trend and can help the firm to drive innovation in relation to its service offering or to do things differently.

For example, a firm may be more willing to contemplate the outsourcing of certain back-office functions if one of its advisory board members has intimate experience of the execution of outsourcing arrangements and can thus guide management through this process. An advisory board can also serve as the firm's eyes and ears in the market and help to make sense of more formally gathered client feedback. Advisory boards in a growing number of firms today include clients.

10. Governance in alternative business structures

Alternative business structures (ABS) allowing for non-licensed professionals to become equity owners in law firms have become increasingly common. The three main purposes of forming an ABS are:

- accessing external capital;
- sharing profits with non-licensed management personnel or professionals from other professions; and
- streamlining the navigation of arcane profit-sharing rules.

For example, the Legal Services Act (2007) has constituted ABS in the United Kingdom; they have been around for longer in Australia and some US states (eg, Arizona) also now permit them.

For ABS, the overall governance considerations outlined above also apply. However, they do impose additional requirements on the firm's management structure. For example, the Legal Services Act has hardwired in two management functions (head of legal practice and head of finance and administration), with tightly defined roles and responsibilities. Today, both regulators and advisers have established best practices on how to organise the management of an ABS for regulatory compliance.

Legal form aside, the basic principles of law firm governance as outlined here, with nuanced differences allowing for business purpose, also apply to an ABS. This is because good governance – that is, good decision making – is simply part of good management, irrespective of the legal and regulatory form chosen.

11. Managing change to achieve good governance

We conclude this chapter with some suggestions about how best to go about changing the governance of a law firm.

The extent of the change management hurdle should not be underestimated – this is because decision making affects the day-to-day working of the lawyers as intimately as a change in the firm's remuneration system. Thus, aspects of change should be prioritised carefully and partners should be brought properly on board by allowing them to contribute meaningfully and not through a cynical 'partner involvement exercise'.

That said, the starting point is usually the establishment of a clear purpose of why a review is necessary, followed by a thorough assessment of the strengths and vulnerabilities of the current governance and how it affects decision making. This assessment tends to take the form of an initial benchmarking of how the firm's governance achieves effective and efficient decision making, which is then drilled down on through a number of means to arrive at a robust gap analysis. In the box below, we suggest a simple framework that can be used for this purpose.

Benchmarking law firm governance – factors to consider:

- Does the firm have defined, effective and clear strategic, tactical and operational goals?
- How cohesive is the firm's organisational culture and how does this manifest itself in the context of decision making in the firm at all levels?
- How clear is the decision-making authority contained in the roles, responsibilities and accountabilities within the firm's structure?
- How well are the roles, responsibilities and accountabilities understood across the partnership?
- What is the degree of conflict among these roles?
- What are the leadership skills of individuals carrying out each role?
- What is the degree of independence and balance among governance bodies, and how is this independence exercised?
- To what degree are priorities placed at the right level?
- How meaningful are the key decision-making protocols?
- To what degree is the formal governance structure followed or manipulated by key decision makers?

Following this assessment, it works best to agree on the *status quo* with the management board and key partner groups or, if appropriate, the partnership as a whole. The project team can then develop a small number of options and – again, with partner input that is appropriate for the partnership's size – select and refine the decision-making framework, DARCI matrix and so on until a blueprint is agreed. The blueprint should be sufficiently detailed so as to be capable of implementation and should in itself provide an implementation plan. The complexity and duration of the design phase and of implementation will depend on the factors addressed in section 2 of this chapter, including:

- size;
- practice complexity and geographical footprint;
- centralisation;
- stage of development; and
- whether the firm is founder led or institutional.

12. Conclusions and observations

At the beginning of this chapter, we stressed that governance is all about effective and efficient decision making. This chapter outlines how good governance can support good decision making in the long term only if it operates as part of an integrated system, working in unison with strategy, organisational design, remuneration and organisational culture.

However, any good decision-making structure comes to life only with and through its people. Any governance structure should focus on the partners and the effective interaction among the firm's partners so that they can get on with their day-to-day business of serving clients and building the firm into an institution that survives them.

Five keystones for efficient business support operations for your law firm

Iryna Nikitina
IOCONS LLC

1. Introduction

Regardless of the jurisdiction in which your law firm is based, how long your firm has been present in a market or how impressive your book of business is, you will be unable to survive current levels of competition without professional managers on your team.

The idea that partners in a law firm need professional managers is not new. Partners themselves frequently recognise that they sometimes fail to combine service to clients with the management of the firm's business.

The COVID-19 pandemic as well as post-pandemic times present a few more challenges for the law firm – the major one being the challenge to change. The professional support of law firm managers is vitally important for partners to be able to cope with these challenges. No partners can do it all on their own.

Law firms, whether consciously or instinctively following market trends, have joined the race to include new administrative positions in their organisational charts and to add new professionals to their payrolls.

However, the final outfitting of a managerial structure and professional team for a particular firm should be unique. There is no universal recipe for how administrative support should be organised in any firm, but this is not a trivial question. The answer should take into account the individual context of the firm and the market – that is:

- the firm's size and number of years on the market;
- its background;
- its business model; and
- its partners' approaches to business development.

The following five-step model can be useful for partners to find the right answers for their own law firm at the current moment of its development:

- Start with a quick audit;
- Manage your expectations;
- Choose a model that is right for your firm;

- Share responsibilities with your professional management team; and
- Track your dynamics.

2. Keystone 1: Do an audit first

Is your firm ready to onboard professional business managers? An at-a-glance readiness audit has two sides: a technical side and a psychological side.

Here are some factors which can signal that your existing system needs to change in some way, possibly ranging from a slight realignment to a significant reform:

- Partners spend more than 20% of their working time on purely internal administrative issues.
- The increase in business administration costs is equal to or higher than the increase in a firm's revenue.
- Partners' administrative responsibilities are on a voluntary basis and are not reflected in the partners' remuneration system.
- There is a high level of partner dissatisfaction with one or more administrative functions.

In order for cooperation with professional managers to be productive and for the investments in them to pay off, partners should honestly answer three basic questions:

- Are they ready to admit that they have limitations in their own competencies in some specific areas, and to trust professionals in these respective areas enough to become their internal clients?
- Are they willing to partially transfer their managerial power to hired professional managers? If so, to what extent?
- What services should be delivered by an internal business team and where should external experts be involved?

3. Keystone 2: Manage your expectations

At an international conference where I spoke at recently, one of the participants – the managing partner of a small local law firm – asked me whether it is possible to delegate all management duties to hired non-legal professionals and get away from the daily routine, in order to focus solely on business development. In my opinion, it is the best illustration of how partners' visions of professional managers have changed and how the level of partners' expectations has risen.

It's a good question. And yet it is still a difficult one, given that law firm partners frequently have their own disagreements and conflicts about how the firm's management functions should be performed.

3.1 The conflicting nature of partner's roles

In their everyday work in a law firm, partners are often forced to play at least four different roles:

- as a professional service provider and adviser to the client;
- as a leader, role model, and mentor for others in the firm;
- as a manager and head of his or her own practice; and
- for equity partners, as an owner of the business.

This constant combination of these three (for non-equity partners) or four (for equity partners) roles causes a natural internal conflict. An important step in a partner's managerial maturity and psychological readiness for fruitful and effective cooperation with professional managers is to identify and accept the conflict in the many roles that he or she must perform.

Obviously, professional managers expect to help partners effectively combine and execute all these roles. What is the scope of that support?

3.2 Trust, first of all

Law firms are partnerships that are created by lawyers for lawyers and, in most cases, run by lawyers for lawyers. Credibility and trust have been, are and will always be a key issue. A non-lawyer specialist in a law firm – even a person of the highest professional calibre – must prove his or her credibility and competence every day, and thereby win trust by delivering solid results.

The starting point (and, frankly, one of the most painful steps) for any partnership in developing or changing the firm's management and administrative support is building trust.

Partners first and foremost need to honestly answer the question: "To what extent are we ready to trust our managers, just as our clients trust us?" It is the only way to:

- formulate clear requirements for potential candidates for management positions;
- define the functional responsibilities for each one; and
- position and frame how they will integrate into the administrative and financial operations of the firm.

Some law firms believe that the easiest way to meet new needs for business management is to identify current staff with management potential and then manage their development and promotion within the company: "Could any of the existing staff cope with this challenge or function or problem?" This reminds us of the need to extinguish the small fires quickly, as well as systematically and strategically to approach the larger management needs of the firm and ask: "Where will we go tomorrow and what skills will we need then?"

One advantage to this approach, aside from the aversions that many law firm partners' have to thinking and planning strategically, is to build sustainable trust in the staff. However, there is sometimes a misapprehension that, for example, a proven human resources (HR) specialist already in the firm, rather than an outsider, could more easily move into a new role because he or she understands how the firm is organised. This is mistaken because, with few exceptions, it sets up that person for failure, for two reasons:

- To simultaneously work and acquire new knowledge can significantly increase the physical toll and psychological pressure on that employee; and
- A thorough knowledge and understanding of a firm's inner workings could actually inhibit the employee in the performance of his or her new duties. Not everyone is ready and able to change overnight the habitual perceptions and habits from previous work experience in the firm and find new ideas and new points for potential development, which normally would be expected in the new role.

So, to build an effective system of business administrative support, it is extremely important to separate the issue of developing trust in an outside professional from the issues that can arise as current employees try to move to new and significantly different roles.

Therefore, as the first and most important step in developing the firm's system of business administrative support and management, partners should overcome their stereotypes about resources and accept a new reality – they have to trust!

Partners can usually see an analogy in the trusting relationships they have already built with their clients. Good partners invest a great deal of time, effort and emotion in building and maintaining these relationships, in addition to delivering high-value legal expertise. The same factors should apply to their role in the firm as 'internal clients' of their business managers. Again, they must learn to trust the managers, just as their clients trust them.

There is another extreme, however. Tempted by peer pressure, some firms hire highly paid professionals without a clear plan. Thus, they often either put unreasonably high expectations on them and simply step aside and blindly trust the new person; or do the opposite, micro-managing, controlling every step and interfering in even minor operational decisions. In either case, mutual disappointment is inevitable. Both trust in a loyal employee and blind trust in a hired professional could work, but are not the most effective ways to build a business support function in your firm.

There needs to be a balance. Success, therefore, is determined by two components:

- a synergy produced by planning and clear understanding of the respective roles of the legal team and the management specialists; and
- mutual trust.

Further engagement of law firm professionals into most of the firm's business processes highlights the issue of trust from sometimes unexpected angles. For example:

- hiring sales managers or account managers for the firm's key clients – very unusual specialists in traditional law firms – can improve the capabilities of the business support team from that of a typical back-office operation to that of a 'quasi-front office';
- adding professionals dedicated to client relations development can open up new opportunities for better lawyer-client cooperation and can strengthen the firm's relationships with clients. Naturally, firms with an 'eat why you kill' philosophy come to this conclusion first; and
- the role of chief operating officer (COO) has undergone major transformations. On the one hand, a number of new roles have been spun off from what was a traditional operations function, such as the responsibility to lead and coordinate innovation (which rests with the chief innovation officer (CIO)) or risk management and compliance. This has permitted the COO to expand his or her focus to include a more direct role in service quality control and client satisfaction measurements.

3.3 The client's perspective

How do clients feel about such transformations in law firms? Are they ready for non-legal professional involvement in the direct line of contact? Are clients ready to trust such professionals without double-proof from the partners' side? In most cases, the answer is yes.

Unfortunately, partners often tend to sabotage such transformations. By empowering specialists with authority in client communications and decision making, partners (consciously or unconsciously) can intrude into the specialists' areas of responsibility, undermining their authority and demotivating them. Whether such sabotage will prevail or only be episodic depends on the firm's managing and senior partners, who should shape and influence the changes in the firm's workplace culture needed for the specialists to succeed.

Managing the firm effectively and ensuring its competitiveness on the market cannot be achieved solely within the firm's ecosystem. There must be a consideration of the interests of all stakeholders, the clients being first and foremost among them. Professional managers can often be a communication 'bridge' between lawyers and their clients, smoothing gaps, fine-tuning business processes to meet client needs better and helping to improve client satisfaction.

3.4 Interaction between partners and professional managers

I would not repeat the truism that even the most talented lawyers prove to be bad businesspeople. It distorts the true nature of things – which, in my opinion, is that most lawyers love their profession, and that law is their life, state of mind and a great source of self-worth and enjoyment. Managing the business is a concomitant induced obligation, which is always supplemental to the main task of practising law. In order to solve the most complex legal challenges, a professional team and a well-honed legal machine should stand behind the partners. The firm's scope of work in progress is in direct correlation to its size.

While a firm is developing and growing, its major investments are, first, in legal personnel; and, second, in the firm's promotion, which is carried out by the partners themselves. A lack of effort and resources to develop the administrative support that this needs usually results in an unsystematic and sometime even chaotic coverage of essential administrative functions.

This is one of partners' most common mistakes: a complete lack of, or inattention to, a systematic approach to their own business. Partners' perceptions of a firm's growth are often somewhat two-dimensional: they see it simply as more lawyers and more fee revenue.

Professional managers can correct this mistake and integrate concepts such as efficiency, a project approach, financial analysis, financial forecasts and other concepts inherent in business success into a firm's operations over a relatively short period of time and at very little cost.

The next important step in systematising the business that can be introduced by professional managers is the formalisation of the firm's policies and procedures. It is this rationalisation of basic service delivery processes that ensures business sustainability, increases operational efficiency and significantly reduces the time required to make operational decisions. Documented policies and procedures keep partners away from micro-management because they know what people are expected to do and what results they are expected to produce.

The final and much more difficult step is for partners to admit the need for change and for a transition to a new model of leadership. The main result of this difficult, responsible and, I would say, revolutionary step concerns the selection of those areas in which partners discover that they can take a step back from their own intense involvement and give way to professionals who, they will come to admit, can do it better.

A major advantage of this approach is the opportunity it gives for professional managers to enhance the partners' competences. Obviously, such a joint team of diversely talented professionals, focused on achieving the same outcome and mutual success, will be much stronger. This is what creates true synergy.

The obvious synergetic effect of cooperation with professional managers more than compensates for a firm stepping out of its comfort zone to pursue efforts to achieve transformations. For one of the firms in which I have worked, the transformation took two years. The investment of time was worth it. Not all of the results were fast, but the most important ones were sustainable in the long term.

3.5 Overcoming inertia: the shake-up

The issue of inertia against internal change in law firms is still on the agenda, although it has reduced in many firms as a result of experiences during the COVID-19 pandemic and what has been emerging in the post-pandemic period. Law firm partners are now more likely to agree – unanimously in some firms – on the necessity for and inevitability of change. In most cases, a serious shake-up is required in order to proceed with the implementation of even the most obvious changes.

This shake-up can be both positive (eg, mergers, business expansion, changes in requirements from a firm's key clients) and negative (eg, losing a valuable partner or an entire practice – often at the same time; losing an important client; or failing to compete credibly in a market segment). A brilliant example of external push to change the model in which law firms were operating for a long time is the COVID-19 pandemic.

Another important factor that law firms must take into consideration is the fast-paced dynamic of both the legal market and its players. The speed of change in the modern legal services market, clients' requirements, the continuous improvement of existing products and the introduction of new products to the market barely allow firms – even those embracing the need for change – to calmly put in place a new structure following all the rules of change management. Changes in law firms are more reminiscent of a repair of a loaded vessel at full speed ahead, rather than during a planned overhaul at the docks.

A professional management team is expected not just to watch and inform partners about current and expected changes, but also to give an assessment of their impact on business, present to the partnership possible scenarios for the development of a situation and offer options to be taken by a firm, so that it can meet the relevant challenges head-on. Management proactivity, which counterbalances partners' reactivity towards external and internal organisational changes, is the result of professional managers giving added value to a partnership or firm.

3.6 Efficiency rules

The economic crisis of the late 2000s radically and forever changed partners' visions of the administrative support function and their understanding of professional managers' roles in legal business development and management. Then COVID-19 came along.

The pandemic has shown how even a good and effective operational support system should not be carved in stone. There is room for change at any moment. Some administrative functions disappeared completely. Many firms laid off dozens of secretaries and assistants. Others had to rely on experienced external service providers to meet increased service demands. Some of these functions were critical if a law firm wanted to be able to continue to delivery services profitably, at a competitive price and during a time when in-house service delivery capabilities were compromised. Information technology, innovation, business process design and practice-area specific services in intellectual property and large-volume document review are some examples.[1] Business development, marketing and client relations instruments went through a complete overhaul, as most of the traditional networking tools and methods were quarantined and appeared to be unavailable.

Partners immediately realised that to change their firm operational model literally overnight while simultaneously managing the growing demand on legal services was an impossible task without professional managers. The pandemic has once again revolutionised partners' thinking by shifting the paramount importance of legal business efficiency from a business school concept to an immediate concern. Moreover, such a change in the agenda has affected the vast majority of law firms, if not all, regardless of their size, length of time in business or geographical location.

The eternal debate about whether the delivery of legal services should be an honourable mission or a business has moved into the arena of optimisation of implementation costs and adaptation to the new rules of the game, dictated by clients and a search for totally new ways of business development to win opportunities in the toughened competition.

'Doing a good job', in general, has ceased to be a competitive advantage. Most law firms now do a 'good job' for their clients. To support competitive advantage, a 'job well done' must now be efficiently organised (in response to budget pressure from clients) and effectively sold (due to the increased competition among law firms). It has also become harder for many firms to keep and develop their accumulated human resources. Addressing this challenge without the professional support of marketers, financiers (and not just accountants), HR specialists and other highly skilled professionals is an unrealistic strategy and a foolish risk.

Sceptical senior lawyers may argue that they can provide or acquire the new knowledge and skills themselves. This is a good argument in favour of partners' and senior associates' 'soft skills', which should be an integral part of their professional development and are important for understanding and managing

1 See, for example, Norman Clark (ed), *Outsourcing of Core Legal Service Functions: How to Capitalise on Opportunities for Law Firms* (Globe Law and Business, 2021) pp5–15 for an analysis of the business case for outsourcing of tasks and functions traditionally performed in-house in law firms.

their business. Several partnerships have gone this way but have lost sight of two important factors.

The first is time. The second is an integrated, full-scale vision of a firm's operations in contrast to a limited and narrow vision of a practice group or practice. Therefore, the timely engagement of external expertise – in the form of full-time, in-house businesspeople or services from external consultants – can be a wise investment in the business.

3.7 The evolving business support function

Market changes and their increasing pace have meant that business support professionals working in law firms are taking on new tasks and facing new requirements in terms of the quality of their service and their professional expertise.

First, professional management must not just perform qualitative functional activities in their area of competence, but also have additional experience in, at least, implementing systemic changes in organisations and managing change within a corporate culture.[2]

Second, the time for acquiring such knowledge has significantly reduced. On the one hand, this is a positive tendency to align the pace of fee earners' professional development with that of non-fee earners; this reduces the notorious communication gap between front and back offices. On the other hand, not all specialists have the time (or the desire or opportunity, due to different reasons and limitations) to progress in their development according to a firm's expected pace. As has been mentioned above, proactivity and outsourcing are important prerequisites for the success of a firm in today's competitive environment; they lead to the natural rotation of the business support team in a period of three to five years.

As a rule, small and medium-sized firms are proud of low staff turnover and are sensitive to news of a 'natural turnover', which should be taken as a new paradigm for the majority of proven staff. In practice, however, during a planned change process, partners quickly become resigned to the idea of staff turnover. There are exceptions to the general rule, but they are rare.

In order to deal with this situation and buck the trend of high staff turnover, partners must radically change two things: the firm's approach to administrative staff evaluation and investment in managers' development.

A regular audit of the business administrative support system and its staff is a prerequisite for a firm's sustainability and future success. Unfortunately, firms often neglect such a simple tool as the annual evaluation of personnel, applying it only to fee earners. So, by their own hand, partners create a 'blind' or 'shadow' zone in their business.

---

2 For further discussion, see the "Leading change" chapter of this book.

Investment in the business support team's development is just as important for a firm's success as the legal team's professional development. Certainly, responsibility for their own professional development should be taken by lawyers and managers themselves. But it is in the interests of a firm to help its team with its development, rather than leaving one person alone with this challenge. With coordinated efforts by employees and employers, this will be a win-win situation.

Summing up these two points, if professional managers' development drifts along by itself, it threatens to become at least a non-systemic and, accordingly, inefficient investment. The lack of a systemic approach and, instead, intuitive guessing of each employee's and administrative team's potential creates a vicious circle of problems directly affecting business development as a whole. In such firms, one hears observations such as the following:

- "We do not know people properly and we do not understand when they need assistance and support in their development."
- "The lack of systemic development of staff means we need to change team members."
- "The team's performance is not sustainable; its efficiency decreases and business processes are affected."
- "The firm's progress is stretched in time; the development itself is in spurts, being artificially limited by particular specialists' level of expertise."

Identifying legal 'stars' and searching for future partners are accepted by partners as natural and are included in partners' agendas by default. The inclusion of screening of future stars on the administrative team's agenda is a pledge for both team and business sustainability.

3.8 Skills expected of business managers

In addition to professional skills in their respective areas of responsibility – such as accounting, HR management or technology – effective business managers in law firms are today expected to demonstrate sophisticated expertise and management skills such as:

- an advanced level of understanding of law firm economics, including advanced skills of financial analysis and forecasting;
- an understanding of the main components of legal project management;
- risk management in the special business environment of law firms; and
- a practical understanding of how to build and support resilience in organisations.

Partners' major expectations of their professional managers (both internal team members and external providers) can be summarised in three main points:

- Professional management should release partners' time for their main business responsibilities – providing client services of the highest quality and developing new business.
- Professional management should deliver a return on investment; otherwise, it is an inefficient use of the firm's resources and, ultimately, the partners' profits.
- The quality of the administrative services provided should build satisfaction and confidence in their internal clients in the firm.

4. Keystone 3: Choose the right model for your firm

4.1 Managers, directors and C-suite executives

When opening a new administrative position, it is important to check on the following points:

- the level of specialist that will be sufficient to cover the current needs of the firm;
- the development prospects of this functional area for the next one to five years; and
- whether this professional should be hired from in-house or whether it is possible to cover the firm's needs with an external provider.

This avoids mutual disappointment, in terms of both expected results and the level of the person's professional engagement.

The starting level of a law firm management system is characterised by the presence of professionals of 'manager' status or below. As a rule, these are good technical specialists in their field who perform their assignments qualitatively and in a timely fashion. However, their vision is significantly limited by their direct functions and current tasks. The leading role in setting goals, perspective and strategic planning at this stage is carried out entirely by the partners.

At the next stage of evolution, functional directors start heading a team of professionals. Partners' leadership in functional processes is significantly reduced; directors are responsible for planning and the effective implementation of tasks assigned to their teams. Partners' workloads in coordinating certain areas are also reduced. These assignments are also taken by directors and it is quite common to have a position of executive director. However, the overall picture of the business is still concentrated in the partners' minds. Functional directors do not always have a complete vision of this picture. Moreover, information about cause-and-effect relationships between partners' decisions and perspectives for the firm's development prospects are not always available to them.

Such an information and communication gap occurs for two reasons:

- Partners do not always verify their decisions in alignment with the

strategic direction of the firm's development and they often therefore make their decisions based on short-term tactics; and
- Partners do not always trust the delegation of purely tactical decisions about operational issues to their functional directors and they keep a minor element of manual control over those functions.

Coordination between partners and functional managers tends to be performed by a firm's managing partner, combining these responsibilities with his or her other responsibilities such as partnership issues and executive functions.

In law firms that are undergoing a 'corporatisation' to their business management structure, there is often a point at which the management acquires features of a large corporation and 'C-suite' executives (ie, chief executives) begin to appear in the organisational chart.

As a result, partners' and professional managers' roles significantly change. First, the pattern of preparing and making decisions by strategic partners radically changes. Second, the communication gap between partner-owners and C-suite managers is eliminated. Third, preparing and explaining cause-and-effect relationships in decision making is heavily shifted to the professional managers' side. And fourth, partners exclude themselves from the firm's operational activities, which become the full responsibility of professional managers.

Partners remain responsible for making strategic decisions about the firm's development, which are then worked through and prepared by relevant professionals.

Along with the management team evolution, a linguistic revolution occurs, from a simple 'support staff' or 'administrative support' to a 'back office' and, beyond that, to a sophisticated 'business support team'. It is obvious that, even from a linguistic point of view, this evolution reflects a significant shift in work approach, scopes of authority, decision making and overall business management, as well as a change in the overall perception of the business leaders.

4.2 The chief operating officer as an operational integrator

My first encounter with the role of COO in a law firm was through an American Bar Association (ABA) book published 1996. Even back then, the authors noted that "there are many strategic issues affecting the way in which law practices typically resulting in the COO's role going beyond a neatly demarked range of the non-legal operations, per se".[3]

3 Caroline Thornlow (ed), *Professional Managers in the Law Office* (American Bar Association, 1996) Chapter 5, pp33–38.

In the early 2010s, a senior management role was the prerogative of large international law firms. However, there has been steady interest among small and mid-sized law firm partnerships in establishing COO roles over the past seven to eight years. This is foreseen as a boost to the efficiency of a firm's operations.

This role is also considered as integrating the legal and non-legal sides of a firm. Every partnership has its own meaning of 'integration'. Thus, the COO's job descriptions and duties will differ from firm to firm. Still, they all have something in common: one more commander in chief along with a managing partner with a holistic vision of the firm's ecosystem.

There are few essential issues to be considered by partners thinking of establishing a COO role in their firm:

- Strategy is and should remain the prerogative of the partners. The task of a COO is to provide a smooth transformation from the partners' strategic plans to tactics and daily operations. Needless to say, it's expected to be done in the most efficient and effective way.
- A senior manager's appearance in a team will either lead to serious transformations in the administrative support within a firm or create an urgent need for such a transformation. It is the COO who is responsible for the firm's business support architecture, the allocation of functions at the firm-wide and office level, and the prioritisation of projects to improve the firm's operations. Partners are better at listening to these recommendations instead of imposing their views or appealing to the historical context ("We used to do it this way here" or "We are used to it here" or "This is how things are done here").
- If your firm is a multi-office one, this is a serious indication for the introduction of a firm-wide COO role. One of the vital skills for the COO of a multi-office law firm is the ability to integrate the firm's function and locations.
- It is critically important to make a clear statement about the partners' expectations from the COO position, as well as managing the COO's professional expectations. It is also paramount to disseminate information about the introduction of such a role in the firm and get feedback from the team. This might reveal new and useful information to the partnership about this position in particular and the firm's internal challenges in general.
- An important aspect is the coordination of work between the functional director (eg, a chief HR officer) and the partner currently carrying the functional load (whether formally designated as a HR partner or informally assigned those responsibilities), as well as their coordination with the firm's COO.
- Key skills for the COO role include coordination, proper communication

and strong implementation skills, plus problem solving and a client-oriented attitude.

- Under no circumstances should the COO be involved in partnership issues and relations, such as promotions, remuneration, lawyer evaluations and conflicts of interest.
- The COO should be invited to partners' meetings in a consultative or advisory capacity.
- The role of a COO in smaller firms can be combined with other senior managerial roles, such as that of a chief finance officer.

The most frequent risks in the teamwork between the partnership and the COO teamwork are the inevitable grey areas in responsibilities and decision making. It might be a good exercise to examine the firm's current organisational chart and consider how a new position fits into it and in what ways it influences decision making. These drawings have proven to be very useful. In addition, a firm-wide decision-making matrix could be designed and approved in order to avoid the risks that these grey areas might cause or aggravate.

There are a few other risks; but these are manageable, such as:

- unclear expectations from both sides (partners and the COO);
- overwhelming one person with two or more separate functions;
- creating an unnecessarily bureaucratic process; and
- a lack of communication among people who have a stake in the decision.

Finally, there are a variety of different models of the COO function within the law firm. Partners should thus consider which model not only meets the firm's needs now, but also is most likely to continue to do so in the foreseeable future (ie, up to the next five years).

4.3 Business support structural models

In 2012, J Weissmann wrote that: "Large law firms are hampered by two things: Their structure and their culture."[4] It would be fair to add: "… as well as their business support structure and culture of partners relations with their senior managers."

One of the most important starting points in the formation of a firm's business support structure is the vision of the managing partner's role and how this vision will be realised, as illustrated below.

4 J Weissmann, "Why Law Firms are Rigged to Fail", *The Atlantic*, 31 May 2012, www.theatlantic.com/business/archive/2012/05/why-law-firms-are-rigged-to-fail/257843/.

(a) ***Full-time managing partner/CEO + COO***

This is the preferred option when decisions about problems and the management of partners' relations are a major part of the workload.

In this case, the position of a COO in a firm's management structure could be:

- an advantage, if the managing partner and COO complement each other in management capacities and personal characteristics. The combined strengths of two individuals can significantly strengthen a firm's internal management structure; or
- a disadvantage, if the COO acts as an intermediary between the managing partner and other members of the administration team, becoming an unnecessary extra link in the managerial communication chain.

Partners frequently rotate the position of full-time managing partner (often every two to three years) to mitigate the impact on the managing partner's legal practice. Therefore, in this scheme, the specific role of COO is also to provide effective support to a newly elected managing partner, while the partner adapts to the new position (see Figure 1).

Figure 1. Business support functions are supervised by COO

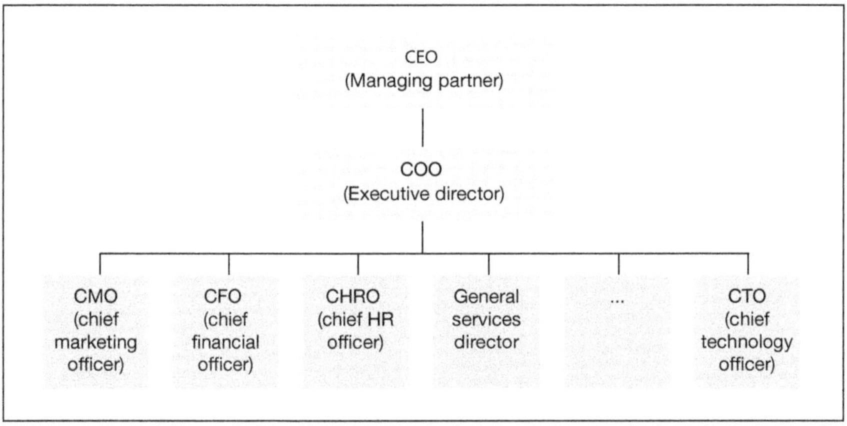

(b) ***Practising managing partner + COO***

Recruiting a COO when there is a practising managing partner in most cases creates additional competitive advantages for a firm.

The main efforts of a COO in this scheme could focus on one of two areas:

- execution, which is a managerial function aimed at the achievement of goals set by the partnership. The most effective way to accomplish this is through the direct subordination of the functional C-suite team to the COO; or

- change management, which is a leadership function requiring the professional manager to be a change agent (see Figure 2). The ideal condition for the realisation of this function is a linear subordination of all C-suite team members to the managing partner.

Figure 2. COO focuses on coordination and implementation of firm's projects (project titles are given as examples)

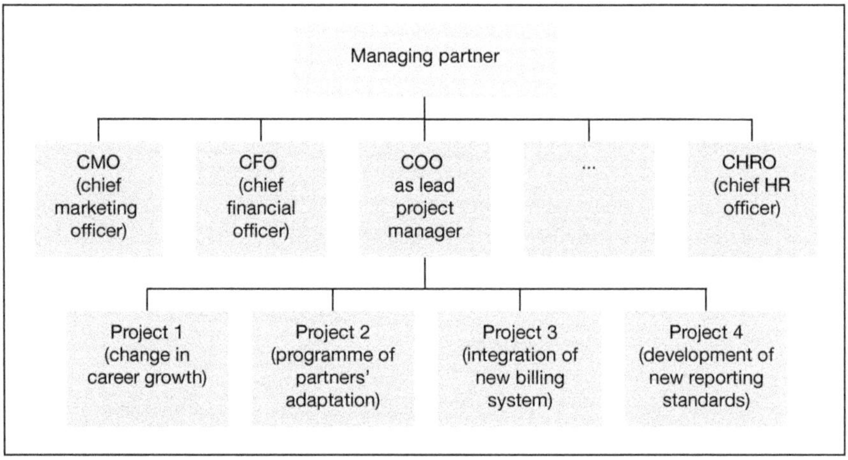

Added value for the partnership and firm would come from the COO implementing an adaptation function as well as a managerial or leadership function:

- to introduce laterally hired partners to the business;
- to raise partners' awareness of the status of changes occurring in business; and
- to help young, newly promoted partners to adapt to their new roles and assist them in finding their unique niche in the existing partnership.

In all the variations listed above, the COO role has a serious mentoring component. For a professional manager in this position, this component requires not only a high level of managerial professionalism and an in-depth understanding of legal business operations, but also partners' trust, knowledge of group interaction psychology, skilled use of technology and effective techniques for implementing changes.

(c) ***Managing partner (CEO and COO) + functional managers***

Regardless of whether an exempt or practising partner manages the firm, a model could be selected in which all functions (including operational) are linearly aligned with each other and report directly to the managing partner.

The business support team could include an operational director or general services director or, more likely, an administrative director. This director's role would likely focus on mentoring or the direct implementation of specific projects that are important to the firm's development at this stage (see Figure 3.)

Monitoring compliance with policies and procedures, keeping track of their relevance and proposing further improvements or radical change where necessary should also be the exclusive competence of an operational, executive or administrative director.

Figure 3. General services director covers essential office management functions

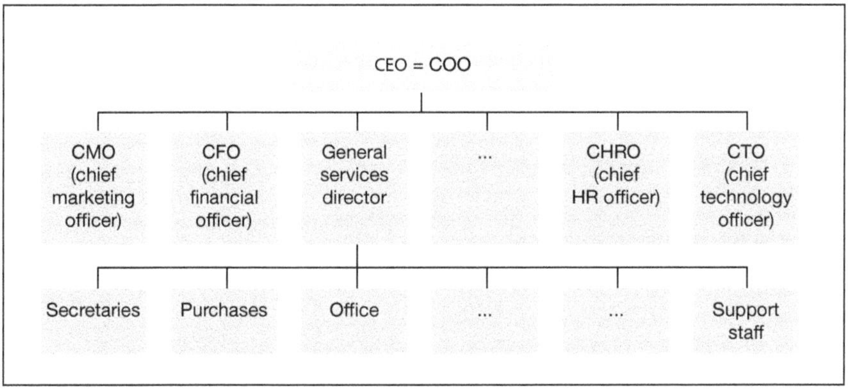

4.4 A few words about leadership

Besides purely professional and functional actions, a firm's employees can be 'partners' in leadership and serve as good role models. These expected 'partner behaviours' include:

- having a long-term vision that will ensure the safety, security and continued existence of the business in the future;
- leading by example, overcoming professional and personal difficulties on a daily basis and thereby confirming the right to continue to be considered a leader in the firm; and
- supporting the firm's corporate culture and values, functioning as 'carriers' of a firm's 'cultural DNA' by demonstrating its values and supporting morale.

How a managing partner and other partners perform these roles frames a portrait of a leader of the firm as perceived by the employees. It will be a benchmark that is followed by the younger generation of lawyers and that frames the behavioural patterns of the firm's future partners.

If hired managers are involved in business management, participate in strategic decision making and acquire responsibilities for the successful tactical implementation of these strategic decisions, their work habits and personal characteristics will have a positive influence on every part of the firm.

If it is accepted that such a 'leadership portrait' is not only about the partners, but also an example for non-partners, the partners will not always have to decide their business problems by themselves, but will be able to take feedback and different points of view from others in the firm. These standards can thus produce a basic list of criteria to use in recruiting highly qualified professionals, both lawyers and non-lawyers.

This is a rather serious mental transformation that partners might need to go through in order for their business to thrive. The results of this transformation will define what the firm eventually gets: a successful management team that operates at the highest levels with the trust of the firm's partners; or the always-anxious administrators who try to manage in an environment in which they will never be seen as equals.

4.5 New kids on the block

(a) Chief innovation officer

According to PwC's Law Firms' Survey, 70% of top law firms now have strategy and innovation roles.[5] It is logical to spin off these roles from the COO functions to manage a massive volume of changes taking place simultaneously. On the one hand, these changes are being initiated by law firms themselves, to resolve internal issues and boost productivity. On the other hand, they are being forced by transformations within clients' internal business processes. And finally, they are being dictated by the market itself searching for operational excellence and the opportunities that legal tech development has opened up for law firms.

These changes are often not part of the general strategy. They could be introduced spontaneously and sporadically as a local response to a particular internal issue. Being layered one on top of the other, in an improvised fashion, many of them might never lead to desired results. What is needed for them to succeed is a strategic vision, not firefighting tactics.

As mentioned, the challenge to change is the main challenge that law firms faced before COVID-19; it escalated during the pandemic and remains even more relevant in today's post-pandemic world.

A totally logical step would be to on-board a professional who has a 'helicopter view' of change and seeks innovations that are beneficial for the firm. Needless to say, this person must have a record of carrying out complex and complicated changes successfully.

---

5 Annual PwC Law Firms' Survey 2019, *Adapting to a New World*, p6. The figure refers to the top 100 law firm by annual global fee income.

(b) *Chief technology officer*

This position is far from being brand new in law firms. But its momentum has increased due to COVID-19 – and not only due to the need to organise remote work for companies in a short timeframe. There are two other important factors that make the chief technology officer (CTO) role critical for law firms.

The first is to ensure sustainable business growth. According to PwC, 80% of the top 10 law firms have identified technology as the key challenge to growth in the next two years.[6] The second is to provide an adequate response to cyberattacks and data breaches. The statistics on cyberattacks and data breaches in law firms are stunning:

- The costs associated with data breaches rose from $3.86 million to $4.35 million on average globally from 2020 to 2022, according to a report recently released by IBM;[7]
- 25% of law firms in the United States suffered from data breaches in 2021;[8] and
- According to the ABA's 2021 technology survey, solo and small firms continue to lag behind larger firms when it comes to their tech budgets, with only 43% of solo firms and 50% of small firms responding that they budget for technology, compared to 65% of larger firms.[9]

Technology will continue to play a crucial role for law firms. Technologies themselves are continuing to develop at a tremendous pace. Do not be surprised to see the COO and CTO roles evolve into a new joint operations and technology role.

(c) *Chief pricing officer*

This is a relatively new role and is still rare. However, three factors suggest that it will grow in importance:

- alternative fee arrangements, which are going mainstream as technology improves legal project management;
- client pressure on fees combined with intense competition in the market; and
- data-driven decisions in the big data era.

---

6 Annual PwC Law Firms' Survey 2021, *Facing the Future with Confidence*, p20.
'Top 10 law firms' here means the top 10 global law firms headquartered in the United Kingdom, ranked by annual fee income (www.pwc.co.uk/industries/legal-professional-business-support-services/law-firms-survey.html).

7 IBM Annual Cost of a Data Breach Report, *How Much Does a Data Breach Cost in 2022?*, featuring research by Ponemon Institute based on breaches data in 17 countries in 17 industries (www.ibm.com/security/data-breach).

8 ABA Legal Technology Survey Report, 2021 *Cybersecurity*, 22 December 2021 (www.americanbar.org/groups/law_practice/publications/techreport/2021/cybersecurity/).

9 *Ibid.*

Having a chief pricing officer appears to be especially attractive to large law firms: a 2019 report by PwC revealed that 63% of the top 100 firms had pricing specialists on their teams.[10] Demand for this expertise is growing among a majority of market players.

4.6 In-house or outsource?

The three roles discussed above could easily be afforded by a large multi-office law firm. But what is the solution for small and mid-sized firms? How can these law firms find the right balance of in-house expertise and outsourced services to cover their evolving needs? This is not an easy question to answer. Even an overview of the issue could be the subject of a separate thorough study.[11]

There are several reasons why this issue is addressed here.

The outsourcing industry has expanded dramatically over the past decade. There is now a much wider offering to efficiently distribute workload between internal and external specialists.

The pandemic pushed law firms to conduct a full-scale overhaul of their operational approaches. In light of the hybrid working mode that has since emerged, there has been a shift away from the previous approach of enlisting external consultants either for simple and clearly structured work or for unique expertise. Now the engagement of external providers often involves their full or partial integration into the firm's existing business processes. Thus, the business support functions themselves become hybrid.

The management of outsourced services must observe two principles to produce the desired results. First, the roster of a firm's needs covered by outsource providers should be regularly reviewed and updated. The panel of providers should also be revised. New players and new offers are appearing every day. Experienced managers sooner or later get tired of working in-house. They often join the outsourcing market, offering their services to a wider range of firms. In emerging markets, a cohort of external consultants is replenished by retired partners. Consulting is one of the career alternatives for them if they still have the energy and passion to share their wisdom with the younger generation of partners.

Moreover, there is a need for control over the effectiveness of interaction between the in-house team and external specialists. As this market develops, the relationship between external and internal specialists gains some characteristics of competition and resembles the relationship between general counsel and law firms. Managing partners and COOs should keep an eye on the issue to avoid minor pitfalls, possible individual misunderstandings, hoarding of work or malpractice issues.

---

10 PwC (n 5), p6. The figure refers to the top 100 law firm by annual global fee income.

11 See Clark (n 1) pp10–13, for an example of an analytical method to identify internal functions that could be high priorities for outsourcing.

Obviously, there is no one size that fits all. Although there are general pros and cons to outsourcing, the best solutions are firm specific.

5. Keystone 4: Sharing responsibilities

In the ideal law firm, lawyers would provide the legal services and professional managers would manage the business. However, for better or worse, the reality is different. It is shaped by the role of trust issues inside the firm and clients' expectations about having partners deeply involved in their matters.

As outlined earlier, any grey areas in dividing duties or overlap in responsibilities could impact on the effectiveness of the management system. Obviously, the main concerns involve coordinating the activities of partners with functional duties and the functional directors.

To start, partners must separate two concepts: the leadership within their firms and the management of their business.

It is not news to anyone that some firms prefer to assign certain functional responsibilities, such as executive oversight of human resources (HR) functions, to partners. Other firms create committees for various internal issues, such as a business development committee, a legal tech committee or a diversity committee. These have been useful and welcome for many years. The only reservation here is that these approaches work best when professional managers collaborate in management decisions rather than having decisions imposed on them.

Clearly, a functional partner is not an arbitrator or a decision-making machine, but rather a pilot through a world of partnership decision making, translating the decisions and their implications into actions in practical terms that the business staff understand.

There are five key areas in which partners and professional managers cooperate:

- strategic planning and execution;
- monitoring the effectiveness and efficiency of the firm's operations;
- shaping the firm's business support functions and supervising those activities;
- risk management and mitigation; and
- being a positive role model for the firm's business management and administrative teams.

It is important to identify four scenarios within each of the abovementioned areas:

- Equity partners make the final decision, but do not take part in its implementation (eg, approval of the company's annual budget);
- Partners are involved in both the decision-making and implementation processes (eg, mid-year budget review or other budget amendments);
- Partners are not involved in decision making, but are direct participants in the business process (eg, a firm's billing cycle); or

- Partners distance themselves from both decision making and implementation (eg, the calculation and payment of taxes).

Mapping your key business processes along with responsible actors will give you a clear and useful matrix. This is the firm-wide decision matrix mentioned in section 4.2. It is an example from my recent mandates. The client is a leading local firm (full service, 10 years in the market, 120-plus employees and described as 'tech-savvy'). The main business processes of the company and their specifications are represented in Table 1.

Table 1. Law firm main business processes and their specifications

Strategic planning	Strategy development
	Budgeting
	Pricing
Strategic execution	Business continuity
	Budget execution
	New projects
	Risk management
Knowledge and business development	Knowledge management
	Business development
	Marketing strategy
Client relations	Client care
	Quality control
	Conflict management

continued on next page

HR	Hiring and integration
	Remuneration
	Learning and development
	Evaluation and promotions
	Separation
Communication	External
	Internal
Information technology	New services
	Release management
	Investments
	Problem solving
Assets management	Office premises
	Fixed assets
Monitoring and control	Quality control
	Firm-wide reporting (monthly basis)
	Annual reporting
Adjustments and improvements	Strategy/goals amendments
	Budget execution

The firm's management structure includes functional directors, the head of operations (as a senior management role) and practice leaders. The highest managerial body is the equity partners' committee.

Here is how accountability is distributed in the management team – for example, in the "Strategic execution" section.

Table 2. Strategic execution

		Equity partners	Practice leaders	Head of operations	Functional directors
Business continuity	Firm-wide operations			X	
	Practices		X		
	Business support			+	X
Budget execution	Corrections (within approved budget) – legal practices		X		
	Corrections (within approved budget) – business support			X	
	Carry forwards within the annual budget – legal practices		X		+
	Carry forwards within the annual budget – business support			X	+
	Excess over annual budget	X			
New projects	Launches within approved annual budget			X	
	Launches over approved annual budget	X			
Risk management	Conflict check	X			
	Security	X		+	
	Emergencies	X		+	

(X) role in charge; (+) in coordination with

To monitor the performance of a particular function, it is necessary to introduce key performance indicators (KPIs) for the main expected results by time periods (eg, quarter/year) or by a specific project. This approach will motivate partners and top management not to fall into micromanagement, but to judge success or failure in accordance with an agreed matrix.

Partners and professional managers, each within their areas of authority and responsibility, contribute through their activities to the functioning of the firm as an integrated organism. This organism has its own dynamics, external and internal. These dynamics must be carefully observed and analysed. The results of ongoing changes should be measured and considered as a possible indicators for further improvements. How should one distribute efforts and share responsibility in such a complex situation?

6. Keystone 5: Track your dynamics

The intra-organisational dynamics among today's legal market players have dramatically intensified due to the need for serious internal debugging and adaptation to the post-COVID-19 environment.

Undoubtedly, partners need a reliable instrument to track and manage their firm's dynamics. Günther Mohr,[12] a specialist in intra-organisational dynamics, proposes a model that, on the one hand, clearly accentuates and highlights priorities for leadership. On the other hand, this model includes a step-by-step guide to setting goals and understanding the role of professional managers in law firms. This model has particular value for the fast-changing world of today's legal market.

Figure 4. Organisation (law firm) as a dynamic system

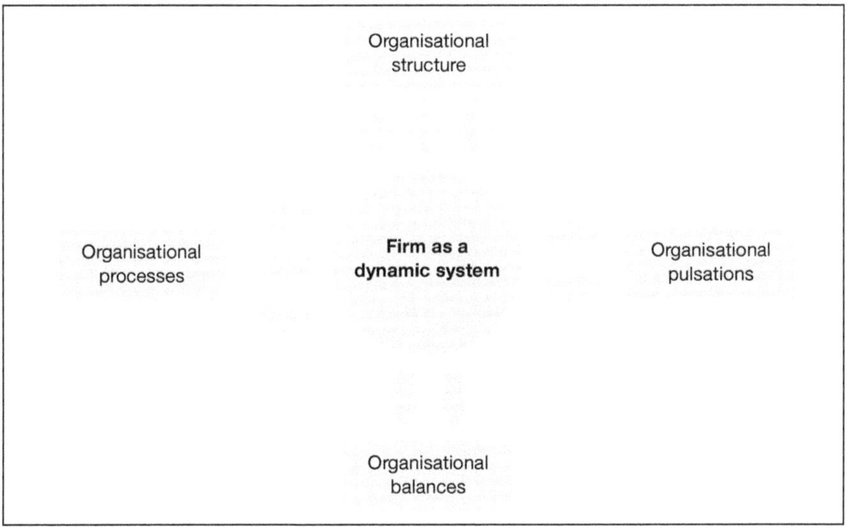

12 Günther Mohr, "Dynamic Organisational Analysis", in Günther Mohr and Thomas Steinert (eds), *Growth and Change for Organizations: Transactional Analysis – New Developments – 1995–2006* (International Transactional Analysis Association, 2006).

Today, a law firm of any size is a complex and highly organised body. Elements of this body, caused by interplay and interaction with the outside world (customers, competitors and the market in general), can be divided into four major groups (see Figure 4):

- organisational structure;
- organisational processes;
- organisational balances; and
- organisational pulsations.

Partners and professional managers are undoubtedly involved in all of these elements and influence the dynamics of the system as a whole. To effectively manage these dynamics, it is important to determine who leads and who assists in each dynamic process.

This is exactly when confusion arises. There are two reasons for this:

- Partners are not ready to give leadership to functional specialists and become implementers and conductors of the professionals' solutions for the benefit of a common goal; and
- Professional managers are not ready to take responsibility for decision making in the spheres of their respective professional competencies.

Either of the above reasons can have a negative impact on overall business effectiveness and can lead to the deceleration of a firm's development and a failure to compete.

6.1 Organisational pulsations

I am convinced that partners' leadership should be focused exclusively on the dynamics of organisational pulsations and, above all, on external fluctuations (see Figure 5).

The slightest changes in the pulse of the external environment (clients, competitors or both) should be recognised and flagged with the appropriate business professionals (eg, financiers, business development specialists, HR specialists).

For instance, partners' observations of changes in pricing policies should be immediately studied by a firm's specialists (potentially in collaboration with external consultants), to propose recommendations to the partners to change the pricing policies when offering services.

The value of this dynamic interaction lies in offering a new approach to pricing services before a client demands it. A proactive approach puts a firm, at a minimum, on an equal footing in discussions with clients; by contrast, reactivity can put the firm in a disadvantageous bargaining position.

Figure 5. Key elements of the organisational dynamic

Pulsations	Structure	Balances	Processes
Internal	Attention	Long-term strategic vision and short-term tactics	Communication processes
External	Roles	Recursivity	Problem-solving procedures
	Relations		Motivation, remuneration & celebration of success processes

As well as any internal changes, parallels identified outside the firm should be analysed. A classic example is employees leaving the firm. This can be an indicator of various shortcomings in the HR policy – for example, the lawyers lack interesting work or the level of remuneration is less than that of competitors. This internal pulsation should contribute to the partners' more sober assessment of the firm's position in the employment market and, consequently, to a review of its approaches to business development.

In maintaining efficient dynamics for the remaining areas – organisational structure, processes and balance – delegating leadership to professional management is the most effective approach.

6.2 The organisational structure

The dynamics of an organisational structure are defined by:

- attention;
- roles and role models; and
- relations.

An old English proverb says: "Energy goes where thought flows." You get what you focus on. To draw partners' attention to specific aspects of the business or changes taking place is one of a professional manager's missions. As mentioned above, partners are not always in the best position to prioritise their attention and focus on the main issues for the business, due to a conflict of interest and the need to combine a business role and business ownership with the role of a primary productive force.

Securing roles in the partnership undoubtedly falls within the partners' exclusive competence. However, it is within a professional manager's competence to give recommendations on how to organise this effectively. This means considering the firm's needs and expectations in conjunction with a particular partner's needs and role model qualities. Again, this assessment requires knowledge and skills specific to professional HR specialists.

While evaluating existing effective connections and relationships and accompanying business processes, it is important to remember why pavements were built at the Ford car plant: putting asphalt on paths made it more convenient for people to get around. Taking into account the fact that even very large systems are inherently prone to self-organisation and building quality internal links, the task of management has been and remains to continually watch out for the moment when a relationship established over many years ceases to be most effective and needs operational change. After all, time is money and permanent efficiency improvement is a competitive advantage in the market.

6.3 Organisational balances

The maintenance of an organisational balance refers to the sphere of mutual responsibility of partners and professional managers.

Two basic dynamics must be tracked and properly supported in order to keep an organisational balance:

- the dynamic balance of long-term vision and short-term tasks; and
- the homogeneity of vertical and horizontal structure and culture.

The first is a key and minimum requirement for a firm's sustainable development. The second is a guarantee of the organisation's integrity as a system.

Carrying out both of these tasks is a serious challenge for professional managers. Each partner in a particular situation is inclined to take more tactical wins here and now for his or her immediate benefit, as well as for the practice and a client, if a firm's policy specialists see no direct conflict of interest. This is a clear pattern of behaviour and is due to several factors, including client retention and the need to fulfil KPIs set for the practice and partners.

In this situation, professional managers are assigned to identify conflicts of interest and to assist partners in making a decision aimed at avoiding any compromise with the firm's main goals.

A no less complicated task for managers involves maintaining a high level of collegiality and cooperation in separate business units and the business in general on the one hand, while preserving the identity and uniqueness of each partner and his or her practice on the other, as a guarantee of diversity in perspectives, attitudes and methods used by a firm in its work. These are valued by clients and allow for different ways of working with different clients, depending on the industry, geography and compatibility of personalities. The sustainable improvement of service quality and systemic quality control itself can be realised within this framework.

6.4 Organisational processes

Last but not least are the dynamics of the three organisational processes:

- communication processes;
- problem-solving processes; and
- motivation, remuneration and 'celebration of success' processes.

Control over the dynamics and decision making in all of the abovementioned components should fall entirely within the hands of the firm's professional management. These processes illustrate the areas in the firm that should be regulated within the framework of formal policies and procedures. On this basis, the management's tasks can be depicted in a kind of cyclical process (see Figure 6).

Figure 6. Professional managers' tasks regarding policy and procedures for sustainable development

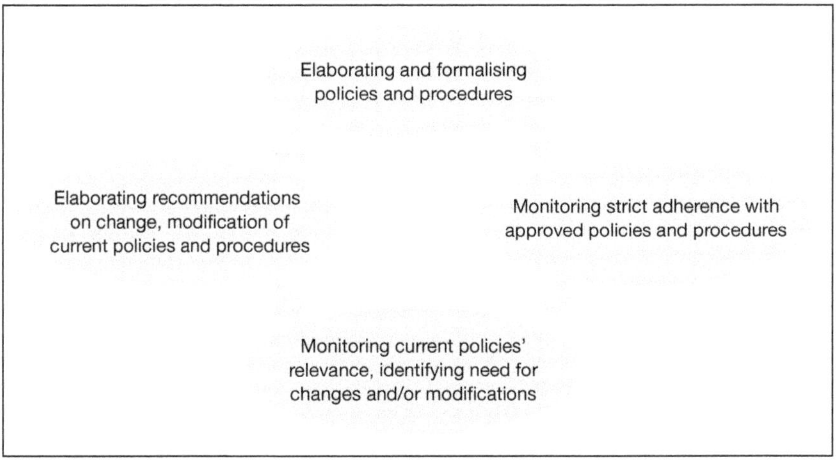

As paradoxical as it may sound to partners, their influence on this part of the organisational dynamics should be kept to a minimum; while the role of management in the dynamics should be kept to strict adherence to approved policies and procedures by all employees. Conveying this message to the partners and securing their buy-in is also the responsibility of professional management.

In summary, a confident approach to organisational matters in the context of constant internal dynamic changes can systematically manage and balance internal dynamics with external dynamics. Certainly, it positions a management professional among competitors trying to build a firm as someone mature and able to maintain a sustainable, familiar and comfortable organisational structure.

Perhaps another important distinguishing feature of the model as a whole is the opportunity for partners and senior managers to see their business from a new angle – through the prism of the process dynamics taking place in the firm – and identify new options for the firm's development and opportunities for new victories against the competition.

Your firm is analysed by your clients, considering not only the level of expertise when outsourcing advisers, but also the level of integrity, the business system and the ability to respond proactively and adapt internal processes to suit external changes.

7. Collaboration for a successful future

The rapidly changing market situation and new challenges that law firms constantly face do not allow partners to simultaneously maintain two adequate levels of focus on high-end quality on both professional and legal, services and managerial effectiveness. Thus, the presence of non-lawyer business professionals not simply to support the firm's operations, but to manage them in a professional manner is vital for an effective presence on the legal services market landscape.

Cooperation between partners and professional managers has never been, and will never be, a simple technical interaction. However, the success of this interaction between these two groups of intelligent, high-level professionals will determine the sustainability of your law firm now and into the future.

Leaders' insights on law firm governance

Norman K Clark
Walker Clark LLC

1. A virtual roundtable

Good governance in law firms is much more than having an up-to-date partnership agreement or corporate bylaws.

As we prepared this second edition of *Good Governance in Law Firms*, we invited a group of leaders from a diverse sample of law firms – ranging from a nine-lawyer boutique in Latin America to a 1,000-lawyer firm in India – to share their experiences and viewpoints on the role of governance in day-to-day operations as well as the grand strategic issues and opportunities. We have compiled their comments in the form of a 'virtual roundtable',[1] which sets the stage for the in-depth discussions of the detailed governance issues that follow in Part II of this book. Together, the members of this virtual roundtable – from large firms and smaller ones, and from different corners of the world – suggest opportunities for better decision making that can reach deep into the internal operations of a law firm, thereby strengthening the foundations for sustainable success in the future.

2. Participants and their firms

- **Borislav Boyanov** is the founder and managing partner of Boyanov & Company, a full-service commercial law firm based in Sofia, Bulgaria. The firm had 38 lawyers at the time of publication; is a member of the World Services Group, Legal Network International and Ius Laboris; is a founding member of the Southeast Europe Legal Group; and is active in the International Bar Association (IBA), the American Bar Association (ABA) and the International Trademark Association (INTA).
- **Ngoc Anh Bui** is the managing partner of VILAF, a full-service commercial law firm with offices in Hanoi and Ho Chi Minh City, Vietnam. The firm had 95 lawyers at the time of publication and is a member of the World Law Group.

1 The participants contributed information, opinions and comments in an online survey conducted in January 2023 by Walker Clark LLC. They had an additional opportunity to review this chapter and revise or extend their remarks before publication, and have consented to being quoted.

- **Hector de Leon, Jr** is the managing partner of SyCip Salazar Hernandez & Gatmaitan, a full-service commercial law firm headquartered in Manila, the Philippines, with additional offices in Cebu City, Davao City and the Subic Bay Freeport Zone. The firm had 140 lawyers and legal assistants at the time of publication. For the past several years SyCipLaw has been the only Philippine law firm with a Band 1 ranking from *Chambers* in all the relevant practice areas.
- **Anthony B Gioffre, III** is the managing partner of Cuddy & Feder LLP, a full-service commercial law firm based in White Plains, New York, with three other offices in the greater New York City area. The firm had 37 lawyers at the time of publication, many of whom are recognised thought leaders in their respective areas of expertise and have prominent leadership roles in bar associations and influential business organisations at the local, regional and national levels.
- **Oscar N Johnson, Jr, KC** is the co-managing partner of Higgs & Johnson, a full-service commercial law firm based in Nassau, The Bahamas, with three other offices throughout the country. The firm had 33 lawyers at the time of publication and is a member of TerraLex; its attorneys also have prominent positions in major international professional organisations such as the Center for International Legal Studies, the IBA, INTA and the Women's International Shipping and Trading Association.
- **Pedro Oller** is the founder and-managing partner of Oller Abogados, a boutique firm in San José, Costa Rica, whose nine lawyers (at the time of publication) specialise in providing public and corporate law services to major national and multinational enterprises. The firm is a member of Legalink and IR Global; and its lawyers are active in professional organisations such as the IBA and the ABA.
- **Cyril Shroff** is the managing partner of Cyril Amarchand Mangaldas, India's largest law firm with more than 1,000 lawyers across six offices in India and one in Singapore. He was named Managing Partner of the Year by ALB India in 2019 and 2022; and he and his colleagues have prominent roles in national and international professional associations.

Our seven participants represent a sample of the prevailing structures by which law firms worldwide are organised:

- Three of the firms are general partnerships;
- Two are limited liability partnerships;
- One is a limited liability company; and
- One is a hybrid structure under local law governing law firms (a registered corporation with unlimited liability of its partners and without registered capital).

All seven participants report that they have not changed the basic corporate structure of their respective firms from one form to another in the past 10 years.

3. Governance and decision making

Defining and managing the responsibilities for decision making are among the most important functions of governance in each of the seven firms represented at the virtual roundtable.

3.1 Which strategic, financial, or other major management decisions have been delegated to an executive, such as a managing partner or management board?

Boyanov: The managing partner is in charge of the day-to-day operations of the firm and the work of its lawyers and employees, and determines the monthly remuneration of the partners and lawyers based on specific criteria (key performance indicators).

The founding partner suggests to the partners the strategy and policy for the firm's development and operations, including for business development and partners promotion.

There is an option to create a formal management board. Currently, we have a *de facto* board which consists of a few active partners who share their views and ideas for the development of the firm. The opinions and views of other partners, employees and lawyers are also considered.

Bui: The managing partner is in charge of the day-to-day operation of the firm/office to ensure the smooth operation of the firm in order to maximise utilisation and efficiency. He also promotes coordination among the partners to initiate and discuss ideas and plans for the firm's operation and development. Business ideas are further discussed among the executive board before they are proposed to the full partnership for approval.

de Leon: Our executive committee (ExCom) has the powers of management and administration over the firm. The managing partner acts as chief executive officer. He or she carries out and puts into effect the policies and decisions of the ExCom.

Gioffre: Our firm is governed by a management group consisting of a managing partner and two management members. The management committee runs the day-to-day operations of the firm and makes decisions for the business to operate. Any major decisions or decisions that require expenditure of over a certain amount must be made by the partnership.

Johnson: The day-to-day management of the firm has been delegated to the managing partner.

Oller: We have delegated budget preparation to the chief financial officer (CFO), which is ratified by the partner committee; and the quality management programme to a committee comprised of partners, an associate, the CFO and the human resources director.

Shroff: The admission of partners, strategic acquisitions and the setting-up of new offices have been assigned to a management board. All day-to-day decisions are made by the managing partner.

3.2 Which major decisions are reserved to the partners, shareholders or owners of the firm?

Boyanov: The following decisions are reserved to the partners:

- changes to the firm statute;
- the acceptance and dismissal of partners;
- the transfer of shares;
- the election of the managing partner;
- the opening and closing of offices;
- mergers and acquisitions;
- approval of the budget;
- the annual report;
- distribution of the profits;
- real estate transactions;
- additional contributions to the capital; and
- other important decisions as provided by the law or an agreement among the partners.

Bui: The most important issues directly relating to:

- short-term and long-term development strategies;
- organisation;
- profit sharing;
- exclusive relations/partnerships;
- admission of new partners (including promotion from salary partner to equity partner);
- election of the managing partner(s) and executive board, if any; and
- the amendment of the partners' agreement and/or articles of association.

While it is advisable always to seek consensus on the decision making, it is also equally critical to limit or avoid deadlock situations in order to move forward, depending on the scale of the firm.

de Leon: The partners:

- elect the managing partner;
- elect the regular members of the ExCom (except in certain specified instances where the ExCom may select a replacement to fill an ExCom vacancy);
- vote on the admission of partners;
- vote on the expulsion of a partner; and
- vote on the dissolution of the firm.

Gioffre: All major decisions are reserved to the partners. The management committee runs the day-to-day operations of the firm and makes decisions for the business to operate. As previously mentioned, any major decisions or decisions that require expenditure over a certain amount must be made by the partnership.

Johnson: Policy decisions are reserved to the partners; and the partners have the residual right to arrive at a decision in respect of any matter.

Oller: Mergers, expansion and promotions are reserved to the partners.

Shroff: The partners make decisions about strategic tie-ups and changes to the compensation system.

3.3 To what extent have your firm's decision-making processes changed over the past 10 years?

Boyanov: They have not changed dramatically. In general, we discuss all issues and take unanimous decisions. We listen more to the younger lawyers and other professionals whom we work with. The firm implements more elements of the corporate management, including greater transparency and authorisation of different committees and groups to decide on certain issues.

Bui: It takes more time and effort to ensure full and active coordination and consultation when the number and seniority of partners increase and the firm grows in scale. The involvement of external professionals in relation to certain law firm management issues is used as a reference for partners.

de Leon: The firm's decision-making process has changed to the extent that the firm implements (and continues to implement) best practices in corporate governance. Examples include the following:

- The ExCom focuses on policies and strategies. To ensure that meeting time is used in the most productive way, items pertaining to policies and strategies are placed at the top of the agenda. With our recent revision of the firm's vision, mission and

strategic plan, there is now a clearer understanding of what the firm's priorities should be.
- In addition to the agenda for the ExCom meeting, the managing partner prepares a briefing paper containing information on the matters that will be addressed during the meeting, which is also sent to the ExCom members before the meeting. In this way, ExCom members can study the issues before the meeting, come prepared to the meeting and make well-informed decisions.
- There is more rigorous documentation of minutes of meetings, policies, processes and procedures.
- There is greater transparency given the sharing of more information with the partners and among the members of the ExCom.
- We have created a risk management committee to assist the ExCom in identifying and managing risks.

Gioffre: Our firm is proud to embrace a true partnership approach. The process has not changed over the last 10 years and neither have the voting rights.

Johnson: They have changed only to enable decisions of greater economic importance to be made by the managing partner, thus freeing up the partners to focus more on legal work.

Oller: We have decentralised most decisions that were focused on partners to the professional staff or committees.

4. Looking forward

4.1 What, if any, changes to your governance and decision-making processes will your firm need to make in order to continue to succeed over the next 10 years?

Boyanov: We have to improve and introduce new systems in order to:
- increase transparency and objectivity in decision making, including for performance assessments, the determination of remuneration and promotions;
- motivate lawyers and employees to play a more active role in working and business development processes, including management and decision making;
- hear the voices of people at all levels of the firm, including young professionals;
- create an ecosystem of partners from other professional sectors in order to satisfy the complex needs of clients; and

- promote the use of artificial intelligence (AI) and other legal tech solutions.

Bui: This is an ongoing and challenging task. Decision-making processes should be more transparent and criteria based. The involvement of experts/professionals on subjects such as AI and legal tech solutions will be needed to assist in the clarification and adoption of relevant policies by firm management.

de Leon: I expect that our governance and decision-making processes will remain the same in the coming 10 years. However, the firm will remain mindful of best practices in corporate governance. It will consider and adopt policies, procedures and processes to ensure accountability, transparency and effective management.

Gioffre: I don't anticipate that any governance or decision-making processes will need to change. I do anticipate, however, that there will be changes to certain operations or business procedures to address market realities and the changing business climate.

Johnson: We will need to continue to improve our decentralised decision making to become more efficient and effective in delivering services to our clients.

Oller: We are looking to implement a more inclusive decision-making process that allows partners and associates to participate, and allows staff to continue to submit their recommendations or make decisions in their specific fields of expertise.

Effective decision making in law firms

Sarah Martin
Martin & Levin; University of Oxford Saïd Business School; Meyler Campbell

---

The decisions that we make as individuals are a reflection of who we are and shape what we become. So it is with law firms. The culture of a firm and the face it shows to the market are the accumulated result of the decisions that its partners have made over the years.

Plenty of academic and business books offer models to help us with our decision making. The one thing we can be sure of is that there is no silver bullet and that decision making is in no small part a question of 'horses for courses'. This chapter aims to help you think through what tends to work best in practice and why, as well as the challenges and pitfalls. It focuses on the more behavioural aspects of decision making in law firms rather than on any formal procedures or governance structures.

I asked senior partners (SPs) from seven very successful law firms to talk about how they make their best decisions. They lead firms in Europe, the United States and Australia. Some of the firms are based in one country, while others are spread across the world, ranging in size from 75 to 200 partners. In their experience there are clearly some things that in practice generally help and other things that tend to hinder both a good decision-making process and arriving at a good outcome.

I was also curious to find out how they align their decisions with their firm's culture and what they want to project to clients, partners and staff about the firm. As one SP said: "Rightly or wrongly, leadership is judged by the quality of the decisions you make about people and strategy and how you handle crises."

It became clear that all law firm leaders can learn a lot from the wise, shared experience of the SPs I spoke to. I have summarised some of their individual viewpoints and most important insights towards the end of this chapter.

1. Decisions, decisions; so many variables

How a firm makes a decision and how well it turns out depend on a wide range of factors, including the type and size of firm, the style of leadership, the economic context and the type of decision. Different types of decision call for different approaches, depending on whether they are strategic, operational, value based, crisis driven and so on.

On the one hand, some of the firms invested a lot of time and resources into their strategic decision making, stating, "We think strategy matters." They mentioned several examples of the range of strategic decisions they had considered: whether to merge, and if so with whom; opening new offices; acquiring a new team; remuneration policy; reducing the number of partners; changing retirement age; and pensions.

However, on the other hand, several of the SPs felt that they made very few strategic decisions. In fact, one stressed that they sought to minimise the number taken:

We believe the fewer major decisions the better; fewer laterals and offices. There are other firms that are far larger and they may make more decisions and faster, but not necessarily good decisions. We have a very narrow strategic focus. We are not prompted to do anything about strategic decisions because our current work is so successful. The phrase "strategic imperatives" doesn't resonate with our partners. But we are one of the most profitable firms in our market, so we assume we must be doing something right by not making a lot of decisions. If you look at law firm profitability movement tracked against major decisions, it is not a good correlation.

In a people business like the law, most of the major decisions will be about the people, whether they are coming in or going out, getting promoted or remunerated or being assessed or supported. For many firms, the choice of new partners is their most important decision.

2. How does it work?

In short, the answer is that decision-making processes work in ways that differ hugely and have evolved to suit the particular firm's size, shape and needs.

Some firms have well-developed governance structures and swear by them: "We have a clear governance framework for the whole firm that provides for where the decision making might be and with whom we consult. It is incredibly helpful."

Others are more fluid: "Our processes are not very rigid; they evolve over time to meet new conditions."

Firms have created different governance structures to fit their context and needs. Some have elected positions for their leadership; others have appointments – some for fixed terms, others more flexible. Some have managing partners while others can't bear the title 'managing partner'. Some have executive teams or committees; others have strategy committees. Some have boards and some include external directors; most do not. Some have one partner, one vote; others have weighted voting rights – although hardly ever, it seems, is a decision taken by vote.

At the centre of those structures is a core group of leaders who often initiate the discussion on major decisions, collect the information and are in charge of the process.

3. What helps good decision making?

Among all these differences, it is not so easy to work out what really contributes to good decision making that is in the long-term interests of the firm. So, I asked the SPs: "What are the most common conditions that are conducive to your best decision making?"

Their answers are very varied. They have had quite different experiences and look at decision making through different lenses.

However, out of the variety, some clear themes emerged about achieving consensus, taking a long view, harnessing good processes and building in checks and balances.

It also became very clear that one major component weaves through everything. That component is consensus building and it is the best place to start.

3.1 Consensus

In practice, it's about taking and shaping views.

Law firms, for the most part, are still essentially a collection of owners. Their cultures and governance structures are very different from companies with CEOs and more hierarchical structures. The consequence is that any significant decision making will usually involve many people and often take a fair amount of time and effort. Sometimes it is a top-down initiative, while at other times it is bottom-up – but either way, consensus is the aim before the decision is made.

Our firm is still very consensus based; we would never simply announce a decision without building consensus first. Our policy is teamwork, consensus building and long-term focus.

Law firm leadership now is about managing people and getting them bought into the vision. Lawyers have to feel like part of the decision and that they have been heard. They need to feel part of the organisation; it takes a lot of time, like herding cats.

If I think we need x then I go out and find the person and make the case to the partnership. It creates legitimacy; everyone gets an opportunity to weigh in. Is it efficient? No!

It works because it is consensus driven. We only come to a decision when the outcome is already certain. It is rare that there are surprises. Things have percolated so much that we only get to a point of consideration when consensus has been reached.

3.2 Building consensus

(a) Appreciation of each other

At the core of the consensus-building process is mutual respect and trust. It involves a great deal of listening and emotional awareness to feel the reactions and the mood. Some leaders allow a reflection period so that everyone feels they could have spoken if they wished to.

> *What drives the firm is an appreciation of each other. We are all invested in the success of each other. I have a couch hour with each partner once a year – an intimate discussion. Our partnership team is a democracy. Certain opinion formers have louder voices than others, but it is all about finding a consensus, discussing and then reaching a conclusion. Is it efficient decision making? No. It's old-fashioned, but very powerful.*
>
> *Listening, so all feel heard and valued as an owner of the business.*
>
> *We have a full debate. As chair, I feel the mood of the room, seeking consensus, take views from all, put the proposal to the meeting and get a rumble of approval.*

(b) No surprises

To build mutual trust and confidence in the decision process, openness is seen by many as an essential ingredient. The importance of transparency in remuneration was emphasised by most.

> *Everything is open, especially on remuneration. The transparent governance system and testing views combine to create confidence and trust.*
>
> *We operate on a 'no surprises' basis, especially on remuneration. Everything is open. This reflects our firm culture: very open, loose, but some structure; partners are very engaged.*
>
> *We make good decisions on compensation – no surprises, deeply engaged, and based on values. There may be a few niggles on the outcomes, but people move on from it.*
>
> *Compensation decisions we do really well. It's a meritocracy. The system went out to all the partners, was well socialised and we got real engagement.*
>
> *Our compensation structure is modified lock-step; it is transparent, so we don't get resentment.*

(c) Persuasion and networks

The art of persuasion is a combination of the skills of the firm's leaders and the use of formal and informal networks. Both are central to the consensus-building exercise. You need to have a champion for the cause who can persuade, but also listen to criticisms and challenges and so improve the proposal.

You also need to find out through different channels where there may be unhappiness or unwillingness. It involves testing the water through the networks to shape the decision and using the feedback to help decide whether to proceed, amend or pull back. As firms grow and move away from their founding generation of partners, these networks become more important for their capacity both to persuade partners to engage and to help build the required trust that leaders are acting in the partners' best interests as a whole.

Telling a lawyer what to do will ensure disaster. It's about convincing people it was their idea. Lawyers are taught to question; they are cynical by nature; they prefer to say no and they don't like change. It is a blend of seeking input and selling the idea depending on the solidity of views of our strategy group.

Building consensus is done through informal networking with other partners, sometimes around practice heads if they are blocking things.

There is a lot of shuttle diplomacy; we want a sense of what the outcome will be. We don't encourage vote taking. In fact, we have never needed to take a vote. If one or two people feel very strongly about something, then it is probably time to back off.

It's good to use networks to know where your problems are and if you think certain partners will be troubled, deal with them first.

We have a chairman. It is not a decision-making role; it is about creating a consensus around a decision. It is fairly drawn out and involves 'hallway chatter' to identify who our opinion leaders are. It is slow and labour-intensive.

(d) Time

Everyone involved in leading the consensus building remarked on their own focus on effectiveness over efficiency. Several partners talked about iterations and the time involved. They recognised that their process takes time and tends to work best where most of the partners are in one place or at least one time zone.

This taking of time to build consensus has a built-in additional benefit for the quality of decision making. We return to this later when we look at the role cognitive biases can play in some major law firm decisions.

Our compensation structure is subjective. It takes 10 months because we interview all the partners.

It has taken five years to build consensus on letting people go.

New partners are a major decision. All partners are involved; there is a full debate. There are no committees. Two weeks later, we make a final decision. We build in reflection time. It doesn't change very much, but it builds in a check and balance on the first wave of decision making and everyone feels they could have spoken if they wished.

Lateral candidates meet with every one of the partners. This may be more typical in the United States.

Most of us started at the same place; this allows the culture to dominate.

Opening the office was three years in the making – building consensus, ensuring all potential pockets of resistance were addressed. It wasn't the firm, but rather certain individual partners saying, "The firm needs to do this," so it was a bottom-up initiative. We persuaded the chairman to recognise it and then finally put it to a vote and all agreed.

The board is responsible for strategic direction. We go through an exhaustive approach. In 2000, we engaged a management consultancy that conducted a one-on-one consultation with each partner. We review our strategy every three years and now have project groups following up on different aspects. We are looking at a range of issues: how you get more profitable, how you build excellence into your reputation, the globalisation of the legal market. Normally we take six months for this process.

(e) ***Fit with core values, culture and brand***

Many firms have put considerable energy into thinking about their values and culture through a highly consultative process. This exercise generates, among other things, a touchstone for decision making. It is like a roadmap or set of signposts that have already been widely canvassed so that decisions can be referenced against them.

Our firm has strong core values: teamwork, innovation, manners and excellence. I can share a couple of examples of good decisions we made using those values:

- *We decided to proceed with a litigation-only brand and pick specific areas of litigation. It was very brave. We passed on other work, but it has been a good decision. We were clear from our values about focus and excellence in our products and services.*
- *We recently considered a lateral hiring that would have been very profitable, but the candidate did not fit with some of our values on teamwork. It was not a difficult decision because it was about culture and fit. It is helpful to have signposts that people follow. We have already had the core values discussion so we wouldn't expect anyone to disagree with the decision.*

It is about core values and focusing on the right people, product and profitability. So many law firms are struggling because they are not offering the right product.

Decision making is a reflection of the firm's culture. There is a fair amount of legitimacy because of our size; we have a tremendous amount of buy-in. Reflection of the culture is shorthand. For example, we have a very open culture: we have full transparency on pay, the work people have done, hours, practice group fees, etc. In many firms this is not so and only the managing partner knows this data and makes top-down decisions with it. That reflects and creates a very different culture.

Fifty per cent of our remuneration decisions are based on performance and weight is given to the firm's values: generosity of spirit, collaboration and passion. It's about brand value, introductions to the firm, research, writing – not just fees.

Our recent overseas office is an example of a good decision because it fits with our brand, our know-how; we have significant work flow and we are harnessing a region with a growth economy.

(f) *Practicality and implementation*

From the beginning of the consensus-building process, it is important to address implementation, to think through the practical steps and impact on the ground. Several partners mentioned the advantages of breaking down decisions into smaller components to make them less threatening and more achievable.

It works well when implementation challenges are addressed in the decision making.

Everyone is engaged and decisions are firmly grounded in the tools we have actually got.

Make it bite-sized and get a good chair for the discussion. When we develop a range of options, they always include something ready to implement.

Even on one of our weaker decisions, we had thought through implementation. Partners here are keen to see things happen. Get stuff in bite-sized chunks. Then it is not too frightening – bite-sized is good. Implementation is then about effective delegation; you need a good team.

You need to create excitement and consensus on implementation too, so it feels like a good decision for all.

3.3 The long view

As well as taking time to think things through carefully, partners are very aware of the long-term impact of their decisions. Unlike companies which are pressured to deliver short-term results by the markets, law firms can take a longer view. The leaders I spoke with talked about the fiduciary role they have to act in the best interests of the firm over the long term and for the next generation of their lawyers.

Our policy is teamwork, consensus building and long-term focus.

For big decisions, it is important to take a moment to think 12 months down the line and think of all the things that could go wrong and what they might be and why.

Recently we made a major decision to move our pension scheme from defined benefit to defined contribution. This required 75% approval. There were many different views on the board. Some of the board members were personally affected by it. In the end they approached it as fiduciaries with the best long-term interests of the firm in mind.

Our appointments committee was originally comprised of the firm's founders and then it self-perpetuates. It appoints the leadership in the firm's best long-term interests. They select the person they think is willing and perceived to be ready, and then they build consensus again, always looking at the long-term stability of the firm.

3.4 Process

As well as developing consensus, the leaders all considered that it was important to have a sound process. Whereas their governance processes varied enormously, they all sought good data with unbiased information and well-thought-out, developed research.

Our trainee appointments to solicitors every year are a big decision. They are the future of the firm. We worked out that there were three individual things they were going to be scored on through the process. We were very careful to be faithful to the process and to make it less about intuition, which is what most recruitment seems to rely on. We paused, reflected and recorded the score before we moved on to the next bit of the process.

3.5 Checks and balances

The consensus-building process has its own checks and balances system within it. Partners emphasised the benefits of these and of the different roles played to test and challenge decisions. Some included boards. They all saw space and time as essential when making important decisions.

Decisions are well made when they are made by a very small number of people and then well challenged.

We use, as an external devil's advocate, a senior partner at a major firm of management consultants. We are engaging him for our succession planning in the firm. It will be an 18-month process; there will be lots of engagement with partners and associates. It is quite exciting – it gives us the capacity to think strategically and be challenged.

The board acts as a check and balance, just by being part of the process. Things have to have been well formulated, discussed and honed before they get to the board. If something comes to the board, you pretty much know it is going to be approved. Part of the pre-meeting activity is consensus building. We would never put something to the vote unless we expect it to pass.

Our managing partner will suddenly say at the eleventh hour, "I don't think we should do it," to push back and test.

We have an annual review where the leadership team is challenged by all partners.

Debate and challenge come from an executive committee of partners. Each member of this committee represents a diverse constituency group of partners whose views they canvass on a regular basis. The quality of the wider engagement and discussion is very dependent on the chairmanship of those constituency group discussions. The executive committee then has cabinet responsibility on its decisions to avoid the mayhem that can be caused by leaks.

4. What hinders good decision making?

Having explored the positive side, I asked the SPs what they found to be the major impediments to good decision making and what tends to derail the process in practice. Some of the problems arose out of the absence of the positive conditions or were side effects of them.

4.1 Lack of engagement and communication

When consensus building has not worked, things do not tend to go well. Partners want to have their say, but often there is also a limited amount of enthusiasm for lengthy consultation processes. So for decision makers, there is a skill to be developed in finding the right balance between engaging people without them losing interest through a consensus-building exercise that is too lengthy. A further level of flexibility is required in times of crisis, when the emphasis shifts to directional leadership, more rapid decision making and clear and timely communication.

Closed minds, lack of engagement – some people think it is management's job and don't engage. Some lateral hires from bigger firms are just not expecting to be told about decisions, never mind involved in them. In their previous firms new partners just arrived unannounced in their groups.

The biggest challenge in practice is process paralysis. The firm is full of individuals who are strong willed and hate process.

Apathy derails the process. As we get bigger, we have to have process and people get bored with it.

Getting consultation wrong or the communication wrong leads to trouble. Also, partners want a strong leader, particularly in a crisis; they want clear, straight decisions. If you leave a vacuum, it will create problems – communicate straight away.

4.2 Time

This cuts both ways. It has been suggested that law firm leaders may be more cautious by nature and tend to take more time over their decisions than most leaders. This can help to avoid some of the problems of thinking biases that corporate boards tend to encounter. However, it can also bring a slowness verging at times on paralysis.

The flipside of the good consensus building is that challenge takes time. We can be quick, but decisions do need to permeate through.

Probably over-thinking and over-analysing is the biggest hindrance. We have so much information we become paralysed. Our current managing partner would rather not make a decision than prejudice the consensus. On one major decision we brought in an outside facilitator because we got stuck. Doing nothing is our biggest Achilles heel.

Our worst decisions are because we have either taken too long or acted too quickly. Lateral hires often bring a lot of time pressure. If it has taken too long, the answer should probably be "no".

4.3 Lack of cultural fit and lateral hires

The hiring of lateral partners or senior associates was the most frequently quoted problem in decision making. Several adverse factors seem to be at play, including an absence of cultural fit, devoting inadequate time to the process, thinking biases and a lack of good information flow.

Our decision to open in another jurisdiction was based around acquiring a new team. We wanted our own team there for our European investors. The problems all arose around the people. They just did not fit.

What we are not so good at is lateral hires sometimes. There is always a bit of bias at work. The biggest risk is cultural fit. It is compounded by confidentiality. Partners don't make the time; they just want it to work too quickly and not think it through.

A challenge is lateral hiring, misreading personality issues – we haven't learned and it is very difficult to call that. It seems odd when you are faced with a CV and references and evidence of their work. But there is a lot of group-think and these decisions are very emotionally driven. It is easy to misread people. We couldn't see that one lateral hire didn't have the force of personality to build a practice using the goodwill in our name.

We have never made a lateral partner hiring.

4.4 Implementation and responsibility

For several SPs the biggest challenge comes in implementing the decision.

We need to introduce accountability to help implementation. For example, I would like to make part of a partner's remuneration dependent on making a person they nominate for partnership successful as a partner.

Who is personally accountable for our new venture? No one, really. We need to have a timeline and be clear about how to continue. For example, we should set a timeframe for our new project, say by giving it three years. At present we are open-ended. We get mission creep. We need to benchmark and decide what success looks like; it is about profitability and the long-term position of the brand. When we were smaller we did not have these issues.

We liked that idea, process came along and the implementation was zero.

4.5 Making decisions for the wrong reasons

If the decision does not fit with the strategy, it often comes unstuck in the long term.

For example, when the decisions have personality-driven issues and are made to meet the demands of or give opportunities to one individual rather than to benefit the firm as a whole. If you become too pragmatic or opportunistic, it is then very difficult to stop something going forward on strategic grounds.

Making decisions that aren't aligned with our brand.

4.6 Cognitive biases in law firm decision making

Another reason why decision making can be less effective is because of the adverse impact of cognitive biases. What are these biases and what role do they play in the major decisions that law firms make?

The brain isn't the rational calculating machine we sometimes imagine. Over the millennia of its evolution it has developed shortcuts, simplifications, biases and basic bad habits ... the brain can be a deceptive guide for rational decision making.[1]

As an increasing body of research shows, cognitive biases come into play to deal with complex situations:

An important starting point for theories of human judgement and decision making has been the suggestion that people have limited capacity for mental work, and in order to deal with a complex and fast-changing world they have developed a number of simple modes of reasoning. These "heuristic" modes of thinking can lead to error and bias.[2]

People are imperfect information processors and "even the brightest people make judgemental errors on a regular basis".[3]

Academic researchers on decision making recommend 'rational' processes that involve specific steps, such as:

- define the problem;
- identify the criteria;
- weight the criteria;
- generate alternatives;

---

1 Charles Roxborough, "Hidden Flaws in Strategy", *McKinsey Quarterly*, 1 May 2003.

2 John A Maule and Gerard Hodgkinson, "Heuristics, Biases and Strategic Decision Making", 18 February 2002, *The Psychologist*, www.bps.org.uk/psychologist/heuristics-biases-and-strategic-decision-making.

3 M Bazerman, *Judgment in Managerial Decision Making* (2006, John Wiley & Sons).

- rate each alternative against each criterion; and
- compute the optimal decision.

The rational decision-making model looks at a logical process that should be made to reach optimal decision making. However, people have limits to their rationality or 'bounded rationality'[4], and we can probably understand decision making better by looking at how it is done in practice rather than at how it should be done. In reality, people are limited in various ways by time, cost, availability of information, usable memory, intelligence and perceptions. These limitations prevent the full use of the rational model and lead to a reliance on intuitive biases. People often 'satisfice', meaning that they forgo the best solution and choose the first alternative that meets their minimum requirements.

Experience shows that people in practice do not always reason in a logical manner. We live in a fast-moving and complex world, with increasing pressures to make important decisions very quickly. In order to cope with this environment people have developed different ways of thinking. Researchers have drawn a distinction between what they have called 'System 1' and 'System 2' thinking.[5] System 1 thinking is our intuitive, fast, unconscious, automatic and emotional system. System 2 thinking is more logical and conscious, is slower and requires effort. We use System 1 the most to cope with the fast pace of life and usually it is adequate. However, people tend to place too much reliance on System 1 thinking and judgemental errors are much more likely to occur when it is used. The need for more System 2 thinking is much greater in major and complex decisions such as strategic decisions. These thinking systems and cognitive biases received widespread attention through the work of Daniel Kahneman (Nobel laureate in economics), *Thinking, Fast and Slow*.[6]

So what are these common bad habits or cognitive biases? How might they apply to law firm decisions? It is important to recognise and understand them to achieve wiser decision making. I explored with the SPs whether these biases were at play in their decisions and how they affect rational decision making in law firms. I asked them to consider whether they had come across six of the most common biases, how often and which were the most important for their firm. Once more, there were many differences in their experiences, but there were some common themes. The most prevalent biases at play were towards the *status quo* and a tendency to seek confirming evidence.

4 HA Simon, *Models of Man* (1957, Wiley).
5 KE Stanovich and RF West, "Individual Differences in Reasoning", (2000) *Behavioural and Brain Sciences* 23.
6 Daniel Kahneman, *Thinking Fast and Slow* (2011, Allen Lane).

(a) Over-confidence or optimism

Human beings generally have a strong tendency to be over-optimistic or confident. Our brains are programmed this way. Optimism and confidence are, of course, positives and they are prerequisites for building any business or profession. However, over-optimism and over-confidence can be disadvantages when making significant decisions. They can lead to unrealistic precision, for example, with too narrow a range of possible outcomes, over-optimistic forecasts and under-estimation of future challenges.

For the lawyers I met, the experience is rather different than for many corporate decision makers. We have seen many corporate disasters following the over-confidence of the latter. Lawyers are known for their scepticism and in general their optimism is more muted. However, in certain circumstances over-optimism seems to kick in and distort decision making, particularly in lateral hiring.

No, definitely not over-optimism; not us.

We are tempered by a heavy dose of realism. We have plenty of 'Eeyores' around here. Decisions go through endless filters. However optimistic people are, there is a heavy dose of realism, so we have muted optimism.

We are never over-confident; we are risk averse.

On the other hand:

In lateral hiring decisions, we have seen lots of biases: over-optimism, confirming evidence and sunk costs. I always say to a lateral, "Be careful what you wish for and with your projections, and have a plan B."

Our new overseas office is a good example of over-optimism on the break-even period.

Yes, we hired a particular partner to build a practice even though we had no basis for it.

Absolutely, it was pretty prevalent. If we had stepped back, we might not have done it, but we were feeling it was all going to be marvellous!

Decisions are not so good when we are carried away with enthusiasm for the project.

(b) Confirming evidence

This involves seeking out information that supports our instincts or point of view, while avoiding or misinterpreting information that contradicts it. It affects where we go to collect evidence and how we interpret the evidence we do receive, leading us to give too much weight to supporting information and too little to conflicting information. Some commentators consider it to be very detrimental:

> *Probably the biggest single problem for human decision making is that when people have ingrained beliefs, they will put a much higher bar for evidence for things they don't believe than for things they do believe. Confirmation-seeking bias, I think, is*

> *what social psychologists call it. Organizations can have amazingly good evidence, but it has no effect on the decisions they make if it conflicts with their ideology.*[7]

Yes. On our overseas office, we didn't research the cultural aspects; we applied European-style thinking. There was some confirming evidence and it's too early yet, but I can envisage sunk costs and escalation of commitment too.

Confirming evidence, absolutely.

Yes, generally when we take references proposed by an individual.

Yes, definitely.

Confirming evidence, yes sometimes and especially when it may confirm the status quo.

(c) Sunk costs and escalation of commitments

> *When you find yourself in a hole, the best thing you can do is stop digging.*
> Warren Buffet.

This bias is commonly known as 'throwing good money after bad'. It shows up when people are tempted to make choices that justify or protect past choices, even when those past choices may no longer be good ones, rather than cutting their losses. When large projects overrun, firms keep investing in them even though the original economics of the decision are no longer valid. Commitment to a project or strategy is often continued or even escalated in spite of strong negative feedback or indications of failure. IT projects are a classic example.

Even though people know that rationally sunk costs are not relevant to a present decision, they still prey on their minds and can lead to poor decisions. People still feel responsible for the previous decision. It requires a conscious effort to set aside any sunk costs for present decisions that have a past. People are unwilling, whether consciously or not, to admit past mistakes. This natural tendency is often exacerbated in business because admitting a previous bad decision is frequently a public matter and can lead to criticism. It is very difficult to make a public admission of poor judgement. It may have costs in terms of money, reputation or status. Lawyers are notoriously reluctant to admit they were wrong.

Yes, lawyers never want to admit they are wrong.

Yes.

Yes, but it depends. If things are going wrong, we will try like hell to get them

---

7 Robert Sutton, in "Prove It: Management needs fewer fads, more reflection", *Stanford Magazine*, May/June 2006.

right. Our core asset is the client relationship – we must defend it at all costs and it's very rare that say we are not going to do so.

Yes, although we are getting better at cutting our losses. When revenues are increasing, it's easier to fill the black holes, but when revenues are falling or flat, we need to pay more attention and be more decisive.

Not really – if we make a mistake, we put our hands up and deal with it quickly. We closed a foreign office and got the key client matters to a competent firm and extracted maximum value; there will be 'nil cost' to the firm.

(d) Status quo

This bias can also influence the decisions people make. It draws people towards alternatives that perpetuate the *status quo*. It operates subconsciously to try to protect people's egos from damage. Taking action involves responsibility and somehow people think that inaction generally involves less responsibility and carries less risk of criticism.

One of the experiments done to show this bias at work asked students to handle the investment of a pretend inheritance. Different groups received their inheritances in widely differing forms of investments with very different risk profiles. However, they mostly left the majority of the money where it was. Their decisions were driven by the *status quo* of the initial allocations rather than their risk preferences.

Yes, very much so. We have a strong need for consensus, so there is an inbuilt bias towards what we know and what is established.

Yes, very much so.

Yes – if any bias applies to us, then it is this status quo. The prevailing attitude is, "if it is all working fine, why change it?"

Yes – in 2002 we bought a firm with a practice that does not fit with our brand; we still have it.

I see this a lot elsewhere. You don't see it here. Part of our core value is innovation. It really annoys me when I ask someone why they have done something in a certain way and they say, "We have always done it like that." I challenge them to think of the best way instead.

(e) Framing

The framing of a decision can bias the outcome. The first step in making any decision is to frame the question or issue to be addressed. The way an issue is framed can alter the whole way that choices are evaluated and a decision is made. It is arguably the most important and dangerous element of the process and often the most hidden. People tend to adopt the frame they have been given, rather than looking at the issue afresh from their own point of view.

It reflects the paramount importance of who is framing and guiding the decision-making process; of how proposals are made and how information is presented. It is often closely interrelated to other cognitive biases as it can set up a *status quo* trap or can introduce anchoring (see sections 4.5(d) and (f)). It may also lead people to confirming evidence (discussed in section 4.5(b)) and help them fall into sunk cost traps (see section 4.5(c)).

Interestingly, only one of the SPs thought this was particularly important. It is unclear whether this is because the bias is so hidden or because there is such a high degree of challenge in law firm decision making that negates it.

Yes – anchoring around first impressions, they count. We give undue weight to first impressions, then fight against them. Unconsciously a lot of weight – instincts, corridor test, appearances, manner – but hopefully we are wise enough to sort this out.

Yes – anchoring particularly around the founders' views. When the founders endorse a view, we see big-time anchoring. The more you get away from the founding generation, the more trust you will need to build as this anchoring bias disappears. We will need greater persuasion that we are acting in their best interests.

Yes, we see anchoring. There is a sub-problem of idleness that goes with it. People trust you as founder. If you say something, they want to agree with you. They assume; they don't do the thinking for themselves – rather they let you do the thinking for them. I try to combat this with more open-ended questions to get them thinking.

Yes, definitely framing is very relevant. I see it in an acute way in litigation; you see it in the corridor discussions of the Royal Courts of Justice. I am very aware of it. It really affects outcomes in decision making.

(f) Anchoring

This bias leads people subconsciously to give disproportionate weight to the first information they receive or initial views that are expressed.

It is well illustrated by another experiment.[8] Many groups of people were asked the following two questions:

- Is the population of Turkey greater than 35 million?
- What is your best estimate of Turkey's population?

They gave half the people the figure of 35 million in the first question and in the other half they used 100 million. "Without fail, the answers to the second question increase by many millions when the larger figure is used in the first question."

It is a particularly pernicious psychological flaw. In experiments, people show this bias even when they see the initial number given by the spin of a roulette wheel.

8 John S Hammond, Ralph L Keeney and Howard Raiffa, "The Hidden Traps in Decision Making", Sept–Oct 1998, *Harvard Business Review.*

There are all types of anchors: initial impressions, estimates, comments from colleagues, stereotypes. Past performance, events or trends are some of the most common anchors in business. People often take an anchor and adjust from it without questioning the starting point. A common example is sales forecasts for future years based on sales in the previous year. Another common area is fund managers using past performance to advertise their funds. While the information is relevant, it often tends to give too much weight to past events at the expense of other relevant factors, particularly in fast-changing environments. Another common area for anchors is in negotiation when a seller names a high sales price so the buyer becomes anchored around that figure.

As we know from the research, high intelligence does not make you immune to cognitive biases. It seems from the interviews that a fair number are recognised as being at play in law firm decisions. On the basis that it is much easier to recognise other people's mistakes and biases than our own, there is a reasonable chance that more biases are operative than just those uncovered by the SPs in our conversations.

The prevalence of the *status quo* bias is supported by an interesting, extensive piece of research[9] conducted in the United States on the psychological make-up of the legal profession. The results are summarised in the table below.

Trait	**Population**	**Lawyers**
Scepticism	50% (the norm)	93%
Autonomy	50%	89%
Abstract reasoning	50%	81%
Urgency	50%	71%
Resilience	50%	30%
Sociability	50%	7% (12% including rainmakers)

The research shows that lawyers tend to be highly sceptical, independent and not very resilient. They do not cope well with failure or setback and do not like to try to move things forward because they might fail. They want to point out the problems in any proposition. This means that there is something inbuilt about the legal profession which makes it slow to adapt and keen to hang on to the *status quo* in the belief that that will create more security.

9 Extract from Dr Larry Richards in the article "Growth is Dead, Part 7 Psychology" (2012), featured on the Adam Smith, Esq website.

The best way to tackle biases is to build awareness of them. One of the SPs had specifically done so by reading some of the materials quoted and discussing them with his partners:

We try to be aware of biases and to counter them. Some of our best decision making comes from looking at how to deal with those decisions that were incorrect. We have a series of meetings and unpick them.

Another way to tackle biases is to build in plenty of time and process to activate System 2 thinking. Lawyers naturally seem to do this in the consensus-building process and this may be one of the components contributing to the success of the law firm model:

Biases are less of a problem if the process is one that evolves over time. I am not sure they are so relevant at the top of law firms as they are in corporate boardrooms. This is not a group of people getting in a room; it is not an analysis of dynamics of a group in a room.

Debate, challenge and a culture of openness are other ways of tackling biases. Although it takes time and energy, the more that these are incorporated into the decision-making process, the less likely it will be that the rationality of a decision is distorted. Introducing a devil's advocate role, as one firm described, is an excellent way to bring in external challenge and legitimise constructive dissent. External board members can play a similar role.

5. Individual leaders' insights on decision making

The chairmanship of discussions and the stewardship of the decision-making process are crucial to effective decision making. The role here for law firm leaders involves a considerable and nuanced skill set.

After discussing all of the important themes above, I asked each law firm leaders to share one insight into effective decision making. Below is a collection of their responses.

5.1 Find the right balance

I find myself juggling a lot between:

- *being prepared to be bold but not being unrealistic;*
- *being pretty directional and building consensus;*
- *listening but not too much; and*
- *being strategic but a bit pragmatic.*

The hardest thing is to decide which initiative to follow through. Every decision has huge inertia. Often nothing happens unless you make it happen, so how hard do you push and when? You have to be thick-skinned. People often want to take a shot at you, but also want you to keep doing it.

5.2 Look at the consequences

Always look at the consequences and think them through.

You are often deciding on the least bad outcome, rather than what is a fantastic outcome.

5.3 Be responsive

Responsiveness is so important; you need a quick reaction time if anything is raised. Don't let it fester. You have to know where your problems are and deal with them first. If you think certain partners will be troubled, deal with them first.

5.4 Be flexible and communicative

We have different processes for different decisions: strategic, operational, crisis. Between the four central people, we have daily phone calls. We have a strong corporate governance system that is well known to the firm. It gives confidence and is helpful when things go wrong in the market.

We have a lot of communication between the chairman and CEO. Since the economic crisis and negative growth, we have had a much more informal style of leadership. Lots of informal catch-ups, no structure – it's changing to a constant conversation, getting more attachment. With 120 partners on one continent, we can do it; it's a point of differentiation and strength.

Different decision making is needed for different types of decisions and depending where you are in the cycle.

You need flexibility in approach. If you have a consensus-driven group, decision-making processes have to reflect the culture. To get legitimacy, you need to get consensus.

5.5 Find the right pace

Too many organisations are slowed down by slow decision making. Ninety per cent of decisions are not bet-the-farm decisions, so get on and make them and let people crack on. People like cracking on and this is how we have cracked on as a firm.

Make time and space for the really important decisions. I picked up from Kahneman to rely less on intuition.

5.6 Display good leadership and open-mindedness

Good leadership means inspiring people to make bold decisions and to get people on side. We need to give people a line of sight from their contribution to overall strategy.

Lots of people come with a pre-existing point of view. We need to be able to say, "I am wrong" and lawyers don't like that. We need an element of modesty.

5.7 Think about your followers

Realise the importance of recognising who is going to follow you and how they think.

Strong leadership needs to have a sense of urgency and show the results of failure to do something in order to beat the status quo.

6. Conclusion

The greatest improvements you can make to the quality of decision making in your law firm often come not from formal governance structures, but from leaders recognising and taking opportunities to improve their decision-making behaviour.

The shared experiences of the SPs highlight areas where they have developed their own leadership and their firms' styles of decision making. They include the softer skills required to create consensus, reflect their culture and successfully implement major decisions. It is a flexible art form.

We know that even big hitters are not immune to cognitive biases. Being alert to them and countering them can avert distortions of rational decision making.

Whereas some advocate that the fewer big decisions, the better, all are clear that if you do take a big decision, take your time if you can – but do not take too long!

This chapter is published as it appeared in the previous edition.

Good governance and partner performance

Lisa M Walker Johnson
Walker Clark LLC

We have the wind at our back, if only we'd pull together to take advantage of it.
Thomas L Friedman[1]

1. Introduction

A common question that the author hears in law firms is: "Why don't my partners just do what they are expected to do?" This chapter starts with the premise that most partners[2] want to meet expectations and succeed, for themselves, their colleagues and their clients – even when the choices they make seem inconsistent with this desire for success.

Let's consider the issue of productivity, a common area of complaint among partners. Productivity in law firms is actually a complex dynamic and the result of many separate factors. Solutions can be found in many different places in a law firm; however, in the author's experience, the principal reason or primary root cause for underperformance is not typically the attitude or work ethic of the individual partners.

This chapter challenges partners to look beyond just telling each other what needs to change. It proposes serious and effective ways to improve competitive partner performance with leadership skills, good governance and quality peer relationships.

Successful change leaders in law firms look for answers every day to better understand problems and conditions that affect the firm's requirements for partner performance and how they as leaders might contribute, for good or bad. Whether they are dealing with problems of underperformance against current expectations or trying to prepare for improvements in knowledge and skills to enhance future competitiveness, leaders stay alert to possibilities. In some cases, partners may want to strengthen already robust performance or build up new

---

1 Thomas L Friedman, "The Way We Were", *New York Times*, 24 September 2013.

2 In this chapter, the word 'partner' denotes any practising owner of a law firm, including shareholders, members and equity partners, according to the corporate structure of the firm. It also includes non-equity partners – that is, those who have the title of partner or something similar, but do not have a financial interest in the ownership of the firm's corporate entity. The professional, management and leadership responsibilities that apply to equity partners also apply to non-equity partners in most law firms.

capabilities. They may want to take advantage of the firm's current reputation and visibility by promoting expanded skills and expertise. Perhaps individual or group performance is jeopardising a firm's profitability, client relationships or the partners' own professional reputations and professional effectiveness.

Whatever triggers the need for change, successful partners start with inquiry, not fixed mindsets. They don't jump to conclusions, prescribe solutions to 'hold others accountable' and assume it's up to the individual partner – or group of partners – to just go forth and 'change!'

Why doesn't this approach work? There are two important reasons. First, when leaders aren't curious about what they don't know, they lose credibility and effectiveness very quickly when trying to lead change – whether on the individual performance level or with full-scale organisational change such as a merger or the firm-wide implementation of technology systems. In other words, partners gradually lose their influence with others. For a leader, the negative spiral can be obvious or subtle; however, the results are the same. As leaders lose their influence, peers increasingly cease to trust their leadership intentions and judgement, even if compelled to comply in the short term.

Partners who don't feel listened to and supported in their own professional development, sometimes even unconsciously, begin to perpetuate a workplace climate of resistance and indifference. They may resist the need for change in ways not always obvious to the uninformed leaders – or even themselves. Even without bad intentions, they disrupt cohesive decision making, contributing to inertia and negative stress during an improvement process. They may refuse to acknowledge the need for change or slow down progress, not investing adequately in needed improvements. They may take a short view or insular approach to their choices without regard for the bigger picture or the longer-term needs of the partnership and firm, withholding key information, expertise and even work. Leaders may end up blaming their partners for these choices and conditions in the firm without realising or accepting their own joint accountability for disappointing performance results.

Second, without inquiry, change leaders cannot anticipate needs or make well-informed decisions. Damaged internal relationships along with poor governance structures and processes impede response times and options. Inadequate information and analysis compounded by poor decisions contribute to failed attempts to make necessary performance adjustments. Superficial responses, while they may have some truth in them, are generally unplanned and spontaneous reactions to problems. They tend to set a precedent that causes professionals to feel that they are in a never-ending crisis environment. Decline in any firm, large or small, and in any market may be gradual but steady when leaders abdicate responsibility.

There is yet another, often unintended, consequence of leadership behaviours that rush to judgement without inquiry. Untested explanations and solutions, including the 'quick fix', or new management trends with promises of easy change usually do little to solve underlying root causes. Problems persist, reinforcing pessimism and a sense of "Why bother?" just when the opposite is needed to compete and perform. Good options become limited. Partners singularly react to problems without understanding them fully, further constricting growth opportunities, market presence and goodwill in the partnership.

The author finds that when partners describe the impact of the working environment on their choices about what they do, these are generally not just 'excuses'. The lack of time or conflicts between client service and internal management expectations are often cited by partners as deterrents to their desired performance. Leaders might not agree with the degree to which a certain motivator or inhibitor should be a factor for others. Their expectations may be affected by whether they share the same concerns personally. However, that isn't really the point. These complaints, real and perceived, provide clues to possible interventions that would reduce performance-related difficulties – not through guilt or coercion, but by taking joint action on mutually developed and agreed goals, even short-term, incremental ones. When partners dismiss and discount each other's points of view and stop listening to learn[3] – for whatever reason they rationalise to make it seem acceptable – they undermine their future resilience as a firm.

2. Can we get better at addressing partner performance?

Partners often ask the author: "Can we get better at addressing partner performance?" They describe obstacles and past practices that make doing things differently seem impossible to them. With over 30 years of experience working exclusively with lawyers and their organisations, the author is cautiously optimistic. On the one hand, partners and law firms have so much going for them when it comes to improving performance and building resilient, successful firms.

Regardless of their national culture, lawyers share many global traditions and values of the profession. They plan, innovate and adapt to changing external demands and trends with an almost universal commitment to service orientation and performance excellence.

International lawyers are generally respected business and political leaders in their communities, with experience in deal making and compromise. They are good at understanding clients, anticipating their needs and responding with flexibility and diplomacy.

---

3 Developing the capacity to initiate and respond to continuous change, individually and collectively, requires significant shifts in partner perceptions and leadership behaviours; these shifts won't happen unless partners listen to learn. See Lisa M Walker Johnson, "Listening to Learn", *Walker Clark World View* (16 June 2018), www.walkerclark.com/worldview-blog/previous-worldview-posts/319-listening-to-learn.html.

Law firm partners are lawyers first. As lawyers, most of them already have the basic intellectual capabilities to be good managers. Through formal training and experience in practice, they develop a set of intellectual skills and values that are natural foundations for handling even very sensitive issues in addressing performance issues with colleagues.

In law school, as well as during their early years in practice, lawyers learn about the requirements to meet certain standards of professional responsibility in the practice of law. These are more than just rules; they are also a set of innate values that, for most lawyers, define a large part of who they are as professionals:

- loyalty to the client;
- integrity and diligence in undertakings;
- truthfulness in communications; and
- the realisation that good advocacy often requires consultation with other lawyers and a degree of professionally responsible collaboration with opposing counsel.

In the law firm setting in particular, lawyers learn that they often need to work in close concert with others in their firm. The 'lone wolf' partner is today as rare and endangered a species as real wolves have become in many parts of the world.

The ultimate deal breaker, though, is whether law firm partners will consistently and collectively do what it takes to turn their strengths, assets and skills inward to create a working environment that is conducive to professional wellbeing and partner performance. There is no reason why partners can't be excellent at addressing partner performance unless they create conditions where they become their own worst enemy. It is a choice.

Helping one's colleagues to perform is an almost universal phenomenon in law firm practice. Experienced lawyers, both partners and senior associates, spend many hours each year – usually unrecorded and unbilled – teaching and guiding newly qualified lawyers in the fine points of technical knowledge and practice skills. This can range from the *de facto* apprenticeships that new lawyers frequently serve in traditional law firms in West Africa, working closely with and learning from an experienced partner, to highly structured mentoring and professional development programmes in large firms operating with a more corporate model.

This is not just mentoring of young lawyers. Law firm partners – at least those in successful law firms – also realise and accept that each of them has a direct financial interest in the success of their fellow partners. Regardless of the structure of the compensation system, partners in these firms support the notion that 'a rising tide lifts all ships', and that it is in their own financial interests to act to improve the performance of a partner who might be falling behind.

The extent to which partners and their formal or designated leaders are willing to understand obstacles to success, ask and answer relevant questions, use tools and methods to identify and address the root causes of disappointing results and make well-informed and well-timed decisions that affect the quality of the total work environment is in their hands. Their choices will determine the extent to which they will be successful in effecting change.

3. Where does good governance come in?

The author has observed that in order to consistently and collectively do what it takes to improve performance, successful law firms use good governance practices. For example, they take a planned and structured approach to partner performance, regardless of their size and unique challenges. This planned and structured approach will look different in every legal organisation and will evolve over time in response to changing economic, market, practice and financial dynamics. There is no one size fits all; however, there are common conditions for success.

Partner performance – along with the performance of all lawyers – involves a complicated set of closely related issues, especially in law firms with a traditional management structure. Partners must manage their own individual and collective performance, as well as providing a developmental and financial infrastructure that supports the performance of non-partner lawyers, such as associates, 'of counsel' lawyers and other billing professionals.[4]

Partners are the principal generators of revenue for the firm, whether through their own billable work or through the origination of new clients and matters. Their performance is critical to the financial success – even the survival – of their firms. Yet many law firms lack even the basic performance management structures and methods that most businesses routinely use to evaluate and develop their senior executives.

As a result, law firm partners approve their own business plans and financial targets, if they have them at all. Leaders often lack the strategic and financial framework within which to reward outstanding contributions, as well as agreed policies and procedures to address substandard performance in the achievement of those goals. In these firms, procrastination about dealing with performance issues is the norm. Incentives and rewards, as well as well-informed responses to performance problems, tend to be improvised and inconsistent, if they occur at all.

Existing and substantial weaknesses in the governance and management of

---

4 This chapter views the relationships among leadership, governance and performance management primarily from the perspective of the partners, with an emphasis on more active and informed partner involvement in internal structures, decision making and the quality of professional relationships; however, the effects and operating principles of strengthening the links between governance and performance reach into every corner of the firm.

law firms create significant challenges to improving partner performance. These weaknesses need not be viewed as obstacles *per se*. No organisation is perfect, any more than any partner – not that that would even be a desirable or realistic outcome. Understanding the need to be alert, successful partners aggressively try to better understand what elements in their organisations and current cultures could potentially help, hinder or derail desired shifts in thinking and behaviour which are at the roots of partner performance. They integrate documentation, collaboration and measurements – for example, "What will success look like?" – into their performance planning, along with a structured change process so that partners know how to participate and what to expect.[5]

Successful firms use a structured performance management system that includes goals and performance measurements. Every performance management system is unique. A systems approach to understanding problems and changing behaviours focuses attention on the total work environment, not just the individual. In this way, leaders can find root causes for perceptions about workplace stressors and better understand lawyers' responses to them.[6] This requires emotional intelligence, as well as cultural capabilities to create a sense of unity and shared purpose within the partnership and among all the firm's members.

This sense of unity and purpose is what helps to create a motivating professional environment where people are willing to learn, contribute, adapt and invest in their future. A sense of purpose is more than a response to "Why are we here?" In resilient law firms, purpose is grounded in partners' beliefs, as demonstrated through their day-to-day actions consistent with those beliefs. Partners are willing to go beyond short-term fixes and aspirations to honestly assess evidence that helps them get to the root of the obstacles to desired performance. Partners go well beyond simply telling others, "Those behaviours are wrong or just not us; stop doing them."

Law firm partners are obviously concerned that the firm should make money on a sustainable basis. However, when their time and energy are focused almost solely on maintaining the business and professional *status quo*, to the exclusion of investments in innovation and future development, the firm is in trouble.

It does not have to be that way.

4. Leadership effectiveness

How well leaders respond to changing conditions with partner performance in law firms has a lot to do with whether they see partner performance as a collective responsibility that requires a collective response.

---

5 For a discussion of an effective structured change process, with three main steps and three conditions for success at each step in the context of performance management, see the chapter "Leading change".

6 Lisa M Walker Johnson, *Stress and Burnout in Law Firms: Leadership Challenges and Choices* (Globe Law and Business, 2022), p184.

Whether leaders think about it consciously or not, their decisions about compensation, development priorities and career progression set the stage for partner performance. Decisions and indecision about internal systems and business and practice priorities impact on the performance behaviours of all lawyers, as well as the quality of their professional relationships.

So, successful law firms address partner performance first by developing and documenting expectations for the leadership behaviours that facilitate performance effectiveness in their firms. They ask questions such as the following:

- "What leadership behaviours will help us succeed in developing high-performing partners and teams, not in an ideal world, but based on where we are right now?"
- "What do our leaders need to know, do and pay attention to in order to get the best results?"
- "How can we improve our decision-making capabilities and effectiveness as a leadership team?"

There are seven areas the author has observed and documented from her work with firms that best deal with partner performance.

4.1 Leaders understand the dynamics of feedback in a law firm and learn the skills to do it well

Almost any reasonable law firm partner would agree that good performance from everyone is critical to a law firm's success. However, many partnerships seem almost to be afraid to directly discuss and deal with unmet performance expectations, especially at the partner level. If the issue of partner performance comes up in partners' meetings, people suddenly become quite quiet. Some partners become visibly nervous or uncomfortable about discussing it further.

Yet the success and survival of the firm depend on the capacity of those very partners to work together to improve and expand their individual and team effectiveness using frequent and reliable feedback from multiple sources.

There are unique factors in law firms that contribute to discomfort in giving each other peer partner feedback, even when firms have performance management structures in place. Some of these challenges are inherent in the practice of law generally.

First, the non-hierarchical organisational structure in most law firms contributes to a sense that "We're all peers." When you see others as peers, you may think "It's not my job" to ask for feedback or to give it to others unless they request it. When partners do not have an agreed and functional[7] process in

7 An unfortunate variation on this situation is the law firm that has these procedures elegantly documented but whose partners always look for 'exceptions' or 'distinguishing factors' to avoid following them. In some instances, this may be worse than having no agreed procedures at all, because of the false expectations and cynicism it produces.

place for discussing and dealing with performance issues, they tend to feel especially uncomfortable talking about it with each other. Ironically, this occurs when they already have the skills and abilities to do it, which they demonstrate with clients – and often with associates – every day.

Second, partners are often expected to produce fee-earning legal work in addition to marketing and business development, leading practice teams or groups, and managing matters, groups and important business functions of the firm. Even partners without management responsibilities are very busy. This limits the time they have available for other responsibilities, such as performance reviews and regular informal feedback. If they do not plan to give feedback intentionally, there is always something else to do that seems to be just as, or more, important. Without planning, partner feedback is usually vague and ill timed. It is often reduced to a critical comment hoping that a colleague gets the message and does something about it; or passing along something that someone else has said to be 'helpful'; or an information dump of saved-up frustrations. Typically, there is no time planned for dialogue, collaboration or agreed next steps.

As 'lawyers first', law firm partners also are subject to values and influences that are characteristic of most lawyers:

- They bring a naturally high sense of urgency to their practice and work. They tend to want to fix even complex performance issues quickly so as not to waste time. They are prone to address performance issues with insufficient planning and little thought as to how they themselves might be contributing to the problem or how they could contribute to a sustainable improvement.
- By training and practice, they tend to be analytical to the point of scepticism. They are much more likely to point out what is wrong than they are to comment on the positive points about their peers' performance or their contributions. This causes some lawyers to confuse feedback with criticism that is inherently negative. Without a specific action plan for improvement – something more than "Just try to do better next time" – lawyers, like anyone else, often become frustrated when they fail to see positive results.
- Lawyers generally don't like to make judgements unless they have all the facts. However, to get to the facts, they must ask questions and listen actively to the other person's point of view, just as they do with clients, before getting to solutions. This component is often missing from discussions of performance issues.

It may feel disconcerting to realise that one person's facts may simply be that person's perceptions of a set of facts that another partner might see quite differently. Yet when partners accept that the performance discussion is more about learning and understanding each other's views than it is about delivering the 'truth' to their peers, it actually makes the conversation more inviting. Partners are less likely to procrastinate when they know that their role is not to pass judgement, but to discuss a problem and work together to agree a way forward.

Partners usually receive more feedback from their clients than they do from each other, even in firms that do not regularly conduct client surveys. The greatest damage to a law firm comes not from poor service delivery, but from a more basic failure to solicit and use feedback – internal and external – to confront reality. Inadequate feedback leads to selective hearing, wishful thinking, distortions of fact and unrealistic expectations of both financial potential and partner performance. Partners become uncomfortable with sharing their different points of view. Accurate and complete information becomes rare, and the reluctance to engage can accelerate the deterioration of decision making and performance for the entire firm.

Inadequate and less than candid communication is a shaky foundation for any business organisation, but especially for one that, like a law firm, is dependent on its most senior people and their relationships with one another for its very economic survival.

Partners, like anyone else, are more willing to buy into a group decision when they are first invited to share their individual reactions on a topic or concern. If partners are discouraged from sharing their own views and experiences before being expected to just 'sign on', they are more likely to persist with "Yes, but…" type responses. The goal, therefore, should be to invite individual partners to differentiate themselves first, looking for differences and similarities. Once individuals have been recognised and others have sought to understand their points of view, it is easier to step back and begin to examine the bigger picture together as a group. Partners can build broader group commitment as their sense of common purpose and shared goals becomes increasingly apparent. Trying to push the 'right answer' on colleagues, without pausing to listen and learn, will convince no one – even if that 'right answer' seems glaringly obvious to a certain few.

To lead any change effort – whether for an entire firm, a group or an individual – leaders need to confront problems. A partner may be behaving in ways that cause negative stress for others, with obvious consequences. Clients might notice and begin to remark about a partner's questionable behaviour in areas that, strictly speaking, are not within the realm of his or her professional ethics or competence. A new lateral partner might fail to deliver a level of fee performance that was expected when he or she first joined the partnership.

Whatever the specific nature of the problem, situations involving partner performance do not get addressed without feedback discussions. Problems are simply ignored or are permitted to lurk below the surface, causing great frustration, demotivation and even cynicism among other partners, lawyers and staff.[8]

4.2 Leaders are aware of the double-edged sword of collegiality

Collegiality and respect for professional judgement are highly valued in most law firms. A natural strength, this may also contribute to partners' difficulties in dealing with partner performance.

Partners often cite a fear of conflict as a frequent excuse for not undertaking a more robust approach to performance management. This may seem like an odd attribute for a profession that is perceived as thriving on adversarial roles for a living. Nonetheless, law firm partners are often loath to do anything or say anything that might appear to be open criticism of one's partner. Understandably, they want to stay on good terms with each other. Professional relationships provide friendships, contacts and invaluable information. They play an important role in one's professional reputation, career advancement and financial success. Therefore, the often-espoused value of collegiality can easily deteriorate into a preference for procrastination – in essence, a code of silence.[9]

Sometimes partners' past experiences cause them to feel that giving feedback, especially to each other, will upset their professional relationships. Past emotionally charged exchanges between partners may have produced unresolved hurt feelings and anxiety, and not just for the partners involved in the interactions. Law firms are vulnerable when these partners have been unable to work through and let go of these hurt feelings, just like partners in a marriage. Their negative thinking about feedback and conflict, along with the feelings that this thinking produces, create a figurative straitjacket around the partnership's ability to grow and compete.

Naturally in these conditions, when their peers underperform, they prefer to adopt a wait-and-see approach, hoping that problems will go away on their own – which they generally don't, even if they slide under the radar. It takes courage to face painful realities or address the 'elephant(s) in the room' in order to learn how to think about and approach partner performance differently; however, with skilled assistance and determination, partners do so every day around the

---

8 For further discussion of the role of feedback in the management of partner performance, see "Feedback and evaluation" in section 5.3 below.

9 The culture of procrastination can manifest itself in many ways. When faced with sensitive problems, such as the unsatisfactory performance of a partner, some law firms feel more comfortable 'kicking the can down the road' for as long as possible, dealing only with performance concerns – and the high levels of stress they can cause – after they have had clearly negative, and sometime irreversible, consequences for the individual partner, the firm and one or more major clients.

When leaders have been unable or unwilling to confront and respectfully work through concerns and disagreements in the past, their behaviours perpetuate norms that continue to inhibit constructive responses. They regularly employ ineffective thinking habits ranging from complete denial that the problem exists to expecting the problem to disappear on its own. Walker Johnson (n 6), p176. See also *ibid*, pp173–181 about the fear of conflict.

world. In doing so, they free themselves and their colleagues to do one thing well – succeed! If they continue to shy away from effectively dealing with partner performance issues, the very collegiality that they so value will slowly deteriorate and, along with it, their hopes and aspirations for the firm.

With a different mindset about feedback, partners learn how to draw on their practice skills, such as compromising with counterparties to close a major transaction or agreeing with opposing counsel to focus the scope of litigation on a set of mutually defined decisive issues. They can choose to use these same skills with their peers, to work through confrontation and disagreement to find workable solutions. They find that these behaviours actually build trust and improve the quality of peer relationships. Rather than talking behind closed doors about others, they talk with others to address and solve concerns together.

Existing skills, combined with the traditional values of the legal profession, form a flexible structure for problem solving that is sometimes almost invisible to most of the participants in the debate. Nonetheless, this framework can guide considerations of even the most sensitive and painful issues to a positive result if partners have the courage to use it.

Skilled external facilitators can help partners to have structured discussions that shift partner perceptions, deepen understanding of options and build commitment to different solutions to performance issues. Human perceptions and behaviour change are complex issues to influence and manage, even for experts. Partners often need help to improve internal communication and performance structures and the quality of their engagement with each other. Frequently they get stuck, focusing on their differences rather than the greater outcomes they want to achieve together. In the author's experience, they unnecessarily leave so much goodwill and relevant information on the table when they go down these rabbit holes of disagreement.

Partners pride themselves on their intellectual competence, for good reason. The law is an intellectual discipline based on logic and analysis. However, when they repress and conceal the effects of anxiety and stress in their relationships, their collegiality suffers anyway. This in turn diminishes their capacity to cope, intellectually as well as emotionally. When partners can think about dealing with possible disagreements as manageable and a natural part of achieving performance together, they feel more optimistic and in control. Confident and successful partners are also more likely to ask for help – for themselves and others – when they need it, instead of avoiding and denying the need to learn how to think about and do things differently.

4.3 Leaders work with different perceptions of the truth

These leaders know that an open approach to the performance discussion is more likely to get the desired results. They advise: "Share your own perspective first, not as the 'truth' but more in terms of what you are observing, why you see it as a problem, and how it makes you feel. Then invite your colleague to talk about the issues as he or she sees them."

They also describe how one of the hardest things for them to do is to stop rebutting someone else who disagrees with them. Instead, they say the better practice is to listen, ask questions and try to put yourself in the other person's shoes.

Another consideration based on their experience is that if you are constantly disappointed with each other's performance or behaviour in a particular area or situation, ask whether your expectations are realistic. Should you modify or change your expectations? Perhaps you can achieve the desired result through a different approach.

The executive director of one of the author's client law firms told the practice group heads in a meeting that he was continuously frustrated by their apparent inability to make the time to understand group financial reports and take the appropriate action in response to reported changes in financial performance. The practice group heads, for their part, also expressed frustration, saying that they were already overburdened by their responsibilities for business development, performing their own fee-producing work and managing the people and projects in their groups. Some of them even believed that it was the executive director's responsibility to monitor the financial performance of their groups and to advise them of any problems.

After candidly and respectfully putting the 'facts' on the table, they decided that both parties were 'right', as they looked at it from their respective experiences. They stopped blaming each other and asked, "What is the way forward for us to get the results that we all want to achieve?"

Rather than continue with a dead-end, frustrating struggle, they decided to focus on finding some practical solutions that could meet their respective needs in the foreseeable future. They proposed some possible approaches and agreed on one.

The executive director, in concert with the group heads, designated financial managers for each group, who were responsible for monitoring financial group performance with the authority to follow up with appropriate action when necessary. In some cases, appropriate action meant little more than tracking down specific bits of information, time reports or client expenses and disbursements.

This creative solution did nothing to diminish the group heads' ownership and accountability for their group's financial performance. If anything, it actually increased their motivation and the likelihood of improved financial performance. It also created a ripple effect in the group, giving others the chance to lead, coach others and improve their business acumen.

This example illustrates the importance of not getting too hung up on form if what is needed is committed action to advance the goals of the firm. By having the conversation about performance and by learning from each other in the process, the executive director and the practice group heads were able to find a successful, pragmatic solution. This was a desirable substitute for becoming increasingly frustrated by inflexible reliance on what each of them expected that others were supposed to be doing.

Rather than clinging tightly to their preconceived opinions about who was at fault, they discovered that their current expectations of each other were not very realistic. This made it easier for them to modify their approach with the end result in mind, rather than focusing solely on who was not doing what. Their willingness to adapt served the goals of the firm in new and improved ways they did not even anticipate.

Interestingly, they were successful not only because they were willing to listen and be flexible. They made the time to search for common ground together. They reasoned, applied critical thinking to a problem, negotiated with each other and made a deal – just as they did in their own practices every day. However, in this case, it was a new situation for them: a performance-related discussion. Their ability to reach an acceptable solution to what was a highly charged emotional issue at the time is a classic example of resilience in law firms. The more frequently the partners have discussions about how to improve performance, the more efficient they become and the more trusting they become of each other and the process.

4.4 Leaders stay alert to blind spots and mental baggage in family firms

Family firms add a special dynamic to many governance-related issues. The fact that one's partner might also be a close relative can substantially affect feedback and frank discussions, for better or worse – especially when sensitive issues involve deeply rooted familial roles and expectations.

Family dynamics can create blind spots, particularly when family members who think they know each other well jump to erroneous conclusions or make inaccurate assumptions about one another's motivations, intentions and capabilities. These untested presumptions could annoy and alienate the other person just when that person's help, cooperation and buy-in are needed most, when dealing with matters of individual performance or managing change.

Emotional residue or 'baggage' from previous experiences might cause a partner to hang on to a grudge or resentment too long, creating frustration and anxiety. Power and control issues that have their roots in unresolved tensions and intergenerational family politics may become exaggerated and difficult to manage in professional working relationships.

It often happens in family dynamics that members hold each other to different – and often unspoken – standards of behaviour, support and contribution. In frustration, they blame each other when their expectations are not mutually met.

This dynamic plays out, often at an unconscious level, when partners under and overcompensate for a close familial bond in day-to-day experiences in the firm. A junior partner may not receive enough visible attention and praise from her senior parent because the partner does not want to be perceived as showing favouritism. A senior partner may be furious that her associate son questioned her judgement in a group meeting, when she would not apply the same standards of deference and compliance to a non-family associate in the firm.

4.5 Leaders take responsibility

Successful leaders assume that partner performance requires a collective response. They accept responsibility for the connection between their decisions and indecision and the quality of the work environment and the professional relationships in it.

They also actively decide which leadership behaviours they will pay attention to and use in order to create the best conditions for partner performance to thrive.

When partners blame others for mistakes or problems, they avoid looking at themselves and taking responsibility for their leadership role and joint accountability. This is not to say that they should not hold others in the firm accountable for their commitments; but they should also not forget to consider their own contributory role in the problem and, importantly, what they can do to help improve a situation and support needed changes going forward.

Taking responsibility means accepting that one has contributed something to the problem, regardless of one's intentions. Often leaders find opportunities to improve how they delegate and follow up. They also realise that their inability to make timely decisions can impact on a peer's stress levels and productivity. Even a person who is only 5% responsible can learn from the situation. A partner can ask: "What could I do differently next time to get a better result?" A problem with another person will be resolved only when both parties accept some responsibility for identifying needed changes and planning how to get better results in the future.

4.6 Leaders view their fellow partners as clients

Communication in law firm partnerships is a two-way process, highly analogous to the lawyer-client relationship. These leaders find that it is useful to consider one's partners as internal clients, in that they receive services in the form of information and feedback. Like external clients, these internal clients also need to communicate their own needs, expectations and supporting information to those who provide the feedback.

Fellow partners are not 'cats to be herded', any more so than external clients. They are serious, competitive, independent professionals who expect to make informed choices in their practice and careers, and can only do so when they have adequate feedback and information to evaluate benefits and consequences – just like external clients. Why would leaders in law firms expect anything else? To expect partners to simply do as they are told is unrealistic and fraught with disappointment for all parties.

The more partners know about their internal clients, like the other partners in the firm, the more likely they are to be able to adjust their approach, when necessary, in order to communicate in a way that is most relevant and inviting to the other person. When we perceive that someone else is sincerely trying to be responsive to our needs and interests, it helps us to feel respected, more relaxed and able to function in a way that is less stressful and more productive. These supportive behaviours can help a partner's internal clients in the firm to be more open to the partner's influence, direction, guidance and assistance. Peers will be more interested, motivated and willing to consider options. These conditions are equally important, if not more so, between practising family members.

4.7 Leaders learn and expand their skills of emotional intelligence

These leaders view the competencies of emotional intelligence as a set of powerful and necessary skills for improving internal communication and relationships in the legal workplace. They are not, in fact, something above and beyond being a successful lawyer; they are the very skills that contribute to lawyers' success every day. Like any other skill, they can be learned, practised, applied in different kinds of situations and measured – not by our mental intentions or stated values, but by the demonstrated effectiveness of the behaviours themselves.[10]

Dealing effectively with performance issues requires emotional self-awareness. It means knowing one's strengths and weaknesses in managing one's own emotions and interactions with others. Lawyers cannot leave their emotions at home when they go to work. Emotions are not inherently good or bad. Sometimes they can be very useful.

However, sometimes feelings and the thoughts behind them can get in the way of effectiveness. For example, when family members are also professional colleagues, partners sometimes find that they react disproportionately to a situation involving another family member, because of prior expectations and events that are not entirely work related. They also may find themselves being overly protective or demanding of family members.

Law firm partners, like everyone else, are influenced by their feelings throughout the day in their decision making, delegation and time allotment, as well as in their focus of attention and in the way they interact with others. Lawyers who are emotionally self-aware and monitor their own stress levels are usually more attuned to the factors that might be impacting on others'

10 For a more extensive discussion of emotional intelligence competencies, see *ibid*, pp161–172.

performance. Self-awareness is thus an essential starting point, for two reasons: it helps leaders to recognise their own thinking and monitor their emotional reactions and responses to the behaviours of others; and it makes them more cue sensitive and empathetic with others.[11]

One important way in which these leaders can become more emotionally self-aware is by identifying triggers: the events or actions that tend to elicit a strong emotional response. When partners know what their emotional triggers are, they can plan how to handle these potentially stressful events even before they occur. Partners have told the author that it is often the very same trigger behaviour exhibited by different people during the day that causes them stress and discomfort or gets them into trouble in relationships. Without emotional self-control, partners may act impatiently, say something they regret or exercise poor judgement that has unwanted future consequences.

Partners can also tell colleagues in advance what their triggers tend to be. In that way, their colleagues are on notice. They are then more likely to give one another the benefit of the doubt and not take each other's reactions quite so seriously – especially when a colleague's unproductive response seems disproportionate to the event. Triggers present challenges even to the most emotionally intelligent people.

The triggers that partners cite most frequently include the following:

- Someone does not perform as expected or presents an inferior work product.
- Another lawyer makes a statement that turns out not to be true, even if the misstatement was unintentional.
- Someone upon whom a partner relies does not follow through on a commitment.
- Someone does not accept responsibility for mistakes, even relatively minor ones.
- Clients show a lack of appreciation and respect for a partner's professional contributions and results.

When partners react to these triggers emotionally, they say they are quicker to judge or blame; less likely to give the other person the benefit of the doubt; more likely to waste time venting to others about the event; and less likely to retrieve a good outcome from the situation.

---

11 Better self-awareness leads to greater alertness to workplace conditions that are causing stress and probably negatively affecting performance. This involves a two-step process of first, recognising the potential stressors; and second, identifying and understanding the observable consequences. Self-awareness is important, therefore, because it makes leaders much better prepared to identify symptoms of stress in their colleagues when they themselves are aware of what stressors affect them. Like anyone else, leaders can get caught in a worry cycle, stuck on one negative thought or obsessed about a particular problem or situation. When leaders are highly stressed, even minor problems can become magnified. *Ibid*, pp46–47.

Recognising the emotional trigger for what it is allows partners to mentally choose to incorporate their emotions in a balanced way, so that they can effectively:

- reason;
- empathise with others;
- read situations accurately;
- exercise self-control;
- resolve disagreements;
- develop client relationships;
- analyse situations objectively; and
- think 'outside the box' with clients and each other.

There is an additional benefit to facing, rather than turning away from, difficult issues in partner performance. Research in group performance in businesses and professions demonstrates that when partners have the emotional competencies to successfully talk about their differences and manage disagreements, this not only builds future trust, but also is a prerequisite for a group to develop its full potential as a high-performance business team.

Partners who have developed their emotional competencies and have the agreed practices and methods in place to address performance issues are far less likely to procrastinate. They are far more likely to take constructive steps with a focus on development and improved results for the future. Optimism and strong collegial relationships prevail in this kind of working environment.

4.8 Leaders use methods and skills to get to the root causes of partner performance

Partners tend to be adept at describing what they perceive as a problem and why it concerns them. They are generally less adept at understanding the reasons why a behaviour or circumstance is occurring or recurring in the first place.

Successful partners know that this is their real challenge and opportunity. If they can get to the root causes of underperformance, for example, they have the ability to make decisions and implement changes that will reinforce positive growth and business results in a sustainable way for the future. If they can't, they won't.

Leaders who want to have more meaningful and candid discussions with their peers about performance issues may need to expand and develop existing skills of enquiry and listening. The nature and purpose of these types of discussions helps partners to choose the behaviours and methods that will most effectively facilitate the interaction. Taking a collaborative approach to understanding and solving problems requires a knowledge of options and skills, the desire to help, plus the will to invest in the development of professional relationships which are the best source of performance-related information.

In addition, using a structured change process, such as that described in the "Leading change" chapter of this book, ensures a disciplined and systematic approach to performance improvement.

5. Governance

Leaders in law firms have influence and control that exceed those of individual lawyers acting alone. They have the final say in how success is defined in their firms. Their decisions and indecision about practices and systems set the stage for individual and team performance.

Sometimes a creative solution to sources of performance discontent between partners may require that they reconsider structural assumptions such as:

- the corporate structure of the firm;
- the expectations, rights and responsibilities – including cultural values and understandings – that might constitute an unwritten 'compact' among the partners;[12]
- the distribution of management authority and accountability among the owners of the firm;
- the capital structure of the firm;
- how the firm manages the financial settlements with partners who leave the equity partnership;
- the relative profitability of the service lines and products that the firm offers;
- the relative profitability of the firm's traditional client sectors; and
- how the firm compensates partners whose books of business vary considerably in terms of fee revenue or profitability.

5.1 Trust: an essential tool in law firm governance

As with any relationship, the constant adaptability of one party without periodic reciprocity may eventually lead to resentment. Trusting relationships are developed over time through the sharing of information, ideas and feelings. Integrity in those trusting relationships requires transparency, compromise and consistent follow-through on one's commitments. The way communication is structured, formally and informally, as well as the practice standards and structures that support how partners deliver services to clients – these are the vehicles for cultivating trust in a law firm. Ambiguity in performance expectations and the systems that make performance possible are a catalyst for breakdowns in internal relationships.

---

12 Sometimes these are summarised in a 'values statement' or other document that is independent of the partnership agreement, bylaws or other 'constitution' of the corporate structure of the firm. Often, like the British constitution, they are unwritten. Whether documented or 'understood', the test of their effectiveness is whether they are demonstrated consistently in the individual and collective behaviours of the partners, and are more than just aspirations or marketing slogans.

Simply reminding oneself to give fellow partners the benefit of the doubt can reduce the desire to be argumentative. Partners say that giving people the benefit of the doubt (and assuming that their intentions are positive) helps them to stay objective. In this way, they keep the focus on desired results rather than on second guessing the other person's motives or blaming them for what has gone wrong. This decreases negative thinking, which is a huge drain of energy and an obstacle to effective performance discussions.

Nonetheless, this is very difficult to do if their internal practices and systems let them down. For example, the flow of relevant and timely information is constantly disrupted by ineffective policies, inadequate technology and competing priorities for partner time. Partners become physically exhausted by time wasters and by having to backtrack in their efforts to respond to client complaints or risks posed by underperformance of others. Their frustration builds and patience runs thin.

The transition of a partner to retirement is another challenge that has serious implications for firm governance and the finances of the partnership.[13] Law firms that have never seriously considered performance standards for any partners, or that have a cultural aversion to discussing individual partner performance, have great difficulty relying on trusting relationships to determine next steps in the performance management of retiring partners. They usually cannot respond efficiently or effectively to requests for alternative career choices for partners, which are becoming increasingly common. The foundations simply are not there.

Expectations and standards of performance for older lawyers, as well as for all partners, must be defined with clarity and flexibility. Will the partner be permitted to shift his or her time and attention away from billable legal work and on to other activities, such as marketing, teaching and representing the firm in the business and professional communities? To what extent will the partner be permitted to make this transition while still receiving a full level of cash compensation? Partnerships that avoid these questions until a crisis occurs undermine trust – an essential ingredient for making quality decisions. They also might unnecessarily lose valuable talent because of their inability to evaluate career options.

Partnerships need to become more flexible in designing options to equity ownership, such as consultancy, non-equity senior partnership or similar partner emeritus status. Senior associates and junior partners will take cues about the viability of their own long-term careers with the firm from what they observe is actually happening with transitioning partners.

---

13 For a more detailed discussion of partner succession management issues, see the chapter "Succession, retirement and beyond".

5.2 Partners and productivity

One of the distinguishing characteristics between successful, world-class law firms and ordinary ones is the level of investment that the firm makes in its people, including partners.

In consultation with hundreds of law firms over the past 30 years, the author and her colleagues have observed a direct correlation between the level of investment in the professional development of individuals and groups and key performance indicators such as:

- productivity;
- sustainable profitability;
- retention of lawyers and paralegal staff;
- client satisfaction and retention; and
- development of new business.

A frustrating aspect of productivity problems is that law firm managers and partners frequently look for the solutions in the wrong places. It may seem easier and quicker to fix a performance problem by assigning responsibility elsewhere – for example, blaming a junior lawyer or 'delivering a message' to one of your peers – rather than actively looking for root causes of performance concerns. Quick fixes seldom get results and usually just builds resentment.

The entrenched view of some partners that people simply cannot change can often be a defensive reaction that blocks growth. It can serve as a convenient cop-out for leaders who are unwilling to understand or accept how, through their actions or inaction, they have contributed to an environment that makes it unrealistic to expect to close the gap between their expectations and a colleague's performance. As a result, some lawyers seldom change because sometimes there is no communicated, apparent reason to change.[14] This is why leaders need to pay attention to signs and symptoms of problems that cause lower-than-expected productivity. Improving productivity almost always involves more than just making other people work harder;[15] it also involves working together to identify solutions and to document plans that are likely to achieve the desired results.

One of the most important challenges to law firms today is to provide a motivating environment for its professional people. Money is not enough. Money is almost never one of the top three factors that associates list as a reason for staying with their current firm.[16] The opportunity to develop future partners

---

14 *Ibid*, p156.

15 See Norman K Clark and Lisa M Walker Johnson, *Sustainable Profitability in a Disrupted Legal Market* (Globe Law and Business, 2019) pp33–45.

16 This conclusion is based on the results of hundreds of focus group sessions and individual interviews conducted by Walker Clark LLC consultants with law firm associates in Africa, the Americas, Asia-Pacific, Europe and Latin America from 2002 to 2021. Compensation is, as one of the associates described it, "the price of admission" to the competition for lawyers. If the compensation opportunity is reasonably

and professional knowledge and skills – in other words, professional development – is always one of the top motivating factors, even for partners.

If partners appear not to be motivated, an internal solution can usually be found in one or more of the functions of performance management. It is very important to remember that partners cannot directly motivate another person. However, partners can and should provide the conditions and incentives that build trust and commitment so that they can open up about what they need, what's working for them and what isn't. Only then can leaders make well-informed decisions about how to respond.

Leaders are uniquely responsible for acting on environmental stressors to minimise these negative consequences for partners' performance. If leaders ignore and diminish the importance of the realities of their colleagues' perceptions of their working experiences and relationships, their colleagues will understandably withdraw and productivity will suffer.

Sometimes partner productivity and overall performance are affected by external factors in their personal lives or an unsatisfactory experience with a client that they feel uneasy about discussing with peers. Partners are often reluctant to ask for help, for a variety of reasons. When leaders can connect one to one, even if they don't know the details, they may be able to help their colleagues to think about their challenges as manageable and a natural part of professional life and the human experience. The message is, "You are not alone and there is always hope." This can result in partners feeling more optimistic and in control of their options, even if the leader simply listens and supports. It also minimises the ripple effect of negative stress throughout the firm.

Productivity concerns do not always require partners to 'fix' the other person. When partners honestly describe what they are observing, explain why they are concerned and seek out their colleagues' input before launching into solutions, they are much more likely to encourage improvement. Leaders may be able to act to remove obstacles to desired performance; however, very often their best role is to encourage and support, creating the confidence and conditions for colleagues to get out of a rut and take necessary actions on their own.

---

competitive in the local market, as it usually has to be, young lawyers make their decisions to join or remain with a firm based on other factors, such as the opportunity to do meaningful legal work for a client; the opportunity to learn from a successful partner; or the presence of at least a general career path that defines what a lawyer must do to advance in the firm. During the economic disruptions during the COVID-19 pandemic from 2020 to early 2022, we observed that compensation was more frequently a consideration that might drive associates or younger partners to leave their current law firm; but continuity of professional opportunity – as expressed in terms of the three major recruiting and retention factors above – remains more important for most lawyers.

Figure 1. Performance as the product of the total work environment

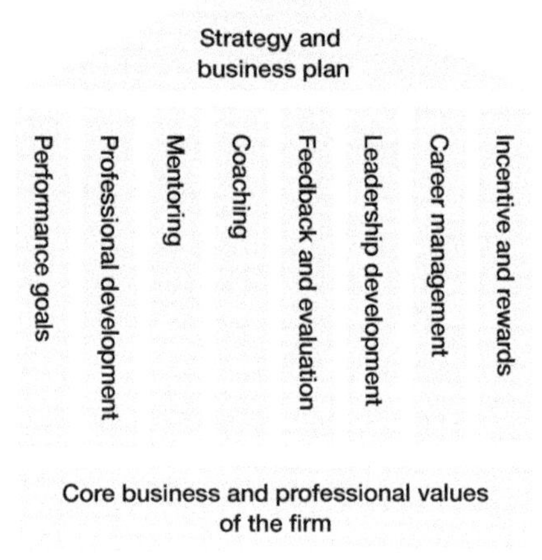

5.3 The structure of a performance management system in a law firm

One way of thinking about the structure of a performance management system is to view it as a complex, integrated and aligned structure of at least eight management functions that are aimed at accomplishing the business plan based on the values of the firm. These eight areas interact, directing and transmitting the core business and professional values of the firm into actions that lead to desired strategic and business results.

Some firms have different names for these eight functions. Some document these functions; others don't. Some firms use these functions only on an *ad hoc* basis, but they nonetheless exist in some form. If a law firm has a performance issue, the underlying causes and possible solutions can usually be found in one or, more frequently, several of these eight functions. Exceptions might be personal matters, including competing familial demands and wellness issues such as physical illness, substance use, mental illness or cognitive deterioration.

There is no formulaic solution or best way to implement or improve performance management in a law firm. Any one of these eight functions might be the right place to start, depending on the needs and unique characteristics of the firm. Even when a direct causal relationship cannot be clearly traced to one of the eight functions, they can function as an 'early warning system', alerting the firm's management and individual lawyers to a potential problem before it erupts into a crisis; and they can also be insightful diagnostic tools to find and address the basic causes. This can lead to highly cost-effective solutions, rather than just superficial responses to mitigate the effects.

(a) *Performance goals*

Partners plan partner development and actions to improve performance by creating and documenting goals and action plans.[17]

Most people do not perform unsatisfactorily because they want to. Even partners have to know what it is they have to achieve and how this will be measured.

Goals are more likely to be achieved if they are specific, measurable, agreed by both parties, realistic and time based. They help to convert business aspirations and good intentions into tangible actions. Performance goals also provide partners with written documentation to guide them in managing time and other resources against the agreed priorities and budget. As such, an effective goal automatically includes an up-to-date action plan for achieving it.

While mistakes can be costly in legal matters, the goal achievement process is flexible and is meant to be used with openness to the unexpected. Some partners may cringe when hearing that. They prefer to set the goal and drive it to closure no matter what. However, in a complex business and professional practice environment, this can be suicidal.

Perfectionistic thinking is detrimental to goal achievement. Bypassing the good while striving for perfection can contribute to procrastination and inertia. An important component of goal setting is the monitoring and reporting of performance measurements so that partners can make informed decisions about what is working and what is not working.

Busy partners may be racing so fast every day that they miss important opportunities or even obvious risks, such as the potential impact of a key contact leaving a valuable client. Performance goals need to allow partners to be open to, and respond effectively to, unexpected events and new information. They work most effectively if the firm's management and the individual partner communicate often enough to keep the goals and the plans for achieving them up to date, agreed and squarely in the context of the evolving strategic and economic priorities of the firm.[18]

Keeping performance goals relevant and up to date requires that they not be put in a notebook on a dusty shelf or saved in an obscure archive directory on a file server and then forgotten. It is important to set aside time for serious discussion about expectations, priorities, goals, development needs and other performance issues. Avoid other distractions during these meetings. This is one of the most effective ways to avoid misunderstandings during the year, as well as disputes, recriminations and distrust at the end.

---

17 See the chapter "Leading change", which creates the context for planning in a change process.

18 This principle is also important in the management and achievement of group goals, such as those in a practice group business plan.

A list of planned activities is not a goal. Goals should be stated in terms of what partners will actually achieve as a result of the planned activities. The activities are the methods or steps that a partner will take to achieve the goal. This is also known as an action plan.

During the course of the fiscal year, the approach to achieving certain goals or the measurements that constitute satisfactory completion of a goal may need to be adjusted in light of new information. Goal achievement can certainly be a 'learn as you go' process for law firms and individual partners. This fact frustrates some partners who expect nothing less than 100% compliance and who view any changes to goals or plans of action as a dumbing down of the process. However, keep in mind the purpose of performance goals when evaluating the need for modifications during the year.

Individual and group performance goals help a firm to ensure that it will:

- achieve the firm-wide business plan;
- create a motivating professional environment for partners;
- focus partners on both developmental and performance priorities;
- expand partners' skills and professional experiences;
- create efficiencies in time management; and
- anticipate budgetary requirements in executing the business plan.

If partners think that the goals are inflexible, unfair, unrealistic, tricky or coercive, they will feel demotivated. Vague or non-existent communications about goals during the year will undermine important professional relationships and lead – particularly for younger partners – to suspicion and distrust about what it takes to be successful in the firm. None of this will help the firm to achieve its business plan.

Because they should be linked, directly or indirectly, to the firm's strategic objectives and business plan, individual performance goals should help to keep a sharp focus on the most important priorities.

To do this, some law firms establish firm-wide goal categories for all partners. These firms select three to five key priority areas each year, such as financial contribution, professional development, client service, business development, quality improvement or profitability. Every partner writes individual performance goals – commensurate with his or her unique roles and responsibilities – that contribute to the firm's initiatives in each of the selected goal categories. Certain practice groups may even select a goal category that reinforces an area of needed attention and improvement for their specific team. All goals are discussed and agreed with the firm's management, such as with a practice group head, managing partner or management committee.

Sharing priorities with others helps to make the goals happen. When partners share goals, this increases accountability and improves motivation and consistency. Partners can coach one another to help everyone stay on track. It is also easier to ask for help from others when they are already aware of their own goals and some of the potential needs and obstacles.

Goals help all partners to focus their mental energy and achievement orientation. Partners tell me that when they have made commitments to their peers in the form of performance goals, they feel highly committed to achieving them – partially because they do not want to let down their colleagues. They say that the goals help with decision making, time management and both their mental and physical stamina. The partners report that goals help them to stay on track: they waste less time and feel more in control of their lives, which reduces negative stress.

Goal achievement must be aligned with financial incentives. Law firms that are starting a goal-setting process will want to phase it in with careful and ongoing attention to the quality of the process and the integration of performance goals with other performance management functions such as career management, annual evaluations and bonuses and compensation. Partners will need skills in setting and achieving effective performance goals, coaching and developing others and leading change.

(b) Professional development

A professional development plan is important, but it is only a management tool. It must be supported by a functioning, serious programme of ongoing professional development that is relevant to the knowledge and skills that partners and associates need to succeed in their practices and in their firms. It must also be aligned with clear goals and rewards.

As one law firm partner noted: "Professional development enables us to take our strengths and get them in the right place – when and where we need them."

Professional development is a central pillar of performance management, for two reasons:

- First, in a profitable, successful law firm, associates must be able to perform sophisticated legal tasks. The partners cannot do everything. Law firms in which partners delegate important legal functions to associates are usually more profitable than those in which the partners try to do all the work themselves. However, to be able to delegate work efficiently, partners must be confident that the associates have the knowledge and skills necessary to do the work competently.
- Second, the associates are the future of any law firm. Some law firms promote associates to partner status before they are ready to perform the duties of a partner. As a result, the performance of these new partners is sometimes unsatisfactory, both professionally and financially. In almost every case, this is because the firm failed to provide the opportunities and support necessary for the new partner to develop skills and knowledge when he or she was an associate. In essence, they set up the

new partners to fail and sadly, in some cases, then blame those same partners for their underperformance.

Development involves more than legal knowledge and expertise. It also requires that associates learn business skills that are almost never taught in law school, such as marketing and sales, client relations, performance feedback, negotiations and business leadership. This is a vital responsibility of a law firm's partners, collectively and individually. However, most law firms forget about these important business skills. As a result, many associates are unprepared to become the kind of agile leaders and owners of a law firm they need to be when they are promoted to partner. It should be no surprise that when these associates are promoted to the partnership, other partners often start complaining about allegedly unproductive partners.

Successful law firms integrate a wide range of competencies, in addition to legal skills, into development programmes, performance appraisals and goal setting. They find ways to identify, observe and reinforce behaviours that are important to the climate of the firm, client relationships, teamwork and the development of future business owners and leaders.

To provide motivation for all lawyers, professional development programmes must be relevant to each lawyer's practice and must be treated by management as a high-priority matter. Too many law firms have professional development plans that look good on paper, but do not operate in real life; or if they do, they are largely irrelevant to the changing needs of the firm's lawyers as they progress through their careers.

Professional development plans are only one part of an integrated approach to performance management that also includes other functions such as individual and group performance goals. A good professional development plan can help to provide a structure in which feedback, both formal and informal, can take place.

(c) Mentoring

Mentoring contributes to the supportive environment necessary for sustained performance in law firms. Law firms that are most successful with performance management and achieve the best business results have an active network of informal and formal mentoring relationships in place.

Mentoring is about more than getting business results. It provides a cultural conduit, integrating new and developing lawyers into the values and client relationships of the firm. Trusted mentors teach the 'secret handshakes', introduce lawyers to key contacts and instruct them in the rules for successful relationships inside the firm, with clients and with the business and professional communities. They help developing lawyers to become resilient, tolerant and politically and culturally savvy. They also help them to learn qualities such as humility and how not to take themselves too seriously.

Mentors teach that our vulnerabilities are not who we are as people. Lawyers do not try to be rigid, inflexible, controlling or difficult. However, it is easy for others to misconstrue lawyers' less helpful behaviours and assign negative motives to their colleagues' intentions. Mentors can provide valuable perspectives about how to process, interpret and respond to colleagues' behaviours. They also help lawyers to monitor their own behaviour, solicit feedback about it and even describe their tendencies to others in advance of problems to avoid misunderstandings.

Quality time with one's mentor may allow a lawyer to explore deeper levels of thinking and self-reflection – important attributes for professionals who need to be ready to deal effectively with ethical dilemmas and change, and to help others through these decisions and their consequences.

One way of thinking about mentoring is to consider the mentoring relationship as one that allows a lawyer to develop self-confidence and insight by frankly discussing situations that have a bearing on his or her professional life but might not necessarily be related to legal work.[19]

(d) Coaching

Coaching and mentoring are two distinct performance management functions, although there may be some overlap. They can be performed by the same person, but there are potential drawbacks with this.

Whereas mentoring includes a broader enculturation into the legal profession and the practice of law in a law firm, coaching is a function that focuses primarily on the acquisition and application at work of specific technical and professional skills. Both coaches and mentors are helping roles[20] that facilitate problem solving, although they might focus on different types of problems or different aspects of the same problem in their respective roles.

Effective coaching relationships identify and resolve obstacles to performance at individual and group levels. They ensure that lawyers have the tools and resources to do their jobs well.

Coaches delegate work so that lawyers have exposure to assignments and experience that will help them to advance in their careers. They also build self-confidence in developing lawyers so they will self-evaluate, self-coach and persevere in stressful situations.

---

19 See Walker Johnson (n 6), pp141–146, for a discussion of the components of effective mentoring components in law firms. The return on investment of partners' time in terms of improved performance by associates is perhaps that highest of any partner activity in a law firm. Yet many law firms – including those which are well managed in other respects – overlook mentoring entirely or implement it in a haphazard way.

20 See *ibid*, pp39–62, for a discussion of the 'helping' roles that partners perform, such as coaching and mentoring, and how important it is for them to understand their options and choices; become more self-aware so that they can effectively help others; consider how their personal biases can affect how they perceive and respond to a performance problem; and think about time differently to build buy-in and reduce procrastination. Helping skills and roles should be agreed responsibilities of every partner.

Coaches can be invaluable resources if they understand the work context and pressures; refrain from judging or pontificating; and can adapt to some extent to the individual learning style and needs of another lawyer.

Both mentoring and coaching can provide important opportunities for partners to work closely with developing lawyers and to plan for meaningful contact with clients. Associates in focus groups worldwide consistently cite working closely with partners and high visibility with clients as being among the top five reasons to stay with their firm. Interesting and challenging work, a relationship with an important mentor and the opportunity to advance in one's career are the other three.

(e) Feedback and evaluation

A lack of feedback leads to selective hearing, wishful thinking, distortions of fact, fear and unrealistic expectations of colleagues and business potential.

How leaders think about the purpose and function of feedback influences how they build it into their professional practices and deal with issues in their organisations. Using the question "Why?" can invite lawyers to think about a situation from a new perspective and challenge assumptions about what they previously took for granted. It can also prompt a defensive reaction when lawyers distrust their leaders' motives and think that the leaders' intentions are to blame. If leaders approach feedback with an adversarial mindset, they might interpret objections and differing points of view as opposition or even suspect disloyalty or sabotage. Their tendency to take offence might result in behavioural choices that exclude colleagues. Effective feedback thus depends on trusting relationships.[21]

Mutual respect among professionals begins with an understanding that we are each responsible for making choices about what we think, feel and do. Partners are entitled to make informed choices about their careers. The only behaviour that leaders can control is their own. What leaders can achieve through feedback is to help partners understand the benefits of change as well as the risks and consequences of not doing things differently.[22]

Sometimes lawyers have logically concluded, based on what they have observed in their firms or among their colleagues, that there is no real consequence to their behaviour that would impede their ability to get what they want out of their working relationships and the practice of law. They perceive no need to change.

---

21 See *ibid*, pp104–114, on how feedback – although essential to improve performance – can also contribute to stress if not skilfully done.

22 Many lawyers find it difficult to view their feedback methods through 'the eye of the beholder', and not just their own good intentions. As a profession, lawyers highly value competence; and it is not easy to give or receive feedback that suggests areas for improvement, especially in the non-technical domain of emotional competencies that they might associate with who they are as a person: "This is who I am; take it or leave it." Such resistance is understandable if a lawyer sees emotional competencies as something separate from being a good lawyer, rather than being a part of it. *Ibid*, p166.

At the same time, these lawyers' leaders and colleagues sometimes do not realise that they have fixed beliefs that set up a self-fulfilling prophecy dynamic for themselves and others: a deeply seated belief that people do not change. This, too, can block any sincere efforts at improvement.[23]

For any kind of performance management to work, partners need to receive feedback and evaluation of their work on a timely and consistent basis. The quality of feedback – its accuracy and reliability – affects the outcomes just as does any other type of data. When the data is credible, it can be integrated into problem solving, decision making and planning with an intellectual rigour and a degree of confidence that would otherwise be absent. Reliable information discourages complacency and, instead, promotes factual corroboration and the timely continuous testing of assumptions.[24]

The professional relationship that one has cultivated with colleagues prior to the feedback conversation, the way that one states the issue or concern and the willingness to ask questions – all of these factors will influence how the feedback is received and the actions that it produces. Asking questions for clarification and understanding is frequently a missing element of many feedback sessions. The partner giving the feedback makes a speech or 'delivers the message', and the person receiving it often silently or verbally rebuts the assertions of the evaluator. Questions and comments are oriented to explaining, rationalising and blaming more than they are to sharing different points of view, learning from each other and finding ways to work together for desired outcomes. Even when the existing professional relationship is otherwise effective, such as between a supervising partner and an associate, treating feedback as essentially one-way communication dramatically lowers the probability of it being productive and achieving the desired results.

There is an art to using questions in feedback sessions.

Of course, transparency is always important when asking questions. Most law firm partners are perceptive people. Most partners will know very quickly whether colleagues sincerely want to learn their point of view or, instead, have their own agendas and are merely going through the motions of asking questions while not really caring about the answers.

In addition, partners will become defensive if they feel that questions are intended to trap them or simply to lead their thinking to the 'proper' predetermined conclusion. Rather than opening up a genuine exchange of ideas, trick questions or leading questions usually elicit minimal answers, given with great reluctance. However, if partners are honest about their views,

23 For a further discussion of the impact of fixed mind-sets about receptivity to change, see *ibid*, pp154–157.

24 Collecting data is an important first step in preparing to give feedback. Without good data from a variety of sources and perspectives, internally and externally, we are only guessing; and if experience is any indicator, we will usually guess wrong. For a detailed discussion of the role of data collection as part of an effective, ongoing feedback process, see *ibid*, pp81–83.

intentions and expectations, the person receiving the feedback will usually respond positively to their questions.

Closed questions can be important for establishing a factual base or for clarifying and obtaining information. While they can be very useful, they are not the best type of question to ask if one wants the other person to open up and become mentally engaged.

An example of a closed question that is usually not very useful is, "Do you understand what I am trying to say?" On the other hand, it may be helpful to confirm a fact by asking, "I understand that you have met with the client about the complaint. Is that correct?"

Open questions encourage the other person to share more information. They give a greater range of possibilities for response. However, if used too early in the performance discussion, before intentions are clear and trust is established, the other person may be uncomfortable answering an open-ended question. It may seem too vague or general, and therefore too risky to answer. Open-ended questions may need setting up so the colleague understands the intention and rationale for asking the question – for example: "Clients have been telling me that they find our new invoices confusing. What are they telling you?"

Other examples of open questions include the following:

- "How do you see the situation?"
- "What ideas do you have about the new marketing plan?"
- "In what ways could we enhance the lawyers' knowledge of the new industry sectors that our firm is bringing into our client base?"

The questions that lawyers seem to like best are those that make them think. These are excellent tools for mentally engaging another person – which builds buy-in – and for obtaining highly valuable information.

These questions encourage lawyers to think by asking them to compare, evaluate, analyse or speculate about two factors or variables. When asked a thought-provoking question, a lawyer might say something like, "Hmmm, let me think about that for a minute"; or "That is an excellent question!"

It helps to plan some of the thought-provoking questions to be asked in a performance discussion. Some may become favourites that can be used regularly. Others might develop spontaneously during the meeting.

Here are some examples of thought-provoking questions:

- "How would you compare X to Y?" For example:
  - "How would you compare the design of our website to that of other firms in our region?"
  - "What is the difference between how you are doing this now and how you did it last year?"
- "What if we did X instead of Y?" For example:

  - "What if we affiliated with them for a year rather than considering an actual merger right now?"
  - "What do you believe would be the two or three most significant consequences with this client if we stopped charging hourly rates and went to fixed fee proposals?"
- "How would you evaluate X and Y?" For example:
  - "Please evaluate the strengths and weaknesses of the two senior associates that we are considering for transfer into your practice group."
  - "Which method for developing business – writing articles or giving presentations – works best for you, and why?"

There is no point in asking questions if we are not going to listen to the answers. Most of us think we are better listeners than we are. A lot of things can get in the way and cause distractions, including our own internal, mental 'self-talk'. Using listening responses – to demonstrate to the other person that we actually are listening – can de-escalate a stressful situation, show empathy and build rapport, help with problem solving and strengthen relationships. Listening behaviours vary according to cultures: they can be non-verbal, such as eye contact; and verbal, such as paraphrasing and empathising.

Effective feedback is not about being nice. It is about being clear and objective. When the performance issue is described in terms of behaviours that can be seen and heard, it is more likely to depersonalise the situation, remove the personal judgement factor and clarify what needs to be done in order to improve. When partners feel that their moral fibre or professional integrity is being questioned – for example, "You have a bad attitude" or "Your behaviour was unprofessional" – the results of feedback discussions are poor and relationships are frequently damaged.

Without frequent and regular feedback, even the best-written goals or professional development or career management plans will fail. Feedback can take place in structured meetings of the partnership and practice groups, as well as in annual or semi-annual performance discussions. To be effective in improving performance together, look for ways to improve performance in the future and do not just criticise shortcomings of the past.

Formal development discussions and evaluations are not enough. Partners need to be adept at giving and receiving performance feedback regularly, in the context of evolving client, legal and business priorities.

An essential step in any feedback discussion is to bring it to closure. Sometimes partners are so relieved to have simply brought the subject up and delivered their message that they want to finish things quickly.

However, just as with a client, demonstrating one's commitment to a plan of action is a critical skill. If partners plan to keep things on track and sustain an improvement effort over time, that firmness of purpose yields results. Agreements should be made and confirmed at the end of the meeting in the management of any performance issue.

(f) Leadership development

Leadership development is especially important in law firms. In most firms, partners are expected not only to market the business and earn fees, but to be professional and business leaders in the firm.

Any law firm can be an organisation with leaders. The most successful firms, however, evolve into organisations of leaders. In a firm of leaders, everyone – from the most senior partner or owner to the most junior clerk – is welcome and expected to speak up, identify problems and contribute to doing things differently and better. Everyone is expected to contribute to a law firm culture that fosters and sustains success.

Making leadership roles accessible to every member of the firm does not dilute leadership. Everyone has strengths that they can bring to bear on different types of situations, at different times, for different reasons.

Leadership is not a philosophy. Instead, it is a set of skills and behaviours that in successful firms creates a motivating environment for performance. Skilled leaders in law firms lead by personal example and by creating the conditions that encourage others to achieve the firm's goals and their own. Beyond that, leaders contribute to the qualities in a law firm that ready it for inevitable change.

Partners have traditionally invested their time and resources in developing specific professional and technical skills. Technical expertise has been their ticket to success. They understandably take pride in their professional reputations and legal competence.

They typically have given much less thought to the skills of emotional intelligence that form the core of effective leadership and business development – even when lawyers use many of these skills every day with clients, as board members and in other roles in their communities.

A consideration of leadership has produced some unfortunate mythology for law firms. There is a widely held assumption that lawyers, by nature, are not good leaders or followers; that they are too impatient or too individualistic or too egotistical to lead others or respond to leadership. This urban legend, fuelled by unskilled leadership and junk science, can wrongly influence law firms to overlook or dismiss the leadership potential that everyone possesses.

The question of whether there is such a thing as a born leader is irrelevant in most successful law firms. Every partner is expected to be ready and able to contribute as a leader in their areas of respective strength, and to demonstrate specific leadership behaviours when the need arises.

Ideally, leadership development starts early in the career of every lawyer. Partners are more likely to improve their leadership skills if they:

- see how leadership skills will help them to achieve their goals and objectives;
- know what leadership behaviours are expected of them by the firm;
- receive feedback from trusted colleagues that helps them to understand the impact of their behaviour on others;
- recognise that the choices they make about their own leadership behaviour will be viewed by their partners as a measurement of their contribution to the firm;
- understand the link between leadership behaviours and performance in the firm, including its business results; and
- have the opportunity to learn and practice new non-technical skills in a supportive environment – one that does not demand perfection and rewards incremental progress through feedback and coaching.

Developing future leaders can involve many types of activities. Doing things together that encourage firm members to identify areas for improvement, problem solve and even have fun together creates experiences that contribute to the qualities of self-confident leadership. These activities are important, and yet somewhat different, in every firm. Here are some examples:

- Some firms use client complaints as opportunities to test the *status quo* and look for better alternatives.
- Staff and lawyers talk about internal work processes together and use problem-solving techniques to find ways to improve client service.
- Partners make time to share insights about specific clients and their businesses in staff meetings, so that younger lawyers learn how to become trusted business advisers as well as technically excellent lawyers.
- Firms offer internal seminars, skills training and 'lunch and learn' programmes for partners and staff to attend together in a spirit of fun and *esprit de corps*.

Some partners say: "Let's just teach leadership skills to the associates. It's too late for us!" However, many partners overlook the fact that they are already leading the associates – sometimes in the wrong direction. Associates take their cues from the top. They will model the behaviours that partners use, regardless of what the partners say. Associates observe and will eventually emulate the accepted practices of leadership (or non-leadership) that they observe in the firm every day.

Law firms must be prepared to say no to non-leadership behaviours that are inconsistent with the values, desired culture and needs of the firm and its clients.

For example, if the law firm has committed to a regular process of performance reviews and coaching and one partner does not carry out his or her responsibilities, that partner needs to understand both the benefits of participating and the consequences of not participating, in order to make an informed choice. In some firms, performance reviews and coaching are considered to be among the basic duties of a partner and dereliction can be grounds for financial sanctions, such as a reduction in shares or discretionary elements of the partner's compensation or, in extreme cases, expulsion from the partnership.

If a partnership is trying to be more inclusive of junior partners in the decision-making process and a senior partner continues to dominate and bully others into submission, that partner needs to know that violating the limits of acceptable behaviour will detract from how the other partners measure his or her contribution to the firm, regardless of his or her portfolio of clients and fee revenue. Sometimes a negotiated resignation or retirement is the only practical option, and the best solution, for dealing with bullies and untempered egos.

If associates are given responsibility without authority, they will become discouraged and frustrated. Partners should ensure that they delegate carefully, assigning formal leadership tasks when associates are ready for them and not just when it is convenient to 'dump' work or responsibilities. If partners delegate authority and then micro-manage the leadership task, they will only increase frustration and ensure that next time, the associate will avoid taking on such a dissatisfying responsibility. Associates need to know that partners value them and appreciate their contributions. They also need to know that partners are willing to help them grow as professional businesspeople and future leaders, not just as technically competent lawyers.

Firms with motivated associates experience higher morale, expanding client relationships and higher fee generation than those firms which do not make a similar investment in the leadership development of their future partners. Acquiring, reinforcing and improving leadership skills is a career-long investment for successful partners and their firms.

The success of the firm in dealing with performance requirements depends on its ability to produce adaptable leaders who can respond to the changing leadership needs of the firm and its partners. Evolving circumstances and performance expectations will require different types of leadership behaviours.

Most of the law firm failures in dealing with partner performance involve one or both of these two problems: partner abdication of leadership responsibilities or a refusal to deal with internal conflicts within the partnership.

Partners can be good leaders and good followers if they choose to be. Sometimes that means relearning skills in a new context. Sometimes it means a willingness to 'look in the mirror' to understand how other firm members perceive one's leadership effectiveness and then make improvements. Once partners organise development goals and plans to improve, they tend to be quite motivated. However, any effort to change behaviours also takes discipline and a sustained willingness to practise, relearn and relearn again.

(g) *Career management*

Career management is the path that enables junior lawyers in the firm to understand what they need to do to be successful. It also ensures that they have the opportunity to perform. It is one of the most important leadership responsibilities of partners and must not be abdicated to the human resources department.

The law firms with the strongest career management programmes usually also have the strongest retention rates and find that talented lawyers seek them out. There are also strong observed correlations between:

- the existence of a well-documented, functioning career management plan – preferably one that includes partners and associates;
- the quality of the firm's management of the growth of its partnership and, in some firms, its management of its equity structure and capitalisation;
- the ability of the firm to execute successful shifts in the traditional career path, especially at the partner level, in order to match individual professional strengths with emerging opportunities in the market; and
- the relative ease and cost effectiveness of the firm's succession planning and transition of senior partners to post-equity roles in the firm.

Embedded in a career management programme is the concept of choice. This enables both lawyers and the firm to make better-informed decisions about career progression and career options. However, to facilitate career progression, the career management programme must be supported by partner modelling of desired behaviours along with training and development opportunities. The starting point frequently is a simple question: "What knowledge, skills and capabilities do we require before we will be confident that we are making a wise decision to admit an associate to the partnership, or to position a senior associate who is not on the partner track as an industry sector expert?"

For example, if a firm wants partners to develop business, it will need to assess associates' skills and provide development opportunities that are commensurate with individual needs and priorities. This does not mean that the firm would benefit from sending its associates on external courses on marketing and sales. Many firms, in the spirit of learning together, participate in internal seminars or do joint calls with partners and senior associates, even if they can't bill the client for all of their time. Partners help associates learn how to write their own business plans and set relevant marketing goals. When lawyers are subsequently rewarded in various ways for their goal achievements and other contributions to the firm's marketing efforts, they realise that they are jointly accountable, together with the partners, for their ultimate success both in the firm and in their careers.

Without such a serious and collaborative approach to the professional development of relevant skills needed to succeed in one's designated professional role or to become a partner, even the most elaborate career development document will quickly be discovered by associates to be a sham.

(h) Incentives and rewards

Partners are more likely to invest the effort to achieve goals when there are clear incentives to do so. Rewards are not always monetary. Partners must also clearly understand the consequences of both performing and underperforming.

For example, incentives that are dispersed to junior partners without clear expectations and without corollary professional development, skills and coaching will likely lead to greater frustration than motivated performance. It is surprising how many law firms will dangle a carrot, such as a bonus for the origination of new work, expecting improved results without making any investment in the business development and marketing skills of the lawyers, all the while ignoring their pleas for help. These junior partners quickly realise that the bonus plan is really a fool's errand and become even more cynical and demotivated than before the incentives were offered.

The importance of incentives and rewards is now recognised as a substantial governance issue, as the basic structures of partner compensation are increasingly being included in partnership agreements – especially in systems that link compensation to a partner's position in the class structure of the partnership. When partnerships make major strategic decisions that affect the roles and responsibilities of partners, one now hears – more than at any other time in recent history – questions about the adequacy of the firm's incentives to motivate partners to meet the new expectations. For example, will the firm's existing structures and policies for partner remuneration provide the motivations that some partners might need to change their individual priorities and behaviours? If not, what is missing?

5.4 Making the performance management system support good law firm governance

It is important to remember that each of these eight management functions is like a lever that can be used to understand causes and find solutions for performance issues in law firms. Partner performance is especially complex because of the many roles and responsibilities that traditional law firm governance places on each partner: owner, business leader, professional supervisor, marketer, public relations representative, manager and revenue producer.

Even small law firms can be very complex systems of policies, practices, personalities, values and taboos. Just as success requires the coordination of the many 'moving parts' of a law firm, performance issues almost never involve only one event, factor, cause or person. As W Edwards Deming observed: "A bad system will beat a good person every time."[25]

A systems approach to understanding problems and changing behaviours focuses attention on the total work environment, not just the individual. In this way, leaders can identify the root causes of problems, which are usually found at various points in the organisation and the ways that it works to impact the thinking and feelings of partners and others.[26]

An often-overlooked part of partner performance is leadership behaviour itself. Sometimes leaders' decisions may make them captive to a work environment that perpetuates their own frustrations and disappointments with performance. Examining the system in which behaviours occur helps partners get to the root causes of problems faster and more efficiently – if they have access to data, information and different points of view. Putting these in place is part of the planning for performance improvement in a change process. A focus on understanding and planning first, then acting to get results produces better sustainable improvements than swatting ineffectively at the obvious symptoms.[27]

Although the system is complex, there are two important starting points for leaders that apply in all situations:

- The first is to understand the concept and process for creating a motivating work environment where professionals can make informed choices.
- The second universal tool in performance management is to reframe performance issues through communication, thoughtful analysis, a tolerance for some ambiguity and an opening of options.

For example, a junior partner is not meeting targets. Many partners will initially state the issue this way: "Why won't George meet his billing targets?"

This question usually also connotes other unspoken pre-judgements and assumptions: "Who does he think he is? We have told him how important it is and he's just not trying!"

---

25 W Edwards Deming, address to the Deming Four Day Seminar, Phoenix, Arizona, United States, February 1993, https://deming.org/a-bad-system-will-beat-a-good-person-every-time/. For more analysis of the role of systems in performance in business organisations, see W Edwards Deming, *Out of the Crisis* (MIT Press, updated edition, 2018).

26 In their rush to find a solution to an urgent problem, anyone – not just partners – can often fail to probe the systems and processes deeply enough. They feel rushed to accept a superficially correct cause and, unsurprisingly, are frequently disappointed by the results they get when they fail to search more deeply. The author recommends the inquiry method summarised as "Ask 'why' five times", first introduced by Sakichi Toyoda, founder of Toyota Industries, in the 1930s. For an excellent summary of the method, see "5 Whys", *MindTools*, www.mindtools.com/a3mi00v/5-whys.

27 For an extensive discussion of the importance of systems thinking in a structured change process (which is what performance management is), see Walker Johnson (n 6), pp183–212.

This sets up a dynamic of blaming George and assuming a lack of motivation on his part. The other partners already appear to have decided the issue or assumed the worst.

What if instead, partners asked: "What is preventing George from meeting his billing targets? We know he understands that this is important, so what could be happening?"

Consider what happens simply by reframing the issue in neutral terms. The whole scope of inquiry expands to take into account all the complex pieces of a law firm. It removes the factor of judgement and the assumed deficiency of the individual, and it also looks at how the firm works.

The most significant causes of many partners' performance problems are factors to which they often have given little thought or analysis, much less tried to resolve. Castigating George without addressing these other factors is unlikely to solve the problem. George's individual performance might increase marginally due to his being motivated by peer pressure or guilt about having let down his colleagues, but this result will only be temporary. The true causes of the substandard performance will remain, notwithstanding George's best intentions. Moreover, the intellectual analysis that reframing permits in George's case could also lead to the causes of and solutions for similar issues involving other partners or associates.

6. Quality working relationships

Unlike many other businesses, which depend on supplies, raw materials, machines and movement of inventory, a law firm must rely primarily on people to achieve its strategic objectives and deliver its business plan. Because of the multiplicity of critical roles that partners perform in most law firms, their performance is especially critical to the sustainable success of the firm. As a governance matter, the partners of a law firm must be able to make executive decisions with a reasonable degree of confidence that they can and will be carried out. An integrated approach to performance management is therefore an essential part of good law firm governance, in that it is the most effective way to ensure that all partners and associates meet their obligations to the firm, to each other and to their clients.

Taking charge of planned change[28] by improving internal communication structures and the performance management system is an effective way to ensure that partners don't take their professional relationships for granted and have the capabilities to perform well. When they develop the leadership knowledge, self-awareness, and skills to do this well, everyone wins!

The question is not whether partners can, but rather whether they will:

28 For a further discussion of taking charge of planned change, see the chapter "Leading change".

- create the conditions, practices and work environment that encourage improved partner performance in technical and leadership roles;
- support partners' efforts to develop the resilience they need to contend with the increasing demands and stressors of the legal workplace; and
- lead with realistic optimism and confidence to future success.

Riding the compensation tiger

Norman K Clark
Walker Clark LLC

There once was a lady from Niger
Who went for a ride on a tiger.
They returned from the ride
With the lady inside
And a smile on the face of the tiger.
Traditional limerick

This chapter addresses five basic issues that each law firm should resolve as part of the process of aligning and integrating the partner compensation structure and policies with the implementation of the firm's strategic direction and business decisions. These are governance issues, not just financial ones. They have a fundamental relationship to how the partners choose to govern themselves and their firm, and only the partners of the firm are in the organisational position to make fully informed strategic decisions about each one. The answers to these questions are always highly firm specific, but each one is universally important to ensure that partner compensation remains a relevant factor in the success of each law firm.

1. Moving beyond carrots and sticks

Compensation is more than a 'carrot and stick' scheme to manipulate partners to do whatever the firm's management wants. Instead, in the most successful law firms, it is an integrated part of a broader strategic understanding by those firms' partners of the components of good governance and the successful implementation of the policies and decisions that the partners make.

It is not easy to achieve such an enlightened state. There are few issues that can so threaten the harmony and collegiality of a law firm partnership as a discussion of the partners' compensation system.

As one managing partner observed: "Whenever I even suggest that we should look at our compensation system sometime – just look at it – I feel like I am climbing onto the back of a hungry and not-too-friendly tiger."

Discussions about partner compensation can be tense. In fact, they usually should be, because important issues are at stake. Nonetheless, these discussions need to take place and should not be avoided. With proper preparation and expert facilitation, when needed, frank discussions about partner compensation can bring a partnership closer together, rather than drive it apart. If left unresolved, a lack of clarity, unspoken resentments and distrust will continue to act as a silent sea anchor, making it harder for the partners to make and successfully implement hard decisions about the firm's future. Partner compensation is seldom the only reason why a firm is not moving forward, but it is often one of the most influential factors.

2. Any compensation system can work well

Or it can be an unmitigated disaster.

The legal profession probably will never end the debate over which works best: lockstep[1] or 'eat what you kill'.[2] That is a false choice, of course, and the issue is much more complex than that. Those who proclaim that nobody uses lockstep systems any more or that 'eat what you kill' is too toxic for a law firm either suffer from a desire to exaggerate in order to make their points or have little experience of different law firms. It is not the purpose of this chapter to participate in or contribute anything substantive to that raucous controversy, other than to say "All of the above" and quickly move on.

The experiences of law firms worldwide, of all sizes and practice specialisms, demonstrate that lockstep (a system under which partner compensation is determined by seniority in the partnership, usually measured by ownership percentage) and 'eat what you kill' (under which a partner's pay is determined solely by the fees produced by the partner individually or by the matters for which one is the billing partner) can each work very successfully in an appropriate firm. Some law firms prosper with lockstep and others are satisfied with the results that they obtain from 'eat what you kill'. Most law firms, however, select a compensation structure that lies somewhere in between these two extremes.[3]

Whether lockstep, 'eat what you kill' or something in between works for any law firm is the result of three practical considerations, each of which is linked to the governance, decision-making processes and day-to-day management of the firm:

---

1 A lockstep system is one in which all or almost all of a partner's compensation is determined by seniority. In some firms, sustained performance over multiple years might be considered as one factor, along with equity ownership and seniority in service, which determines a partner's 'rung' on the lockstep 'ladder'.

2 'Eat what you kill' describes a system in which all or almost all of a partner's compensation is determined by the fees that he or she personally produces or, in some firms, supervises.

3 The trend in recent years has been for hybrid systems that recognise short-term performance as well as long-term contributions to the value of the enterprise. When well crafted to be consistent with the professional culture and business priorities of a law firm, these can reinforce the benefits of lockstep and 'eat what you kill' while avoiding or mitigating the possible negative effects. For further discussion and examples of the components of such hybrid systems, see Norman K Clark, "Table manners: rewarding performance without 'eat what you kill'" in Michael Roch and Polina Pavlova (eds), *Partner Remuneration in Law Firms: A Guide to Reward Structures, Performance Management and Decision-Making* (Globe Law and Business, 2016) pp73–86; and Paulina Pavlova, "Hybrid systems and contribution-based meritocracies: the golden mean?", *ibid*, pp87–94.

- Does the partner compensation system meet the business needs of the firm? In other words, to what extent (if at all) does the partner compensation system support the firm's specific needs with respect to issues such as:
  - client retention;
  - profitable management of cases and matters; and
  - succession planning?
- Does the partner compensation system provide incentives for and reward the behaviours that directly support the delivery of the firm's business plan? For example, if the business plan assumes that there will be an improvement in cross-marketing activities, the partners should consider whether the partner compensation system supports, obstructs or is irrelevant to cross-marketing activities in that firm.

  Some firms with lockstep systems might not need to introduce specific rewards for cross-selling, because of a strong cultural consensus among partners that 'a rising tide lifts all ships'. Firms with performance-based compensation systems, however, might need to introduce origination credit or some similar specific financial reward to overcome partner objections of: "Why should I give up my fee-earning time to sell work that my partner will do and for which he or she will receive all of the financial reward?"
- Is it fair? This is by far the most frequently asked question. It is a common reference point for partners who might have vastly different views on every other aspect of a proposed compensation system.

All three are issues that can be decided, in the long term, only by the partners; and all partners must participate in the decision.

3. Five good governance issues for partner compensation

Because this is a book about law firm governance, and not financial management, the primary concern of this chapter is how to review, adjust and manage partner compensation systems as a matter of good governance. The focus is on the decision-making process about compensation, rather than the relative merits of specific compensation features, components, structures or substantive financial results. In other words, what are the best practices for governance of partner compensation?

There are five questions that should be answered before a law firm attempts any changes – even a tweak – to its partner compensation system:

- "What behaviours do we want to promote and reward?"
- "Are there any significant differences among practice areas, in terms of the economic factors that drive their respective levels of financial performance?"

- "Will the changes actually work?"
- "Will the system be fair?"
- "What further adjustments must we be prepared to make?"

Whenever a law firm tries to omit or gloss over one of these issues, the results are usually disappointing and sometimes might even make things worse.

3.1 What do we want to promote and reward?

This is the heart of any partner compensation system in a law firm.

The compensation system must do more than just pay people for their work. Instead, it must incentivise business behaviours that the firm needs for sustained success, such as fee generation, marketing and the professional development of oneself and others.

Partners must ask, and periodically revisit, this question. The answers to "What do we want?" should remain in view as guides to ensure that the ensuing discussions about the details stay within the line of sight of the agreed purposes of partner compensation. Otherwise, it is so easy for a group of partners to lose their way and waste their time.

(a) Asking uncomfortable questions

All partners need to participate in this discussion. Even if the firm has been in operation for more than 100 years, the answer to "What do we want?" must be relevant to the current group of partners and the current needs of the firm.

Some of these questions can be profound. For example, how does one measure the business value that a partner contributes to a law firm? Partnerships that favour lockstep compensation systems might answer this question by reference to a partner's long-term investment of intellect, effort and assumption of business risk. Partners that prefer to base compensation exclusively or primarily on financial performance are often culturally predisposed to define the value of a partner in terms of his or her recent and current financial contribution to the firm, typically measured in terms of fees produced and originated.

The danger of not asking basic questions such as this is that, over time, younger partners might enter the partnership with significantly different views from the senior partners about the value of a partner and how that value should be recognised. When disconnections such as these arise, the continued existence of the partnership and the firm could be in jeopardy.

The significant number of law firms that have difficulty retaining their younger partners is evidence of this. The views of the younger partners about what they desire from a career in a law firm, in terms of both financial rewards and intangible benefits, might be substantially different from those of the older partners who still retain control of the firm.

Asking the hard questions about what partner compensation should reward might produce uncomfortable discussions and might also expose longstanding unspoken grievances. However, there is too much at stake not to ask them.

How to use the partner compensation system to respond to substandard partner performance is another sensitive question. Law firms with lockstep compensation systems tend to be alert to the first signs of declining performance in a partner. They make appropriate inquiries without delay and take action to correct the underlying issues, if possible. Firms with partner compensation systems that are performance based, even if they are not pure 'eat what you kill' structures, tend to rely on compensation to function as the principal motivator for partner behaviour. Either approach can work; but whether in a lockstep system, 'eat what you kill' or a mixed compensation system, it is critically important that partners investigate, agree on and understand the answers to the following questions:

- "What specific, observable behaviours do we expect?"
- "How will we measure the effects of those behaviours?"
- "What, if any, specific incentives do we expect our compensation system to produce?"
- "What will we do if a partner fails to perform to our expectations?"

It is very important – not only as a financial issue, but as a basic governance principle – that the partners get this first question right.

(b) A new emphasis on partner profitability

An emerging best practice in performance-based compensation is the shift in the understanding of the concept of the financial value of a partner from fee production to profitability. This concept injects into a partner compensation system certain issues and values that might be new to many law firms, but that have significant long-term importance for how the partners govern themselves and their firm.

One of the traditional flaws in performance-based partner compensation is that too much emphasis has been placed on gross revenue – productivity measured by fees collected – with not enough attention being paid to profitability. In an earlier time, when most large clients were not as fee sensitive and most legal markets not as intensely competitive as they are today, revenue was a reasonable – even if occasionally inaccurate – measurement of individual performance. This was related to a general – and not entirely incorrect – notion in many law firms that if the firm collected enough money, it would be profitable. Cost and non-financial measurements of productivity were less important and, in some instances, disregarded unless they exceeded fairly relaxed ranges of variation. Assuming ever-increasing revenue from year to year, most law firms could rely on crisis-to-crisis improvisation to manage any serious issues that might arise with respect to anything else affecting the firm's bottom line.

Things began to change in the 1990s in most legal markets and now appear to have changed forever for most law firms. The firms that are managing the new economic and competitive challenges most effectively are those that have begun to emphasise profitability, not revenue, as the most important consideration in assessing a partner's economic value to the firm.

As one managing partner in a law firm in North America asked about one of its top fee producers during a review of the firm's profitability: "She brings in a lot of money each year; but does she make any money for her partners?"

For this reason, performance-based compensation systems are starting to evaluate a partner's performance not just on fee revenue (which is, after all, still a big part of profitability), but also on the profitability produced by the way in which a partner manages his or her book of business. This includes the measurement of a set of economic indicators, not just billable hours recorded or fees collected. These new indicators might include the following, among others:

- The fully loaded operating cost of the partner's practice: Formulas and factors vary among law firms, but this indicator is essentially the average operating cost to produce one hour of billable legal work (even if the fee is not billed on an hourly basis).
- The professional compensation cost incurred to generate the fees in a partner's book of business: This can be especially important in work performed on a non-hourly fee basis, such as a fixed fee. If work is delegated to lower-paid associates, this will produce a much lower compensation cost and contribute to better profitability than if the partner does all the work himself or herself.
- The costs of collecting overdue fees in matters supervised by the partner: These can vary significantly among partners and therefore are a reasonably accurate measurement of a factor in assessing the relative profitability of partners.
- The old accounts receivable attributable to the partner's book of business: Like collection costs, these can be a reasonably accurate measurement of how profitably a partner manages his or her matters and resolves any billing disputes arising from them. The most frequent measuring point for 'old' accounts receivable is 120 days, but periods as short as 90 days or as long as 180 days might be appropriate for various practice areas, depending on the nature of the engagements and the payment policies of clients. Nonetheless, the effectiveness of a partner in managing accounts that have gone beyond the agreed age is another useful indicator of the relative profitability of partners.

This analysis has greater implications than being merely a new and different way to display numbers on a spreadsheet or a clever new formula to determine how much partners are paid. By focusing on specific indicators of the profitable management of a partner's book of business (including, of course, fee production), law firms are challenging their partners to reconsider their roles, responsibilities and accountability in the business. Such a consideration of specific factors in the profitability of the management of a practice necessarily raises new questions that are important to the continued governance of a law firm partnership. Whether or not a law firm decides to introduce profitability considerations into its partner compensation system – or to have a performance-based system at all – partners should consider, in a well-informed and organised way, some difficult new questions that have profound importance for the governance of the firm, such as the following:

- "In our law firm, to what extent are the profitability indicators specific to one practice area or partner? Stated another way, do we expect too much of some of our partners and not enough of others?"
- "What should be each partner's responsibility and accountability for addressing specific weaknesses revealed in the profitability indicators for his or her book of business?"
- "To what extent, if at all, would it make sense for our firm to adopt multiple sets of performance standards for partners from different practice areas?"
- "Going one step further, are firm-wide financial performance expectations – whether measured by fee production, billable hours, profitability or any other customary performance measurement – still relevant at all for our firm?"

3.2 Are there any significant differences among practice areas?

Not all practice areas function in the same way. There can be profound differences in the profitability management techniques that are effective in a high-volume practice and those that are more appropriate to a practice that consists of a smaller number of long-term, complex engagements. Periods of economic disruption – especially those triggered by unexpected crises such as a pandemic or war – can make these differences even greater.

This variation in profitability is a fact of life in many law firms. Live with it. Do not ignore it.

The first step to managing variability in financial performance among practice areas is, of course, to try to detect it. Some law firms resist financial analysis by practice group. As the managing partner of one large New York law firm told the author: "We never look at the practice group financials. We don't even produce those numbers. It would be too destructive of our collegiality."

Nonetheless, if significant economic differences exist, ignoring them – even for the sake of collegiality – will not make them go away; nor will it mitigate their effects on the culture of the partnership. Partners in firms with performance-based partner compensation should agree on the extent to which, if at all, significantly different levels of financial performance, based on the respective economic structures of the practices, should be addressed in the partner compensation system. In some firms, a willingness to recognise and make allowances for structural variations in the underlying economics of practice areas and partners could be the single most important factor in maintaining a consensus that a performance-based partner compensation system is fair.

In partnerships that consider themselves to be 'all one team', these differences should be identified so that all partners have a full understanding of the level of financial contribution that they can reasonably expect their partners to make to the team. This is especially important for firms with lockstep systems, to avoid resentment of partners who might otherwise be assumed not to be 'pulling their weight'.

3.3 Will the changes work?

Answering this question requires more than a simple spreadsheet. Instead, the firm's management should develop an interactive working model of the proposed system, usually documented in a spreadsheet that will allow the partners to manipulate the variables and to see the real-world financial results that changes to the compensation system could produce for the firm and for each lawyer.[4]

Sometimes a firm will go through as many as 40 or 50 models and variations on them before the partners see a structure and compensation factors that will produce the results they want. Lawyers usually enjoy manipulating variables and observing the results; and this exercise can remove some of the stress from the discussion. It can also help to depersonalise it, because its focus is on a system rather than an individual. This process can be very time consuming; but for most law firms, it is the single most important factor in producing a partner understanding and acceptance of the compensation system.

"Will the changes work?" also involves the extent to which the proposed compensation system will actually promote and reward business behaviours – such as fee generation, marketing and the profitable management of matters –

---

4 When the author's firm, Walker Clark LLC, advises on changes to partner compensation systems in law firms, our working model typically projects forward at least 10 years, and sometimes as long as 20 years, to take into account the effects of the retirement of senior partners and the admission of new partners. Sometimes a change that appears to work well over the next two or three fiscal years might produce undesirable results later.

For changes to a partner compensation to work, they also should integrate into the firm's succession planning. In firms in which distributions from a profit pool are a major component of a partner's total compensation, a working model can also suggest the increased levels of fee production and profitability that will be necessary to produce a sufficiently larger body of profits to continue to maintain and, one hopes, increase each partner's level of compensation.

which are top priorities for the long-term business success and professional culture of the firm.

A holistic approach is best. Even if the compensation system appears to provide handsome rewards for changed partner behaviours, other factors might undermine the firm's efforts. Remember that although defects in the partner compensation system are often the principal reason for the disappointing implementation of important decisions in a law firm, they are seldom the only reason.

For example, if a compensation system rewards partners who bring new clients to the firm, does the firm also need to improve the partners' marketing and sales skills necessary for successful client development? Offering origination credit when most partners lack marketing and sales skills usually rewards only those who are already good at cross-selling, and does nothing to improve the performance of their relatively unskilled colleagues. This only frustrates the people at whom the incentives were aimed, as they quickly realise that the new rewards are unattainable for them. Instead of incentivising partners to hit new levels of achievement, the overall effect of the new origination credit scheme is to make the desired behaviours – increased marketing and sales efforts by partners – even less likely than before. Even worse, it can create overdependence on a small group of rainmakers to maintain and increase fee revenue.

Some law firms have introduced, as a specific component of partner compensation, the extent to which a partner achieves his or her individual performance objectives,[5] which in some firms are defined in an individual business plan that is published to all the other partners. However, unless those goals are reasonably specific, clear, measurable and realistic – and agreed to be such by the partner who is expected to achieve them – this part of the partner compensation system frequently produces more disputes and administrative burden than it does benefits.[6]

3.4 Is it fair?

Fairness appears to be one of the common values that are characteristic of lawyers everywhere. Thus, fairness might be the most important consideration for law firm partners as they consider their firm's partner compensation system,

5 See Clark (n 3), pp79–83.

6 This can be especially difficult with respect to goals for the origination of new clients. For example, if a partner meets a lawyer from a foreign law firm at a conference and that lawyer later refers a client to the partner's firm, should the partner receive credit for 'originating' that new client? In some law firms, the answer will be "Yes"; in others, it will be "No"; and in still others it will be "It depends." For a law firm that wants to provide a financial reward for origination, it can often be simpler but equally motivating to base it on the achievement of a goal, resulting in an increased share of a profit pool, rather than to pay a cash commission as a percentage of the fees produced. Nonetheless, documentation of which activities will count towards the achievement of an origination goal, as well as which will not, is essential. *Ibid*, pp80–82.

as well as other governance issues. To be successful, a compensation system must be perceived as fair. Law firm partners will sometimes agree to aspects of a partner compensation system to which they have significant reservations if they are satisfied that, overall, the system will work fairly and will produce reasonably fair results.

Is the partner compensation fair to each partner individually and to the partners collectively? This question usually arises in two contexts.

First, are the methods and measurements used to determine each partner's compensation – whether based on seniority, equity, fee production or any other factor – reasonably clear and equitable? In some firms, fairness also includes a sense of reasonable flexibility to permit adjustments in response to special situations, such as the need to offer an attractive compensation package – at least initially – to a laterally recruited partner who brings a large book of business or a new area of expertise to the firm. Not only should the rules be fair; so too should the possible exceptions.

Second, does the compensation system produce individual results that are not unfair to that person? To what extent are the partners willing to accept a system that in some years might produce individual compensation that is disappointing but nonetheless agreed by the recipient to be reasonably fair?

In both contexts, most law firm partners are satisfied if there is 'rough justice', rather than mathematical precision, in partner compensation systems and results. For this reason, some law firms with compensation systems that are primarily formula-driven allow for discretionary adjustments to avoid clear injustices in individual cases.

A compensation system that is fair can continue to motivate, encourage and reward dedication to the firm even through the worst financial times. One that is unfair will open the door to partner departures upon even the slightest financial downturn.

3.5 What further adjustments must we be prepared to make?

No changes to a partner compensation system – even a simple one – work perfectly from the start. As a law firm gains experience with the new system, the partners frequently notice possible minor adjustments and improvements that are either necessary or advisable. There are three situations that seem to arise more frequently than others and that often require a well-defined response: not too little, not too late, but not too much.

(a) Corrections to respond to unexpected financial injustices to individual partners

Sometimes a partner's unsatisfactory performance is the result of the professional structure, systems and processes that shape how he or she practises law, and not due to personal shortcomings or bad attitudes. These frequently arise when the compensation system fails to consider or misestimates the effect of fundamental differences in the economic factors that drive the financial performance of different practice areas. Of course, a system that is perceived by partners to be fair will already address individual issues unrelated to performance, such as illness, that affect a partner's compensation.

(b) ***Responses to unexpected business performance***

In the short term, these unexpected developments usually include events such as the unexpected departure of major fee-producing partners, practice groups or clients. Although there might be early signs that these disruptions are possible, they are often true surprises. Longer-term factors in financial performance, such as the general business climate or financial trends in the industry sectors of the firm's major clients, are more predictable and should have been considered by the partners before agreeing to the changes.

In either situation, it is a worthwhile investment of the partners' time to ask some tough 'What if…' questions. For example, how would the partner compensation system be affected in the following situations?

- One of the most productive rainmakers leaves the firm;
- The partners need to buy out the interest of one of the founding partners;
- The firm loses one of its most valuable clients;
- One of the firm's most reliable clients files for bankruptcy; or
- One of the firm's most important practice areas becomes more price sensitive and competitive over the next two or three years.

Anything that affects the firm's revenue or profitability could have a significant and disrupting effect on partner compensation.

(c) ***Adjustments in response to incorrect planning assumptions***

In an uncertain economy, the assumptions that were made at the beginning of the year might be completely inoperative within six months. One of the most common problems arises from advance distributions in the nature of monthly salaries. In theory, a partner's monthly draw should be set at an amount that makes it reasonably probable that the partner will also receive an additional year-end profit distribution. However, in recent years, some partnerships have been very reluctant to decrease partner draws during the year – even when it was becoming apparent that the firm's financial performance was insufficient to produce profits for year-end distribution and that some partners would be overdrawn on their compensation accounts.

The tenth or eleventh month of a fiscal year is too late for the partnership to decide what to do about overdrawn compensation accounts, at least without risking significant short-term rancour and long-term distrust. These plans should be made and agreed by the partnership in advance. Delaying them frequently means that their ultimate resolution will create greater personal hardships and longer-range negative effects on the firm.

4. Why compensation is a governance issue

The issues involved in any successful partner compensation system are those which test the effectiveness and long-term sustainability of the governance of a law firm. Partner compensation can also be a powerful governance tool, which dramatically increases the probability of partnership decisions on a broad range of issues, from the admission of new partners to retirement and possible post-retirement roles with the firm. Deciding on what is needed for an effective compensation system should also lead to consideration of some of the most profound and fundamental issues of law firm partnership – particularly those that define and provide direction for the responsibilities and accountability of each partner.

How a law firm partnership manages partner compensation as a governance function is highly specific to each firm. Although the five key questions proposed by this chapter are universal in their applicability to law firms, the specific answers for each firm are the product of unique factors, such as:

- the nature of the practice;
- the perceived responsibilities of partners in the firm;
- how the partners define how they add value to the firm; and
- the strength of their professional values, culture and aspirations in binding together individual partners in a common enterprise.

Partner compensation and partnership structure

Martín Carrizosa
Lawyer

1. The strategic and governance contexts

A partner compensation system, if set and periodically adjusted to meet the changing needs of a law firm, can be a powerful tool in long-range decision making and strategic implementation. The experience of our firm, prietocarrizosa,[1] demonstrates the importance of considering compensation not just as a division of profits, but also as one of the most important features of how we govern ourselves and how we achieve sustained growth and profitability.

At the time we conducted this exercise, the firm was a mid-sized, full-service law firm in the hotly competitive legal market of Colombia, one of the fastest-growing economies in the Americas. The legal market is dominated by a small group of similar firms which are home to some of the best lawyers in the Americas, including partners who are well known, well respected and well positioned in the business community and political circles. The Colombian legal market is further strengthened by smaller boutique-style practices and offices of foreign law firms. I use the word 'strengthened' because the competition from these firms outside the circle of the major Colombian firms makes all of us better and stronger.

Our firm grew rapidly in the first two decades of the 21st century, like most of the other larger law firms in Colombia. The presence of foreign clients increased dramatically. While we competed harder than ever before for good legal talent, our firm had to plan our first transition from the founding partners to the next generation.

2. Traditional values and evolving needs

As with many law firms in Latin America, our partner compensation system had traditionally been a modified lockstep model, with a significant base salary paid to each partner and the remaining profits distributed according to equity. We never favoured the 'easy in, easy out' approach with regard to partner capitalisation requirements. Our partners paid for their equity participation as a multiple of the firm's earnings before interest, taxes, depreciation and

1 The firm is now part of the regional law firm of Philippi Prietocarrizosa Ferrero DU & Uría.

amortisation. On retirement, they sold their equity participation either to the firm or to the other partners, according to the terms and conditions of an equity purchase and sale programme agreed by all partners and the firm.

This equity-based system made our partners focus on the long-term profitability, sustainability and growth of the firm. Partners believed that their purchase of shares in the firm was a sound investment over the years.

Our system worked reasonably well because it supported concepts of mutual respect and professional parity that had always been important parts of our partnership culture. We kept the base salary at the top of the market in Colombia because we recognised the need to provide financial security and good financial opportunities if the firm was going to attract and retain top-quality partners.

After a period of very rapid growth, both internally and in terms of our market presence in Colombia and internationally, we realised that we needed to consider whether our partner compensation structure required improvement in order to continue to support our strategy and the implementation of our internal governance and management initiatives. Because we felt that these questions had strong strategic implications, as well as practical governance ones, we engaged external advisers to assist us.[2]

For us, partnership compensation was about more than how we should split the cake at the end of the year. It also involved how we would move forward for years to come.

3. Our strategic priorities

There were four strategic questions to be asked regarding our traditional partner compensation structure, as follows.

1) Would our partner compensation system continue to attract and retain the best partners?

We realised that, by itself, offering lots of money is not an effective recruitment or retention strategy. Our partners and our associates were telling the firm's management committee that, while generous salaries were attractive and appreciated, they expected more from their professional lives in our firm – particularly opportunities to:

- develop and perfect professional knowledge and skills throughout their career at the firm;
- work with and learn from colleagues – not just in the first few years, but for their entire professional lives;

2 We engaged the consulting firm Walker Clark LLC, which had previously advised us on internal management and strategic implementation issues arising from our governance system and management structures.

- participate in serious, important and interesting legal work;
- contribute in tangible ways to the growth and success of the firm;
- build a nest egg for the future; and
- especially for senior associates and recently admitted partners, receive financial acknowledgement for extraordinary contributions to the firm's business success.

2) Did we need to modify the partner compensation structure to provide incentives for individual performance?

Nobody in our partnership wanted to move from our modified lockstep structure to 'eat what you kill'; but some of the younger partners, who did not have enough equity points to receive substantial distributions of the residual profits, wanted an opportunity to increase their income. Introducing a performance-based element of some type seemed to be a logical adjustment to our traditional structure; but to what extent could we introduce performance-based compensation without risking undesirable changes to our traditional partnership values of mutual respect and teamwork?

3) Did our traditional system support the needs of our firm to continue to grow and improve, across multiple dimensions, in order to remain competitive with other excellent domestic firms that offer essentially the same services to the same groups of potential clients?

In our partnership, there was always a general recognition, held to varying degrees by each of us, that 'a rising tide lifts all ships'. However, aside from this general philanthropic principle, we could not identify anything in our partner compensation that incentivised individual partners to work unusually hard to make extraordinary contributions to the firm, such as earning an unusually high fee or concluding a strategic initiative with great long-term importance (eg, opening a new office in another city or developing a new practice area). At best, our traditional system was irrelevant to these needs. We had to conclude that the traditional compensation system, which did not support those needs as adequately as we would have liked, could actually be a long-term obstacle.

4) Did our traditional partner compensation system reinforce and communicate to the partners and to the firm the values and commitment that are the core of our partnership culture?

We took our partnership culture seriously. It was a driving force in our firm's business performance, not just human resources jargon. This was an area in which we thought that our existing structure was working well. The approximately equal salaries paid to all partners reinforced collegiality as a value with economic consequences, not just a vague 'feelgood' notion.

The high salaries that we paid, compared to the other major firms in our market, were part of an implicit compact between the firm and each partner, in that we expected each partner to dedicate 100% of his or her available working time to the firm's business and to our clients, with no 'side businesses'. This rule made our firm significantly different from most other law firms in Latin America, where side businesses are common among law firm partners. However, in the case of our firm, it reinforced the levels of focus, commitment and persistence that accounted for our growth into one of our country's leading law firms, and that we would need from each partner in the future.

Our traditional compensation structure, with its equity-based distribution of part of the profits, also recognised the respect and value that we attached to partners who had invested this focus, commitment and persistence over the years.

4. Meeting today's and tomorrow's needs

Our adjustments to our traditional partner compensation system reflected what we believed was a careful approach. We tried to preserve the strengths of the existing system, such as the high base salaries and equity-based distribution of residual profits. We introduced a sharply focused performance element, which produced good results and a strong, flexible platform to meet future needs in our highly competitive, fast-changing market. This resulted in our partner compensation system having three components.

4.1 Salary

We continued to distribute a substantial portion of our profits – currently slightly less than half – to our partners as draws in the nature of a salary. Although a high salary by itself does not guarantee success in recruiting or retaining top talent, we took the pragmatic view that it is 'the price of admission' to the market for the best legal talent.

4.2 Extraordinary performance pool

We created an extraordinary performance bonus pool in which partners who substantially surpassed their performance goals could receive shares. Currently, we set aside a small but significant portion of our total profits for distribution to partners who have earned shares.

One of the most difficult and at the same time most interesting issues in creating this bonus pool was determining what constitutes 'extraordinary performance'. This is when one really gains insight into the thinking of one's partners about what is important to them. As a group, we learned a lot about ourselves and each other in these discussions, most of which were informal. We recognised the danger of setting the threshold of 'extraordinary' too low, because then almost everyone would get shares and what was intended to be 'extraordinary' would actually be 'ordinary'. We also knew that we could not set the qualification too high, because lawyers quickly know when a stretched goal is unrealistic and therefore not worth the effort, no matter how lucrative the theoretically possible reward.

We recognised that the performance for which shares would be rewarded could and should change from year to year, to reflect changing priorities for the firm. We limited the eligible achievements for the pool to extraordinary financial performance because it is the easiest to measure and remains a significant priority for our firm. Theoretically, other eligible achievements might include originating new clients or matters, cross-selling and other major strategic contributions.

The compensation system was a powerful set of tools for the use of the firm's management committee. As we expected, the 'young stars' in our partnership responded well to the extraordinary performance bonus and made up a significant portion of the pool's participants.

4.3 Distribution of residual profits

After the payment of salaries, extraordinary performance bonuses and other bonuses to fee earners and staff, we distributed the remaining profits to our partners in proportion to their equity in the firm.

Succession management is one of the major governance issues confronting law firms in Latin America. We expected that over the next 10 years, we would see a significant adjustment in the ratios of the equity of the most senior partners to junior partners. Two factors were driving this, as for most other law firms in our region:

- the retirement of founding partners, who usually hold the largest equity in the firm; and
- the overall growth of the partnership as more partners moved into the bottom of the equity structure and began to purchase equity under the equity purchase and sale programme.

We chose this equity-based system because:

- it recognises and reasonably compensates the efforts made by partners in building the firm;
- it aligns partners in their collective effort to create the firm's value;
- it allows younger partners to grow their equity interest in the firm; and
- it allows partners to build their own nest eggs for future retirement.

5. More than a knife to cut the cake

Our experience demonstrates that a law firm compensation system is more than just a knife used to cut the profits 'cake' each year. Its more important function is as a tool that helps the law firm to support the achievement of long-range strategic objectives, as well as to respond to shorter-term priorities that are needed to deliver the business plan.

No matter how energetically law firm partners might praise or condemn the various models for partner compensation, no single system will meet the needs of every firm. Perfection in this area will always elude most law firm partnerships. What is really important is to agree on a structure that is 'just about right'.

Getting it 'just about right' means finding a combination of features that will support the achievement of a firm's most important strategic goals and business priorities, rather than be irrelevant to them or – even worse – work against them. It also means finding a compensation system that preserves the parts of the partnership culture that continue to support business performance and reinforces the changes that might be needed for future success in a rapidly evolving competitive context.

We believe that our success was based on the following cornerstones:

- Prune, rather than slash and burn: Some law firm partners become so frustrated with the irrelevance of their partnership compensation systems that they want to throw everything out and build an entirely new system. This usually results in too much work and puts at risk some features that might actually be unrecognised strengths. Ironically, many of these 'zero-based' projects produce compensation systems that are almost identical to those that were discarded.
- Identify what you want to achieve: Partner compensation systems are part of a much larger management system. A good system should provide incentives for the types of actions that the firm needs from its partners. This is why the first question that should be asked when considering improvements to the compensation system is: "What do we as a firm want to achieve?" Many law firm partnerships cannot answer this question. That is a strong indicator that they are not ready to start tinkering around with their partner compensation system.
- Listen: The most valuable input into a project to improve the partner compensation system comes from the firm's lawyers, not from its accountants. Management committees frequently charge ahead with compensation changes based on their own assumptions about what their partners want – or, more accurately, what their partners should want. This wastes time, because the uninformed product seldom works, even if a majority of the partners can be convinced to accept it.

This is not a project that can be completed on a weekend partners' retreat or by management decree. It requires careful consideration of what is important to the firm and active participation by all partners. In short, what we did is not as important as how we did it.

Partner appraisals: what does the managing partner need to know about partners' performance?

Aku Sorainen
SORAINEN

1. Introduction

Corporate values are important, but they are only ideas unless they are practised every day. The values at most successful modern law firms tend to be quite similar; where the differences lie is in how these values are implemented in practice. The way in which these values are practised every day across a firm sets the foundation for its culture. If the culture is strong – as it tends to be in many successful and well-established law firms – the question for the most senior leader in the law firm, often the managing partner, is how he or she will maintain it. If the firm is younger or less established, or has recently opened new offices or expanded into different countries, the question is how to build a strong culture.

Many law firm leaders would include strengthening their culture among their highest priorities, as this helps to promote alignment among the partners. Better alignment towards the achievement of mutual goals increases efficiency, collaboration, know-how sharing, overall work quality, client satisfaction and profit; and finally, it makes the work much more fun. Alignment strengthens the culture and *vice versa*.

Alignment is important; but it may contradict the need of some partners to maintain their autonomy and independence. This is sometimes apparent when the culture in the firm is evolving: some partners may find it difficult to adjust, while others may find it natural. Cultural evolution is a constant change management process that the managing partner must lead and manage carefully. If done properly, the partners will become aligned in acting as role models, representing the firm's culture and achieving mutual goals, which are usually described in the strategy

In the years since the global financial crisis, law firms – at least in Europe – have paid much more attention to becoming more professionally led and managed. Those managing partners whom I have met over the past decade have shown much greater interest in management and leadership than they once did, when these obligations were often seen as merely diverting their attention away from client work. We are no longer living in times when the typical description of the managing partner's role was "being a lamp post in the midst of a crowd of dogs"; or when – as legendary law firm consultant David Maister explained in his 2006 article entitled "Are Law Firms Manageable?"[1] – most law firms were poorly managed and the only reason that they succeeded was because their competitors were being managed equally badly.

Whether the managing partner's role is to create the right culture and build alignment among partners or just to maintain the culture and level of alignment, the managing partner will benefit significantly from access to plenty of information about each partner's performance – that is, how the partner is managing his or her business case, leading his or her team, collaborating with other partners and ultimately contributing towards the development of the firm. The typical point at which to discuss the partner's performance is during the annual partner appraisal process.

High-quality information about partners' performance from many different angles is perhaps even more important in a law firm than in any other business. This is because partners have multiple roles, led by the managing partner, who is in charge of implementing the firm's strategy through them; but at the same time, they are also owners of the firm and collectively exercise power over the managing partner. The tendency is for many law firm partners to question everything, be highly sceptical, dislike being managed and resist feedback.

In order to successfully lead and manage, a managing partner must not only be very convincing in delivering his or her message, but also back up that message with correct and convincing facts The mere opinion of the managing partner, without supporting facts, seldom results in desirable changes in the firm.

If the managing partner can successfully implement a reporting system that produces correct and convincing information, it is often surprising how quickly the firm will start to produce what is being measured, since "you get what you measure".

There are different practices among leading law firms in terms of the kind of information that is collected for the partner appraisal process. Some great firms still look only at basic financial performance data, such as the personal billings and generations of a partner. In other firms, the partners additionally spend a lot of time writing personal annual activity reports in advance of the annual partner appraisal, which are then filed away. In still other firms, the partners are asked to complete a lengthy questionnaire about what they have done that year, which other partners have helped them most and what they plan to do the

1 David Maister, "Are Law Firms Manageable", 2006, https://davidmaister.com/articles/are-law-firms-manageable/.

following year. Finally, there are some firms with sophisticated systems that track various types of performance and activities, with annual activity reports generated almost automatically or with the help of the business services team. The partners spend little time reporting on the past year, but rather focus on making plans for the next year.

The aim of this chapter is to suggest what can and should be measured in a law firm which has a more sophisticated partner appraisal and remuneration system than the simple 'eat what you kill'/cost-sharing system or a pure lock-step system. In many pure lock-step firms, it is typically considered sufficient if a partner performs in a way that ensures he or she is not left behind by others; the partner's exact performance is less relevant. Modern law firms, however, are increasingly implementing either a modified lock-step system (with additional bonuses available) or a managed lock-step system (where equity points may remain unchanged, increase or even decrease). The result of these changes is that a managing partner – assuming that he or she is also leading the partner appraisal process – needs much more detailed information about each partner's performance, behaviour and actions in order to conduct constructive, effective and meaningful partner appraisal discussions. This need is perhaps even more important in managed lock-step firms, as in modified lock-step firms bonuses are typically paid for purely financial contributions and there may be less need to measure other aspects of performance very precisely. Interestingly, there are also pure lock-step firms at the top of the market which are very attentive to partners' individual contributions, as otherwise the top performers may become discouraged if the mediocre performance of other partners is tolerated. Leaders of such firms need the same amount of information as leaders of sophisticated managed lock-step firms.

In the author's experience, it is useful to measure a wide range of key performance indicators (KPIs) and other performance indicators and then focus on what is most relevant for each individual partner (usually, the highest and lowest areas of performance are most relevant).

2. Developing and maintaining strong client relationships

Normally, one would expect that the partner appraisal process would begin with 'simple' financials, such as billed hours, generated revenue or profit. However, in a culture and strategy-driven firm with a modified or managed lock-step system, financials can be considered a 'hygiene' factor and need not be the first thing to be looked at. Instead, the process should begin with clients. Without great client service and strong client relationships, a law firm cannot maintain a leading position in any practice area, business sector or jurisdiction. No matter how successful a firm might be, clients can never be taken for granted. So, what can we measure to assess the strength of our client relations? Consider the following, for instance:

- Focus (or premium) client revenue, measured against the results from the previous year and those of the partner's peer group: This indicates the strength of the business relationships that the partner has developed with these key clients and revenue trends in comparison with the previous two years and his or her peer group – that is, those partners with similar seniority in the partner remuneration system. These benchmarks (previous two years and peer group) can also be used for most other comparisons, as they will help to identify longer-term trends, which are more important than specific performance in a single year.
- Total amount of business development/client relationship management (BDM/CRM) hours registered for focus clients: This indicates the effort that the partner has put into developing his or her focus clientele, and his or her ability to mobilise other partners and lawyers in developing these relationships. This is especially relevant if the revenue from this clientele is decreasing for some reason.
- Total client portfolio revenue: This indicates the depth of the partner's relationships with the firm's existing clientele and the revenue trends from those clients.
- Total BDM/CRM hours registered: This indicates how much time the partner has invested in developing existing relationships beyond his or her focus clients, and in building future business streams and valuable contacts for the practice group and the firm.
- Revenue from corporate group clients: These tend to be the firm's 'crown jewel' clients, as they often receive services from multiple practice groups. A successful group relationship partner must coordinate the activities of several relationship partners and make an active effort to link different companies under a single group in the firm's practice management system. This makes it much easier to conduct conflict of interest checks and identify more cross-referring opportunities.
- Revenue from cases secured by the partner: While partners are encouraged to introduce associates and other partners to the firm's clientele, they must also stay close to certain clients and generate work from them. This indicator reveals how close the partner actually is to some of the firm's clients. It also measures market perceptions of whether the partner is considered a leading expert whom clients trust.
- New clients secured by the partner and revenues generated from them: This indicates how entrepreneurial the partner has been in attracting new clients. It also enables the managing partner to assess whether the new clients are in line with the firm's strategy.
- Sector group revenue: This measures the development and market penetration of the sector group in which the partner is a leader or member, and the prevailing revenue trends.

- Outbound referrals to clients, other law firms/accounting firms/ investment banks and similar: These should also include 'attempted referrals' – that is, those which did not materialise due to a conflict of interest or other reasons. It is not only corporate clients that appreciate their lawyers providing them with business leads and referrals for other high-quality service providers; foreign law firms, accounting firms and investment banks may value these even more, and may be an important sector group for the firm. The firm will thus benefit from the active pursuit of leads for outbound referrals, especially where this is done in a coordinated and disciplined manner.
- The ranking of the partner and his or her practice group in international legal directories: Usually, every partner is expected to become a publicly recognised professional in his or her field of practice.
- The number of new and updated contacts of the partner in the firm's CRM system: This measures not only the entrepreneurial drive of the partner in expanding and updating his or her network and becoming known in the market, but also how disciplined he or she is in adding new contacts to the system and updating old ones – otherwise, they have little value for the firm. There is a good saying about the relevance of updated data in the practice management system: "Trash in, trash out."

3. Empowering, engaging and developing people

It is difficult to state whether clients or people are more important to the firm, as these are the twin pillars on which it stands. Enthused and engaged top professionals tend to attract top clients and vice versa.

Partners should take good care to attract, inspire and develop people if they want to win the war for talent, which is perhaps becoming even more intense than the war for clients.

A firm can measure most people-related aspects of performance by conducting an annual engagement survey. This is an interesting tool, as it measures how people feel about their working conditions. It is different from a 360 review, which aims to collect feedback from people about other people. In many ways, engagement surveys may provide more useful information than 360 reviews, as the latter are occasionally used by some people to throw dirt at somebody they dislike. A well-organised engagement survey can provide information about the following:

- The partner's ability to engage people: This also provides a good indication of the partner's leadership skills by indicating how engaged, motivated and loyal the members of his or her primary practice group are.
- The creation of a working culture characterised by trust and openness: This measures the 'soft' skills of the partner and his or her ability to

cultivate a positive and healthy working culture within the practice group.

- Being a role model and a good example for others to follow: This measures the partner's attitude and ability to work successfully in cooperation with others, and to be a liked and respected leader. In particular, it measures how people perceive the partner in supporting the firm's culture.
- Coaching, mentoring and training younger colleagues: This measures the commitment of the partner to invest in developing and raising new talent.
- Personnel turnover in the practice group for reasons other than parental and study leave, compared against the average in the firm: This may indicate the satisfaction of practice group members with the leadership of the partner. It also indicates whether the right people are being recruited into the practice group.
- Diversity: Where the practice group exceeds 15 to 20 people, increased attention should be paid to diversity. A firm should hire the best available talent for each job, regardless of gender, race, sexual orientation or disabilities which will not hinder the person from performing well in the relevant role. By comparing diversity between different practice groups and offices, some interesting trends may be discerned, which may serve as the basis for a constructive discussion with the head of the practice group or office.
- The extent to which practice group members have reached their annual billing target: This indicates how well the partner has organised work in the practice group and managed workload volatility and headcount. It also provides some guidance on how to interpret the engagement survey results. Often when people are 'underwater' for a long time, with too much work, their engagement reduces. Engagement also tends to reduce when people don't have enough work.

4. Managing, sharing and developing knowledge

Being one expert among many others is not a competitive advantage, since all leading law firms have experts in every field where demand for advice is high. However, being a leading expert in the market does afford a competitive advantage. That said, from the firm's point of view, having an individual leading expert is also a high-risk factor: what will happen when he or she retires or moves elsewhere? For the firm, the most valuable expert is thus one who systematically develops best practices in managing, sharing and developing knowledge across practice groups, sector groups and offices. However, such initiatives are far too often overlooked at law firms and are typically delegated to less experienced lawyers and knowledge management coordinators. While those individuals can help to manage and share knowledge, the most senior lawyers must innovate and develop knowledge. For example, who should be involved in automating a full-scale complex corporate or real estate share purchase agreement?

Obviously, this should be done by those with the best knowledge of these transactions. Knowledge management coordinators can undertake the technical automation work and help to set up the questionnaire. The partner's role is to ensure that as much knowledge in the practice group as possible is institutionalised and remains in the group even if many people leave the team. It goes without saying that it is mandatory to manage, share and develop knowledge if the firm wants to increase the efficiency and quality of its service. The following could be measured in this regard:

- Systematic sharing of best practices and debriefing, and recording of best practices in a useable and useful manner: This measures the partner's leadership skills in focusing the practice group towards improving work efficiency, discipline and profitability. It also gives a good indication of whether the practice group has the right attitude towards increasing its long-term competitiveness and that of the firm. Finally, this shows whether a partner exercises well-honed judgement and effective process management skills: whether he or she is working smart and consistently sharing and developing knowledge to ensure that it becomes part of the institutional knowledge of the firm.
- Training attended during the year and the cost involved: This measures how much the partner is investing in himself or herself with the aim of becoming or remaining a leading expert.
- The use of templates, precedents and automated documents by each practice group member: This measures the partner's leadership skills in focusing the practice group towards improving work efficiency, discipline and profitability. It also indicates which lawyers in the practice group have the right attitude towards increasing its long-term competitiveness by working with standard tools; and confirms which lawyers are storing their favourite precedents and templates on their own laptops and using them from there, thus hindering know-how sharing and the overall development of the practice group's tools.
- Effort to promote the development and use of new tools: These might include process maps, flow charts, clause libraries and automated documents. This indicates the partner's ability to innovate, consolidate the practice group's know-how, improve work efficiency and profitability in the long run, and invest in strengthening the competitiveness of the practice group and the firm.

5. Creating a strong culture of collaboration

Ever since Heidi Gardner's famous book *Smart Collaboration* was published in 2017,[2] most modern law firms have understood the abundant potential of increasing collaboration; but they have struggled to figure out how to enhance it and how to measure it. It goes without saying that the partnership system and the firm culture arising from the partnership system provide either a strong foundation for enhanced collaboration or a strong hindrance to it. Fully integrated true equity partnerships (regardless of whether they are modified, managed or pure lock-step) tend to have the best conditions for creating a culture of strong collaboration. The following can be measured in this regard:

- How much the partner encourages collaboration, as indicated by an engagement survey: This measures how practice group members feel about the partner's attitude towards developing a culture which encourages people to collaborate.
- BDM/CRM meetings conducted with partners from other practice groups: This measures the partner's attitude towards developing a culture in which cooperation rather than internal competition is a priority, and whether the partner shares his or her contacts and business rather than trying to keep them to himself or herself.
- The outcome of a questionnaire in which partners are asked to name those partners who have provided them with the most leads or cases or otherwise helped them the most during the previous year: Cross-referred work indicates how much a partner is referring cases to other partners – those who either are better experts for the case or have more resources to take it. Meanwhile, cross-supervised work indicates how much the partner who is in charge of a case uses members of other practice groups on that case.

6. Driving and supporting important projects or showing leadership beyond the practice group

In order to ensure market leadership, a law firm must continually invest in projects and initiatives which keep it one step ahead of the competition. Ideally, each partner should be ready from time to time to make a voluntary and extraordinary commitment to a new or otherwise important area for the firm. Wider contributions to the firm can also be made by showing the right attitude and 'spirit' in everyday work which helps to strengthen the firm – for example, by improving its processes.

Almost all other data can be collected from a well-organised system automatically, but these other firm contributions will need input from the

---

2 Heidi K Gardner, *Smart Collaboration: How Professionals and Their Firms Succeed by Breaking Down Silos* (Harvard Business Review Press, 2017).

individual partner before the appraisal team can form an opinion about the partner's performance in this category. The following could be looked at:

- The shaping and driving of strategic projects which may have a major positive impact on the firm's future: The long-term success of the firm depends on the partners' ability to understand the big picture, their sense of responsibility and their commitment to building a strong, successful and resilient firm. Examples of this could include leading a client experience workshop or reforming the lawyers' bonus system.
- Execution of commitments beyond the respective practice group which provide value for the firm: This measures the partner's ability to focus on the successful execution of tasks and roles beyond the practice group which have long-term value for the firm, but which usually are not urgent or do not provide an immediate noticeable impact or result. One example of this could be a partner helping to build a new sector group.

7. Building and sustaining a profitable practice and maximising the financial contribution

Finally, it is time to look at the financials more carefully. A law firm doesn't share partners' billable hours or revenue, but rather profit. The trend of profit growth reflects the long-term success of the firm, and that of its practice groups and various offices. In the short term, however, profit is subject to market volatility and even geopolitics, as we clearly saw during the writing of this chapter. And it is not only the overall firm profit that can be volatile; profit also varies across different practice groups and offices. The following could be measured:

- Practice group revenue and profit, adjusted according to how much a team has collaborated (eg, revenue/profit from cross-referrals and cross-supervision which is above or below average): This adjustment is very important to support the culture of collaboration, as otherwise this sends mixed messages to the partnership – "Please collaborate and send work to other partners, but we still measure just your own practice group's profit!"
- Revenue and ideally profit from cases supervised by the partner: This indicates how busy the partner has been in comparison with his or her peer group. This figure alone doesn't say much, but it becomes more revealing when reviewed alongside other information – for example, does the partner share work enough with other partners? Is the revenue generated in line with the expected profit? Are the revenue and profit in line with BDM/CRM efforts? Did the partner have enough time to make other firm contributions and develop knowledge?
- The profits of the partner's office (ideally adjusted for collaboration if the firm has more offices): In the medium term, the amount of dividends

that the firm pays to partners in any office should typically be in line with the profit that the office generates, so that it is not subsidised by other offices or supporting other offices too much for too long.

- Revenue from, and the number of, personal billable hours: This measures how 'hands-on' the partner is in conducting client work while building his or her technical skills over time. Revenue from those hours indicates how judiciously the partner is in choosing the highest-value producing work for himself or herself. In my opinion, this is more of a 'hygiene factor' and billable hours are most relevant in assessing how well the partner is building his or her technical skills. However, for many great law firms, a partner's personal billable hours and generated revenue from those hours still rank among the very top priority KPIs: the more the better. But why should a partner do anything that he or she can delegate to others? A partner should always focus on doing the work that has the highest long-term value for the firm and its clients. Very often, the highest long-term value is created by taking care of client relationships; leading people and projects; improving processes in the practice group and the firm; innovating and developing knowledge; and doing things which help to scale the practice group or the firm, rather than constantly trying to 'reinvent the wheel'. That said, however, building one's technical skills and eventually becoming a leading expert takes a lot of billable hours. Subsequently, as the partner becomes more senior, fewer billable hours are needed to maintain those skills and the achieved position.
- Average work-in-process during the year: This measures the attitude of a partner towards invoicing clients on a regular basis. A good standard is not to exceed six weeks' workload.
- Supporting revenue management team: The firm's revenue management team could be asked to provide feedback about the behaviour of the partner towards assisting in the invoicing process and collecting overdue receivables. This measures the attitude of the partner towards supporting the collection process and is an important part of his or her overall financial discipline.
- The practice group's total billed hours: These indicate the practice group's market share, the competition environment and the trend in work volumes – up or down.
- The practice group's invoiced average hourly rate: This indicates the practice group's market share, the competition environment, the trend in rates – up or down – and how well the partner has been able to 'sell' the practice group's fees to clients. It also indicates how work is distributed within the practice group and divided between more junior and senior members. This indicator is viewed in connection with the practice group's profit.

- The average time it takes for practice group members to register timecards on the system: A good standard is within 24 hours at the latest. This measures the discipline of the practice group in ensuring that all hours are properly and timely registered. Studies show that if hours are registered late, as much as 30% of the used time is forgotten and not registered at all.

8. Supporting the firm culture

The firm's culture has the potential to set it apart from its competitors and provide it with a special competitive advantage which is almost impossible to copy. In addition, culture often plays a strong role in attracting the right people to the firm and helps to maintain their engagement and loyalty; while conversely, those people who don't share similar values often leave. The way in which a partner behaves and makes often even very small decisions either will accord with the firm's values or will not. People will notice and remember the partner's behaviour and decisions.

Although this embraces many other categories – and perhaps even to some extent repeats certain categories that we have already looked at – it may still merit individual attention. Typically, all partners are at least successful in this category if they are successful in other categories. However, it may be that a partner who has a strong business case and is highly regarded by his or her own practice group members is behaving badly towards people in other practice groups or offices, but this doesn't come up in the engagement survey or financial reports. The appraisal team could form its own opinion about the behaviour and integrity of a partner and how well he or she is supporting the culture across the whole firm. It is good practice to discuss with each partner what he or she believes sets the firm apart from its competitors and what is genuinely distinctive in the market.

9. Summary

Each law firm has its own preferred KPIs and other performance indicators; and as long as the culture is strong, the partners are motivated to perform well and the partnership is aligned, there is no pressure – or even need – to change them.

However, if the firm needs to strengthen its performance, increase alignment among partners or strengthen the culture – or do all three simultaneously – then it may be advisable to develop the KPIs and the reporting system. In order to obtain proper information easily and consistently, and to avoid the risk of mistakes, it is advisable to automate reporting systems. It is also good practice to present information using graphs and colours, so that viewing reports is as easy as possible. Such reports make it easy for the managing partner to quickly identify those indicators that he or she needs to deal with (ideally each partner should have a personal 'dashboard' which immediately shows those indicators to which he or she should pay attention). Naturally, the managing partner should appoint the right people from the business services team to organise the collection of the data if it is not yet automated. While some indicators may be rather objective, others are based on quite subjective judgements. Hence, it is important that a wide range of indicators are looked at simultaneously, as together they can form a comprehensive picture of a partner's performance without the need to rely too much on any one indicator alone. Most of the indicators above will produce correct information if correct data is entered in the system.

The question thus remains: who should be responsible for entering the correct data in the system? If the firm's partnership at large agrees that all processes, behaviours and actions described above are useful and beneficial for the firm, and will help to strengthen alignment and promote the right culture, then it is obvious that the firm should be able to measure how well these processes are adhered to, what actions are being taken and how the partners are behaving. Partners are the ultimate owners of the firm and the firm's interests are their interests. Hence, each partner is expected to cooperate and ensure that correct and complete data is recorded in the firm's system; otherwise, it is not possible to measure whether the firm is achieving its objective. For example, if the partnership agrees that outbound referrals are important and should be made in a coordinated manner that will be of greatest benefit to the firm, then it is the responsibility of all partners to ensure that every outbound referral they make is correctly recorded in the system. Whether each partner records them personally or with the support of an assistant is not important.

It is beyond the scope of this chapter to discuss the pros and cons of different compositions of the partner appraisal team, the remuneration committee and the appeal process where a partner is not satisfied with the outcome of his or her appraisal.

Last, but not least, good plans and a good reporting system help to identify the 'dynamos' from the 'cruisers' and 'losers'; and make it easier for the managing partner to do his or her most important job: inspiring professionals, finding out what motivates each individual and keeping on pushing those buttons.[3]

3 David Maister, *Maister Moments*, podcast series, Dynamos.

Governing risk

Norman K Clark
Walker Clark LLC

1. The business case for risk management in law firms

Poor risk management policies and procedures are among the most serious vulnerabilities in the efforts of law firms to sustain profitability. In some instances, unmanaged risk has a greater impact on profitability than any of the other, more noticeable issues in contemporary law firm financial performance: more than clients' increased price sensitivity; more than increased competition; and more than ever-escalating compensation expectations by associates and partners. In some law firms, especially small and mid-sized ones, ineffective risk management can have a greater effect than all of these other issues combined.

Ineffective management of risks can produce costs that are seldom itemised in a law firm's financial reports. Some firms discover that the time and effort that they expend in collecting old debts from their clients can often be worth more than the uncollected fee itself. Moreover, the older accounts receivable become, the less likely they are to be collected at all. Inadequate quality assurance measures can also produce substantial financial risk, with rework – doing the work again to correct mistakes that should have been detected and corrected the first time – by itself accounting for as much as 40% of fee write-offs.

This chapter reviews the three most common forms of risk in law firms today. It presents countermeasures that are used by some law firms to address specific risk issues. Unfortunately, most law firms respond to vulnerabilities with crisis-to-crisis improvisation. This chapter therefore concludes by presenting typical features of an integrated, firm-wide system of risk management as a high priority in law firm governance, requiring the ongoing attention of all partners, and not just those persons in the firm with financial management responsibilities.

2. The three forms of risk in law firms

Law firms are subject to three principal forms of risk in their operations:

- financial risk;
- client service risk; and
- professional responsibility risk.

The relative importance of each of these areas might vary from firm to firm. For example, a firm could do a magnificent job of managing its financial risks through simple tactics such as credit screening of new clients, advance payments and close attention by partners to collections. At the same time, it could be undermining all of these good efforts in the area of financial risk by failing to address serious vulnerabilities in the area of client service risk, which produce unacceptably high write-offs. Moreover, all of a firm's risk management policies and procedures could be nullified by lapses in professional responsibility, resulting in professional indemnity claims from clients, which in turn can cause unplanned expenses, increased insurance premiums and possibly even a reputation for unprofessional conduct.

Therefore, even though the following pages discuss each form of risk separately, it is important to adopt a holistic view of all of the areas of potential risk in law firms.

2.1 Financial risks

This category addresses the risk that the client will not pay the agreed fee. It excludes, by definition, fee disputes arising from dissatisfaction with the services or work product that the client received. It involves two varieties of non-payment:

- clients that are simply unable or unwilling to pay the fee; and
- clients whose payments are slower than the agreed timeframe.

There is a wide range of precautions that law firms can take to mitigate financial risks or to avoid them completely. The most common ones include the following.

(a) Creditworthiness evaluation of new clients

By definition, the basic financial structure of the lawyer-client relationship is inherently risky. A lawyer or law firm promises to deliver professional services over a period of time in return for the client's unsecured promise to pay the fee. The strangeness of this proposition is heightened by the fact that most law firms are very reluctant to make any inquiry at all into the client's ability to pay the fee or credit record, for fear of offending the client at an early stage of the relationship.

Some types of transactions also involve substantial financial risk to the firm if the deal is not closed successfully. In effect, by taking on a new client for a high-risk transaction, based on nothing more than the client's promise, the law firm is joining in the client's speculative venture.

Both of these propositions describe what most lawyers would agree is highly imprudent business practice; but the fact is that this is how most law firms in the world do business. They happily trust the client's word until there is an event – usually unrecoverable and irremediable – that demonstrates that the firm's trust has been misplaced.

One of the most fundamental governance questions for any law firm is: "Whom shall we serve?" All law firms should have documented standards and guidelines, such as inquiry thresholds, which are estimated fee amounts at which the firm requires an evaluation of the client's ability to pay and creditworthiness.

(b) Substantial advance payment

When a case or transaction is likely to extend over many months, most law firms will request a significant advance, non-refundable payment. This can help the firm to mitigate its loss, in the form of unbilled work in progress and accounts receivable, if the client terminates the engagement prematurely.

As with most risk management measures, advance payments are something that many lawyers require almost instinctively. However, many firms – and most small firms – have no standard policy about when to require an advance payment and in what amount.

As the partner in one small law firm once memorably told me: "We have no policy about this. We just act on instinct. After a while, you just know what's the right amount, if anything."

The problem arises, however, when different partners have different 'instincts' and no one in the firm is making these decisions based on objective facts.

(c) Written terms of engagement

Although most law firms document new instructions or a new project, these engagement letters frequently lack a thorough recitation of the financial terms of the engagement. This can be a significant vulnerability, because vague or unaddressed terms in the engagement documents are one of the most common sources of fee disputes. Moreover, under the principle that vague terms in a document should normally be construed against the author, these disputes are ones that law firms seldom win.

The best practice is to issue a standard letter with complete terms of engagement in every instance. No client is too big or too small to be exempt from this risk management procedure, which protects the interests of both parties.

(d) Universal timekeeping

Universal timekeeping is a policy by which all fee earners, without exception, record all working time, without exception. Universal timekeeping is a highly effective tool to measure and diagnose potential problems in productivity and profitability. It can be a powerful tool to manage financial risk by documenting the work that the firm performed for the client, whether in the obvious situation of an hourly rate or to demonstrate the fairness of a fixed fee. To be effective, however, universal timekeeping should include the persistent enforcement of three basic rules:

- Every fee earner, without exception, records time;
- All time is recorded, both billable and non-billable; and
- Only a partner may write off time before it is billed and then should note the reason for the write-off.

The most common reason for not recording time is expressed in two words: "I forgot." By contrast, one mid-sized firm in Latin America observed that it had improved fee revenue for hourly work by more than 10% in one year, due almost entirely to a shift to universal timekeeping.

(e) Collections roles and responsibilities

Whose job is it to collect overdue bills from clients? In some firms, the billing department or finance department has the primary responsibility. In others, partners are responsible for the collection of bills that are past a certain age. But in many law firms, even large ones, these roles and responsibilities are not clearly defined.

Partners' responsibilities are one of the basic areas of attention in law firm governance. One of the fundamental responsibilities of any partner in any business is to exert one's best efforts for the financial performance of the partnership. Consistent with this duty, the role of partners in the collections process should therefore be defined by agreement of the partners, documented and enforced.

(f) Addressing potential financial risks from other partners

The above examples relate primarily to external risks arising from inadequate definition and documentation of the lawyer-client relationship. Law firms can also be vulnerable to a subtle, but potentially more damaging, financial risk arising from inadequate agreements and documentation of the roles, obligations and privileges of partners.

Some of these risks could also be considered professional responsibility risks, as they might give rise to serious issues concerning conflicts of interest or misuse by a partner of a client relationship, to the detriment of other partners in the firm.

The nature and extent of these risks from other partners vary from jurisdiction to jurisdiction, but they should be evaluated and addressed as necessary. Modern partnership agreements, or annexes thereto, should address and document clear guidance on issues such as the following:

- To what extent, if at all, may a partner engage in outside business activities, either directly or through a member of his or her immediate family?

- To what extent, if at all, may a partner use or refer to the firm's name or other brand identity in his or her outside business activities?
- To what extent, if at all, must a partner account for income from external sources such as teaching, publication, arbitrator fees, speaking honoraria and compensated service as a member of a board of directors?
- To what extent, if at all, must a partner communicate to the other partners any investment opportunities offered by the firm's clients, although not necessarily during the course of, or related to, a matter on which the firm has been, or is likely to be, instructed?
- To what extent, if at all, must a partner make a confidential disclosure of his or her financial interests to prevent possible conflicts with the interests of the firm's clients or with the interests of the firm itself?
- To what extent, if at all, will a partner be restricted in the practice of law after withdrawing from the partnership and ceasing practice in the firm?

2.2 Client service risks

Client service risks arise when the firm fails to meet client needs and expectations. This produces financial problems in two dimensions that compound to have a serious impact on profitability:

- Firm resources – often at partner level – must be diverted from fee production to correct the mistakes, most of which should have been avoided the first time; and
- The client is highly unlikely to pay for the additional work to correct the firm's mistakes.

Client service vulnerabilities can also jeopardise a firm's reputation in the legal markets in which it competes. The quality of client service, as reported by clients themselves, is one of the most important elements in competitive rankings in reputable legal directories. Therefore, vulnerabilities in client service can not only damage relationships with current clients, but also lose engagements from potential clients which will eliminate the firm from consideration because of a poor reputation in the firm's local market or a low ranking in an international legal directory.

How can these risks be managed? Unfortunately, most law firms learn the lessons of managing client service risks the hard way, after a client service failure has cost the firm a major client. The better approach is to identify the vulnerabilities in the firm's client service processes before they can deteriorate into crises and to implement quality assurance procedures that reduce the probability of them becoming problems.

The process is easier than it might seem. Some law firm practice groups have been able to make dramatic improvements in client service, and in some cases have saved highly dissatisfied clients, in as little as two or three afternoons of work. The steps involved are as follows.

(a) ***Step 1: Identify the indicators that are most important to the client in its evaluation of the quality of the legal services that the firm delivers***
These often vary among practice areas or industry sectors, so do not assume that 'one size fits all'. This also usually requires interviews or brief surveys with major clients, especially the unhappy ones. Even the most dissatisfied client will usually appreciate the effort that a firm takes to understand and confirm its needs and expectations. This single act of approaching an unhappy client, by itself, can save the relationship.

(b) ***Step 2: Identify the major processes, procedures or tasks by which the firm delivers the service***
The basic tool used in this step is a simple flow chart.

(c) ***Step 3: Identify the critical processes***
These are the processes, procedures or tasks that have the greatest effect on meeting the client's most important needs and expectations. A simple matrix is usually the most effective analytical tool for this step. If there is a serious quality assurance vulnerability in a law firm, it is usually in a critical process. Improving this process – even if all others are left substantially unchanged – can produce dramatic improvements in client service and in the profitability of the delivery of the service. The two usually go together.

(d) ***Step 4: Consider what can go wrong and why***
What are the most common errors, mistakes or reasons for rework in the critical process? What are the most frequent causes of errors? Consider not only the probability of an error, but also the seriousness of its consequences. Errors with relatively low probability but very serious consequences if they do occur should not be dismissed.

(e) ***Step 5: Agree on actions to reduce the most frequent causes of errors or to eliminate those causes completely***
These frequently involve four areas that many law firms overlook:

- improved communication with the client;
- improved consultation between junior fee earners who are doing the work and their supervisors;
- documentation of the completion of certain actions that relate to the client's most important needs and expectations; and
- periodic review of the file and records by supervisors or, in the case of partners, a periodic peer review.

(f) *Step 6: Document the new procedures in a quality assurance protocol*

This almost never requires the publication of a thick manual, which is most likely to gather dust on a shelf. For example, the finance litigation group in a major English law firm was able to document completely its quality assurance protocol, covering four types of case, in a single document of 16 pages.

(g) *Step 7: Collect information about the performance of the new quality assurance measures*

Have error rates decreased? Has client satisfaction improved? Has the profitability of the work processes in the new risk-managed process improved? This data should be reviewed after approximately 90 days to identify any further refinements and adjustments that are needed.

2.3 Professional responsibility risk

The most common example of this type of risk is having to pay a claim for professional malpractice. Even a relatively simple lapse in professional responsibility can have very expensive long-term consequences. An entire firm's reputation can be marred by the acts or omissions of a single partner. Moreover, the incident can produce an unplanned expense to satisfy the deductible from the insurance coverage, as well as ongoing additional costs in the form of higher insurance premiums.

People make mistakes, which could be minimised by considering them as ordinary business risks. However, in the professional responsibility category, there is a large gap between the substantial immediate and short-term financial costs on one side of the equation and the usually nominal costs of managing the risk on the other.

Perhaps the three greatest producers of unnecessary professional responsibility risk in law firms could easily be avoided almost completely, as discussed below.

(a) *Inadequate conflicts checks*

A startling percentage of small law firms – including in developed and presumably sophisticated jurisdictions – have no conflicts information or checking procedures other than the memory of the oldest partner. Even in firms that have conflicts-checking policies, procedures and systems, partners frequently ignore them, having the apparent authority to open any new file without complying with any internal requirements, such as a formal engagement letter, advance payments or a conflicts check.

In an era when sophisticated conflicts-checking systems are available at a reasonable cost and are relatively easy for even the most technologically challenged (or resistant) partners to use, there is no good excuse for any law firm to continue to be exposed to this risk.

(b) Inadequate central calendaring

The single most frequent cause of professional indemnity claims remains missed deadlines, resulting in the dismissal of a cause of action or the expiration of a business opportunity. In most of these cases, the failure was one of simple oversight: "I forgot." Missed deadlines are also a major source of client dissatisfaction.

Some law firms have discovered that mandatory use of a common electronic calendaring system as part of the firm's matter management procedures can eliminate missed deadlines almost entirely, provided that the senior leadership of the firm reinforces the rules. These systems are inexpensive and easy to use, and have powerful reporting capabilities. There is no good reason not to use them.

(c) Inadequate institutional guidance on professional responsibility issues

Who decides the difficult questions of professional responsibility, such as whether the firm is conflicted out of a potential engagement or what the ethical course of action is in an uncertain situation? In many law firms, there is an assumption that it is the responsibility of the managing partner or the senior partner; but the honest answer usually is: "Nobody."

As a matter of good governance in a law firm of any size, one or more partners should be formally designated as responsible for professional responsibility issues and guidance to the firm. These assignments should be documented in the firm's corporate documentation, such as the partnership agreement or an annex thereto.

There also should be documented procedures to resolve professional responsibility issues within the firm. Demonstration that a law firm had such procedures and that one of its partners or employees relied upon them, even if with erroneous results, can sometimes be a mitigating factor in disciplinary actions by regulatory authorities arising from client complaints.

3. An integrated governance structure to manage risk

Most risk management efforts by law firms fail to deliver their full potential benefits because they are usually produced through crisis-to-crisis improvisation, rather than through an integrated, systematic approach that is centrally managed as part of the firm's major governance functions.

Law firms that are effective in managing the risks of legal practice usually have governance structures, policies and procedures in place. There are four cornerstones to successful risk management practices:

- The partnership itself closely monitors, manages and enforces risk management, rather than abdicating responsibility to a bright young associate or to senior business staff;
- The risk management policies and procedures are documented;

- The risk management policies and procedures are regularly tested; and
- Lawyers, especially partners, who do not comply with the firm's risk management policies and procedures are subject to sanctions.

How these four cornerstones are shaped and interlock varies with the characteristics that define the specific risk environment of each law firm, such as:

- the jurisdiction's regulations of the profession;
- customs of practice;
- client base;
- practice specialties; and
- workplace culture.

However, each one is present and observable.

3.1 Partnership responsibility

Law firms with good governance treat risk management as a partner-level responsibility and priority. There is direct management 'line of sight' between a partner and the functioning of the various risk management policies and procedures in the firm.

Rather than taking a piecemeal approach to engagement letters, spelling errors in documents, conflicts checks and calendar management, for example, these firms consolidate and integrate responsibility for the risk management programme under a single partner or small group of partners. Although some functions might be delegated to associates and staff, the responsibility and accountability for a successful risk management programme remain at the partner level.

Some firms assign some specific risk management functions, such as conflicts checks or the opening of new files, to a single partner for supervision. Partners with similar oversight responsibilities for other specific risk management functions are sometimes designated as a standing committee of the partnership.

With respect to client service risk, some larger firms with well-developed quality assurance programmes have created 'quality councils', which supervise quality assurance activities. These groups are almost always headed by one or more partner and frequently include the managing partner, at least in an *ex officio* capacity.

Although the structural forms should vary to suit each firm's specific needs, the definitive point is that risk management should be a governance function, managed by the partners as part of the firm's overall governance, and not an operational function run by the staff.

3.2 Documentation

Documentation of all risk management policies and procedures is important for at least three practical reasons:

- It eliminates confusion about what the policies are and reduces the risk of them being applied inconsistently;
- It provides a reference for ongoing evaluation of the risk management system; and
- It publishes firm-specific rules of professional conduct for lawyers in the firm, providing clear standards for which they will be accountable.

Although some firms combine all of their risk management documentation in a single volume, the more practical approach for most firms is to publish the policies and procedures as a set of standard operating procedures. This makes it easier for junior fee earners and staff to find relevant guidance when unsure of how to proceed, rather than having to search through a large binder of materials to find the one or two provisions that answer the question.

3.3 Testing the system

The firm should regularly and periodically test the risk management policies and procedures to ensure that they remain relevant and are being followed.

One of the simplest but most effective ways to evaluate a law firm's risk management programme is through an internal review tool known as a management control review. This process focuses on the major risk management policies for each of the three forms of risk.

For example:

- in the area of financial risk, management control reviews could focus on:
  - policies for the acceptance of new clients;
  - financial and creditworthiness checks of new clients;
  - compliance with policies and procedures regarding engagement letters; and
  - responsibility for collections;
- in the area of client service risk, the reviews could look at:
  - compliance with risk management protocols;
  - missed deadlines; and
  - error reporting and analysis; and
- in the area of professional responsibility risk, the management control reviews could study:
  - compliance with conflicts checks;
  - compliance with calendaring requirements;
  - missed deadline reporting; and
  - compliance with procedures for guidance on professional responsibility issues.

A management control review asks five basic questions:

- Are the relevant risk management policies, procedures and rules stated in writing, clearly and unambiguously?
- Are they being observed consistently? If not, what are the reasons or justifications for deviations from policies, procedures or rules? People do not usually ignore or violate the rules without good reason. If non-compliance is detected, the firm needs to know what factors are preventing compliance.
- Do any such deviations pose a reasonably probable risk of fraud, waste or abuse of the firm's funds, or of client funds in the firm's custody? If so, there could be a substantial and potentially costly professional responsibility risk. A specific internal audit of the vulnerable functions is usually highly advisable.
- Overall, is the process meeting its desired purpose to reduce the specific risk that it is intended to manage? It is helpful if the firm has some simple measurement of relevant results. For example, if the policy is intended to reduce missed deadlines in delivering documents to clients, has the number of missed deadlines actually gone down?
- What changes, if any, are required at this time? If the risk management policies and procedures are well informed and thoughtfully designed, this question should produce recommendations for refinements and adjustments, rather than major revisions.

Most management control reviews take one day or less to complete, but a small law firm should attempt no more than one or two reviews per month. They should always be conducted by a partner, who typically samples matter files and related administrative documents and interviews people who have the most frequent contact with the specific risk management policies and procedures that are being reviewed. The results should be submitted to the managing partner or some other partner who has been formally designated as responsible for the firm's risk management programme.

The management control review is also an excellent mechanism for ensuring that other areas of the firm's operations – such as finance, human resources, marketing and facilities – are complying with the firm's policies and are meeting the expectations of external clients and internal customers of the process. The purpose of the management control review is not to catch people in non-compliance, but to identify improvements that will make the risk management programme even more effective.

3.4 Lawyer accountability

Risk management is not just partnership responsibility; in well-governed law firms, lawyers are individually accountable for compliance. Lawyers who refuse to cooperate with risk management policies, or who undermine the firm's policies in their comments to partners, associates or staff, risk being sanctioned by the partnership. For example, firms that have universal timekeeping requirements might withhold draws or salary payments until the time records are up to date. A partner who fails to comply with policies for financial management of his or her matters or who generates an inordinate number of client service complaints or professional indemnity claims might be penalised by a reduction in profit points or expulsion from the firm.

The sanctions and reinforcements should be customised to suit the circumstances and professional culture of each firm. What is important, however, is that the management of the firm must be ready to show that its risk management policies and rules are serious and will be enforced. Notions of collegiality and professional friendship are important, but they are not worth leaving the firm vulnerable to risks.

4. Risk management as a core governance competency

Why has risk management become an important governance issue in law firms? The short answer is the need for sustainable profitability in uncertain times. Law firm partners have realised that risk management can be a reliable, cost-effective diagnostic tool to address subtle but profound causes of poor profitability – factors that seldom appear on a balance sheet or profit and loss statement.

Law firms have also learned that, although improvised responses to specific risks are usually better than nothing at all, risk management policies and procedures must be coordinated and integrated into a common firm-wide system if they are going to meet their full potential.

This has involved several paradigm shifts. Simply stated, the traditional view which dominated most law firm partnerships for years was: "If we keep our fees high enough, we will make money." In recent years, however – and especially since the global financial crisis of 2008–2010 and again during the COVID-19 pandemic of 2020–2022 – law firms have been challenged to redefine notions of law firm financial performance in terms of anticipating and managing risks, with new attention focused on a more comprehensive understanding of the intricacy of profitability in the delivery of legal services, as well as the challenges of financial sustainability of law firms in a quickly changing, hyper-competitive market.

Risk management, which used to be a concept that most lawyers dismissed as something primarily for accountants and actuaries, has moved from the back room and into law firm partnership meetings. Increasingly, risk management is regarded with the same sense of high priority as capitalisation, partnership structure and the admission of new partners – as one of the central issues and core competencies of good governance.

Succession, retirement and beyond

Lisa M Walker Johnson
Walker Clark LLC

1. Introduction

Retirement is an important life transition for any professional. For senior lawyers, the prospect of leaving the practice of law, as well as the partners and close professional friends with whom they have worked closely for many years, can be a complicated and difficult transition that some welcome and others dread. Evolving expectations about what constitutes a satisfying career increasingly influence partners' choices to stay or to leave the legal profession. The increased lateral movement of partners among law firms for various reasons is also pushing law firms to evaluate old paradigms about retirement. Whatever the reason for partner departures, they can be traumatic for the partners who are left behind. Whether expected or unexpected, the departure of a partner can have serious impacts on the firm's client base, management and financial health.

For this reason, retirement not only is a major milestone in the professional life of a lawyer, but also can be an arduous test of the strength and resilience of the governance policies and structures, professional culture and relationships among the partners of the firm. Firms and lawyers that plan for partner transitions in advance typically manage partner retirements much more effectively than those that rely on case-by-case improvisation.

This chapter investigates the governance implications of succession planning and, specifically, retirement departures from two points of view: that of the individual partner and that of the firm the partner leaves behind. Both perspectives must be considered for succession planning and retirement to be managed well. The firm's policies and practices with respect to succession planning, retirement and possible post-retirement roles for partners should take into account the personal challenges and ethical choices that this transition to 'life after the law' can bring. Each partner also needs to plan his or her own transition well in advance – mentally, emotionally and financially.

Retirement from a law firm is a complex process. Why does retirement appear to be more difficult for lawyers than for most other professions and occupations? How should individual lawyers and their law firms think differently about the role of, and options for, senior lawyers who are approaching, have reached or are well past the customary retirement age?

2. Changing expectations about the 'golden years'

Less than a generation ago, age 50 was considered to be the peak of one's professional life – the time to start reaping the benefits of one's career. For most people in Western cultures, full-time retirement was no more than 10 to 15 years away. In some countries, retirement from the law in one's 50s was not unusual.[1]

Dramatic advances in medicine and education, as well as economic change and frequent uncertainties in the past 20 years, have changed much of that. In most countries, a much larger portion of the population are living active, healthy working lives into their 80s and 90s[2] – some by choice and some by economic necessity.

Longer, healthier active lifespans have produced two significant and opposing trends in law firms. Some partners are remaining active in their firm longer. It is not unusual to find active equity partners still practising full time or almost full time at age 80,[3] especially those who are founding partners of their firms. The counter-current, however, is that opportunities for a longer work life have encouraged more partners to work hard and retire from their firm early – sometimes in their 50s or even late 40s – to pursue other activities in the law, government, academia or business. The emergence and acceptance of remote working in the early 2020s have made this more feasible than ever before.

3. Having too much fun

In many countries, it is the lawyers from their 50s to their early 70s who drive financial performance and continue to hold respected leadership positions in their law firms. At 1,500 billable hours per year, one 70-year-old

---

1 The concept of being 'old' is also rapidly evolving, being challenged by life expectancies that have almost doubled since 1900. Old age is often a social construct associated with a change of social or economic roles and activities, such as reaching a mandatory retirement age. See United Nations Population Fund, *Ageing in the Twenty-First Century: A Celebration and a Challenge* (2012), www.unfpa.org/publications/ageing-twenty-first-century.

2 The global population is getting older, with people aged 65 and older constituting the fastest-growing segment. According to data compiled by the United Nations, by 2050, one in six people in the world will be over age 65 (16%), up from one in 11 in 2019 (9%). By 2050, one in four persons living in Europe and Northern America could be aged 65 or over. In 2018, for the first time in history, persons aged 65 or above outnumbered children under five years of age globally. The number of persons aged 80 years or over is projected to triple, from 143 million in 2019 to 426 million in 2050. United Nations Department of Economic and Social Affairs, Population Division, *World Population Prospects 2022* (2022), https://population.un.org/wpp/.

3 For example, the American Bar Association (ABA), which has the largest database of lawyer demographics (1.3 million lawyers) in the world, has reported a steady ageing trend in the American legal profession. The median age of licensed lawyers in the United States increased from 39 to 46.5 between 1980 and 2021. In 2021, nearly 13% of all US lawyers – one in eight – were 65 or older. See American Bar Foundation, *ABA Profile of the Legal Profession 2022* (2022), www.americanbar.org/content/dam/aba/administrative/news/2022/07/profile-report-2022.pdf. The UN and ABA data suggests that there is a 'bulge in the python' of lawyer populations – in developed countries at least – that will produce a record number of law firm partners who are now reaching the traditional retirement age range of 65 to 70, but who are likely to continue in active practice well into the 2030s and possibly into the early 2040s.

partner said recently: "I am having too much fun to even think about retiring."

The 'fun' derives from sources inside the law firm, as well as being part of the legal profession. There are close ties between a lawyer's active status in a law firm, with the opportunities it brings to serve on corporate and civic boards, and the respect that he or she enjoys as a leader in the community. When a senior partner leaves a law firm, he or she is leaving behind more than an office, other partners and colleagues, and must also say goodbye to an extended 'family' of business, legal and professional friends.

As with other successful people in business and the professions, lawyers' 'golden years' can be truly golden. Rather than follow the paradigm of the mid-twentieth century of retiring at the earliest opportunity, more lawyers now want to keep practising their profession – not because they have to, but because they realise that they are in one of the most satisfying times of their professional lives. The personal lives of the most senior lawyers are also continuing on an upward trajectory and present few, if any, compelling reasons to consider complete retirement.

These factors produce the two countertrends noted above. Some partners are still having too much fun or making too much money to want to leave their law firms. On the other hand, after 25 or 30 years of hard work, other law firm partners have accumulated enough financial security or professional experiences by their 50s that they are ready to take on new roles or expand existing ones (eg, grandparent, chief justice, politician, philanthropist, professor, ambassador, business owner, world traveller).

As a result, each law firm must be fully prepared to manage these fluid, evolving and somewhat unpredictable dynamics:

- the partners who want to, and can, remain active and productive long beyond the traditional retirement age; and
- those who want to leave early for personal reasons or to move into the next phase of their active professional lives.

4. The risks for law firms

The risks of ignoring succession planning and retirement issues are well known in law firms. The departure of a partner, even when expected,[4] can impose a substantial financial burden on the partnership to fund the buy-out of the departing partner's interest. Some firms structure their capitalisation requirements in ways that either:

- mitigate the short-term financial impact of buy-outs, through the

4 The possibility of 'unexpected' departures – such as to accept an in-house position in a corporate law department or a temporary assignment to a government or diplomatic post, or to move to another law firm; or even the unexpected death of a partner – can and should be anticipated in a law firm's planning.

mandatory gradual sale of a partner's equity beginning several years before a presumptive retirement date;[5] or
- avoid those problems completely, by token capitalisation requirements such as 'easy-in/easy-out'.[6]

However, prudent succession planning also requires that the firm adopt and enforce policies and procedures to ensure that:
- the departing partner's responsibilities for management and professional supervision are competently passed over to other lawyers; and
- long-term client relationships that the departing partner nurtured over the years are transferred to others in the firm.

The risks to the financial performance, client base and effective management of a firm can be significant – even when the firm adopts and enforces clear, thorough and well-documented policies and procedures to manage them. A firm must also consider the indirect risks that arise when, as a result of weak or non-existent succession planning, senior associates and junior partners do not see clear benefits to progressing with their careers in the firm, compared to taking what appear to be better long-range opportunities elsewhere. Without planning, however, whether a firm can manage these risks becomes mostly a matter of *ad hoc* cleverness and good luck.

5. The need to discard outdated paradigms

Writing a succession plan and tweaking the partnership agreement will not be enough for most firms to manage the new challenges and risks of this fluid retention and retirement environment. Successful management will also require that firms:
- discard outdated assumptions about how a law firm partnership should be structured;
- confirm the roles and responsibilities of equity partners; and
- define what constitutes a 'career' in their law firm.

Except in family firms, the traditional pattern of career management in law firms has included a strong 'up and out' preference in the tenure of partners. Once a partner reaches a certain age – usually assumed to be in the early to mid-

5 For example, if the firm has a presumptive retirement age of 65, an equity partner must begin to sell back to the firm a stated percentage of his or her equity each year upon reaching age 60. Another variation is to execute the purchase of the departing partner's equity at the retirement date, but to spread the payments over an agreed number of years.

6 For example, upon joining the equity partnership, the new partner is required only to make a token cash payment for his or her interest in the firm. Some firms require the new partner to execute a promissory note, payable to the firm on demand, to cover unexpected short-term requirements for capital. Upon leaving the firm, the partner receives only the nominal amount that he or she actually paid to purchase shares or equity, plus any outstanding short-term loans to the firm.

60s – best practice has favoured a variety of succession planning strategies, most of which were intended to move senior partners out of the equity partnership so that the next generation of partners could assume leadership of, and greater financial benefits from, the firm. This trend became especially noticeable in the 1990s and early 2000s, as record numbers of young lawyers joined law firms, established themselves as successful practitioners and began to be admitted to partnership. The prevailing presumption was that older partners would move out of the partnership to provide adequate profit distribution opportunities for their younger colleagues.

The problem with the up-and-out model today is that it no longer fits a profession that, while becoming younger, is also growing older at the same time. This is a paradox; but it makes little, if any, business sense to jettison an otherwise productive partner who wants to continue to contribute to the firm just because he or she is 'too old'. Moreover, as discussed previously, the definition of 'too old' is changing rapidly.

Moreover, the up-and-out 'escalator' no longer travels in a smooth, steady upwards trajectory. Rather, its operation is complicated, and in some instances disrupted, by the increased lateral movement of equity partners among law firms – especially since the global financial crisis of 2009–2010. Some partners now jump off the escalator later in their ascent, while others jump on much closer to the top than would previously have been customary.

The implications for multi-generational law firms are substantial, both in the short term and over the next 10 to 30 years. Although some senior equity partners will gladly trade their share of the profits for the more predictable income and lack of risk inherent in non-equity partnership, others will be unwilling to cash in their equity until much later. Likewise, younger lawyers might have to make a choice between a longer wait for equity partnership or moving to another firm in mid-career.[7] Increasingly, these lawyers are selecting the second option.

Law firms will also need to understand the measurable, but currently unmeasured, economic value that older lawyers can contribute to the firm in areas other than fee earning, such as a greater investment of their time in

---

7 Senior associates, in particular, want to be able to tell clients that they are partners and to be perceived as advancing in their careers. Most of them crave greater professional responsibility, the opportunity to lead other lawyers in matters of increasing importance and complexity, and the chance to earn more money. They also seek greater visibility with the firm's clients, which can create opportunities to generate new work and give them practical experience in business development activities with a high return on investment.

Some law firms use non-equity partner status to retain senior associates. Non-equity partners frequently point out four benefits to this approach:

- the professional status that the title of 'partner' communicates to clients and to the legal and business community;
- the opportunity to lead more sophisticated matters;
- significantly higher compensation; and
- many of the financial and other benefits of being a partner in a law firm, but without the financial responsibility and risk.

marketing and business development, especially with the firm's important client sectors and major clients. Such efforts increase the probability that when senior lawyers finally retire, the major clients that they serve will transition smoothly to the next generation of partners. Otherwise, unless a client relationship has been 'institutionalised' before a senior partner leaves a law firm, there is a high probability that many, if not most, of the clients that partner served will go elsewhere, often in as little as 12 to 18 months.[8]

Keeping older partners active in client relationships, even after they formally withdraw from the equity partnership, is a highly effective way to prevent such an 'emigration' of clients. This sometimes requires that partners become more flexible in designing alternatives to equity ownership, such as consultancy, non-equity senior partnership or partner emeritus programmes.

Leadership expectations and standards of performance for partners must be defined with clarity and flexibility. This could be a challenge for many law firms that have never seriously considered performance standards for any partners, or that have a cultural aversion to direct communication and feedback about partner roles and responsibilities – particularly when performance becomes substandard or otherwise does not meet expectations.

6. Letting go is never easy

Even with the ability and desire to work into one's 70s, 80s or even 90s, there typically is a time in most lawyers' careers when they intellectually realise that it is time to let go. Ageing affects everyone, even lawyers. Denial is a natural psychological defence against fears and anxieties that all lawyers – all people – have about ageing and retirement, even when it is a planned change and one to which they are looking forward. Retirement can be a potentially sensitive topic for lawyers – perhaps more so than for other people, because it is linked to perceptions about professional competence and performance.

Why do partners hang on when even their own logic convinces them that they have 'paid their dues' and should spend more time with friends, family and the non-legal activities that they enjoy best? Why is the reluctance to move to the next phase in one's personal and professional life such a gut-wrenching process for many lawyers, but easier for others?

The unique psychological and social factors that contribute to the progression of a lawyer's career also produce specific factors that affect, and can sometimes inhibit, optimism about the transition from full-time practice in

8 This is based on observations and consultations by Walker Clark LLC since 2002, while advising law firms about succession planning and management. We have found insufficient evidence, other than anecdotes usually arising from isolated incidents, to support the frequently heard complaint that law firm clients generally are 'less loyal' or 'more fickle' today than before. Instead, we have observed a strong correlation between weak or non-existent succession planning and the loss of clients upon the departure of the partner who was principally responsible for those client relationships.

one's law firm. These factors also present some significant risks – not only for the senior lawyer, but also for the firm.

Even partners who are retiring because they choose to do so often resist, often unexpectedly, 'retiring gracefully'. There are at least 10 frequently observed forces driving and influencing these struggles.

6.1 Purpose and personal identity from one's work

This is one of the most powerful forces affecting a senior lawyer's transition out of a law firm. It is much more pronounced among those men for whom their life is their work, but women are by no means immune.

Lawyers often identify themselves with their professional positions. This is typical of men in contemporary Western culture. An overidentification with their success as a lawyer might lead some partners to perceive their value solely through that lens. The job comes to represent not only what they do, but the essence of who they are. Any suggestion that there is room to expand or improve this narrow view goes to the core of their self-identity and self-worth.

Professional colleagues and clients often dominate their relationships outside the office. These relationships are vital to feeling 'in the loop' and to maintaining a sense of self-importance, purpose and power.

Both men and women achieve a sense of purpose through their close relationships with clients and professional colleagues – unmatched in most other occupations.

At the same time, social expectations of men and women differ, which can have positive and negative effects on retirement. Women, in general, are more likely to view their jobs as just one element of who they are. For women lawyers, other aspects of their lives typically take up too much time to permit total identification with their careers. The author has observed that women tend to make more time, by preference or circumstance, for relationships and activities not directly related to their professional practice. They often describe to the author how important the care and empowerment of others is to their core values, both personally and professionally. Women may, in fact, have more integrated and fulfilling careers, and may already feel a greater sense of purpose when they reach retirement.[9] This can make the transition easier.

On the other hand, women partners may have less flexibility to invest in new directions on retirement because societal expectations and family responsibilities have a disproportionate impact on their time, resources and options.

Women who waited until their 30s and 40s to have children, which is common for professionals, frequently find themselves caring for young children and ageing parents at the same time. In the United States, for example, 65% of

9 See Sally Helgeson, *The Female Advantage: Women's Ways of Leadership* (Doubleday, 1995).

older persons who require long-term medical care rely exclusively on family members to provide that assistance; and 66% of those in-home family caregivers are women, with a substantial impact on their availability to work outside the home, accept promotions or continue in full-time employment.[10]

For women in law firms, the shift to a work-at-home practice during the COVID-19 pandemic from 2020 to 2022 had mixed benefits. While enabling them to be more responsive to family members who needed their assistance, that proximity also resulted in distractions and obstacles to managing their professional work. The deterioration of the social safety net and healthcare services in developed countries in particular, such as the United States, means that balancing the needs of ageing family members at home and one's professional responsibilities to a law practice is a challenge that is likely to continue.

This role of the professional woman as a multi-generation caregiver is complicated even further by the trend – particularly in the United States, but also observable in other countries – of children and grandchildren moving back home to live; and of more people in their 40s, 50s and 60s assuming primary responsibility for the care of their grandchildren.

6.2 The desire to maintain control

Information – in the form of technical legal expertise, contacts in the business community or knowledge of a client's business – is the chief source of some lawyers' power in their firms. This can make a senior lawyer suspicious of the interest of a junior partner in, for example, learning more about the senior lawyer's clients. Sometimes senior partners are reluctant to share knowledge because it may feel as if they are diluting their value to the firm, as well as weakening the source of their personal identities. As long as a senior partner retains knowledge, he or she can hang on to the myth that "No one can ever do this as well as I can."

The fear of loss of control is what drives many partners who say that succession planning is impractical because of the assumption – which is part egoism and part denial – that there is no one else in the firm with whom their clients would be willing to work. Confidential interviews of clients – including with those which have had long, close professional and personal relationships with one partner in a firm – frequently expose this supposed reluctance as highly exaggerated and easily overcome by a gradual transition of the responsibility for client relationships.

10 See "Women and Caregiving: Facts and Figures", National Center on Caregiving, Family Caregiver Alliance (2015), www.caregiver.org/resource/women-and-caregiving-facts-and-figures/; and Lynn Fineberg and Rita Choula, "Understanding the Impact of Family Caregiving on Work", AARP Public Policy Institute (October 2012), www.aarp.org/content/dam/aarp/research/public_policy_institute/ltc/2012/understanding-impact-family-caregiving-work-AARP-ppi-ltc.pdf.

Moreover, except in very small firms or extremely highly specialised practice areas, there is usually a junior partner or senior associate who can do the non-delegable work just as well as the older partner.

Just as a client's fears of eventual death should never prevent a lawyer from advising him or her to execute a will, no law firm should allow a partner's dread of 'professional mortality' to prevent it from discussing candidly and making prudent plans to keep the clients after the partner retires.

The habits of traditional legal practice, in which partners tend to practise individually, and not usually in teams, might also contribute to their reluctance to give up information and knowledge, which are symbols of professional power in the firm.

Letting go of this knowledge and a valued close relationship with a client – even as part of an effort to transfer the client relationship to younger partners and to keep a client after the older partner retires – can appear threatening: "Once they have this information and the client's confidence, the firm won't need me and I will get pushed out." This is not necessarily a fear of being expelled from the partnership, because this rarely happens. Instead, the older partner frequently fears being excluded from the flow of important information, especially financial, and from vital decisions. This suspicion can be aggravated by the traditionally competitive and individualistic nature of most law firm partnerships.

The desire to use knowledge as a weapon to retain control – or, if not control, then influence – can have serious consequences for a law firm transition. For example, key information needed by the whole firm, not just the one senior partner, can be withheld as a conscious or unconscious ploy to sabotage, or at least slow down, that partner's transition out of the firm.

Hoarding information, work or client relationships can actually be counterproductive for a senior lawyer. Overburdened with work, a senior partner has less time to redirect professional energies into alternative activities, such as coaching and developing others in the firm, business development or personal development of outside interests. There is also a long-term cost: senior partners who do not invest in building business development skills in their colleagues foster a 'cult of the rainmaker', which makes the entire firm overly dependent on the activities of a few partners. Unless the firm has already developed effective plans to transition client relationships from the rainmakers to other partners – to institutionalise the client relationship and move from a 'my client' attitude to an 'our client' attitude – it will probably suffer a significant loss of business from the clients whose relationships one partner hoarded.

6.3 Loss of personal prestige

Many senior partners enjoy great personal prestige and professional status in their law firms, their communities and the business and professional associations to which they belong. They frequently fear that any reduction in their activities – even while remaining affiliated with the firm as a consultant or attorney of counsel – will cause them to lose their prominence and with it some of their sense of self-worth.

6.4 No clear succession of leadership in the firm

If a law firm has not taken succession planning seriously, some senior partners might fear that everything will 'go to hell in a handcart' once they leave the firm. This can be an especially powerful force in the decisions of a founding partner, who might see the law firm as the only lasting legacy of his or her professional life. The lack of a succession plan – even an informal or undocumented one – can also make the retention of experienced associates and senior associates more difficult, because they often perceive no realistic opportunity to assume leadership roles, manage client relationships and advance.

6.5 No bridge to life after retirement

A career in a law firm can be all-consuming. Lawyers whom the author counsels frequently complain that they have no life outside the firm because of:

- the unrelenting pace imposed by clients' needs and expectations;
- the perceived inability to take a break during the day;
- working vacations rather than real holidays;
- little spare time for hobbies and family life;
- a feeling that they need to be 'on call' 24 hours per day;
- the lingering effects of stress-producing conditions in the firm;
- not enough time for reflection, including about legal matters;
- the inability to detach from work and the related nagging sense that there is always something not being done; and
- no opportunity to pursue personal or even professional development.

Although practising law is intellectually stimulating, lawyers often complain to the author about social isolation. Personal relationships with family members and friends often suffer as a result of neglect over the years, while the lawyer focuses intently on establishing prominence in his or her firm and in the profession.

Some senior partners may have viewed the work – and even the people in the firm – as simply a means to an end, without holding any intrinsic personal value that could be sustaining in the long term. For many lawyers – partners and associates alike – legal practice becomes a series of finite tasks and achievements, with few long-term benefits. This intense focus on solving the problem at hand for the client, combined with the tradition of virtual solo practice – even in large law firms – can also make it more difficult for a lawyer to develop full and rewarding long-term personal and professional relationships with others in the firm.

The end of a partner's long career in a law firm can often bring the realisation that he or she has not cultivated skills and developed expanding professional interests that would bridge into other areas of meaningful, continued post-partnership contribution to the firm, or the application of his or her knowledge and experience to other worthwhile activities in the legal profession or in the community.

As a result, partners may discover that opportunities that might be available to others are, for all practical purposes, closed to them, because of a lack of investment in them over the years.

6.6 Financial concerns

In many countries, including some with the most developed economies, the financial crises of the early 21st century have almost wiped out personal retirement funds, which many older lawyers had always assumed would be adequate to support their retirement. A significant number of these lawyers have started second families and are responsible for young children. Many of the older lawyers – a higher proportion than would have been observed in the 1990s – are postponing retirement or considering part-time practice rather than retiring completely from the legal profession. Their firm's compensation system and capitalisation structure sometimes create a financial disincentive for partners to retire or even to reduce the hours they work.

6.7 The desire to remain mentally active

The practice of law requires a level of thinking and analysis that is not available in many other occupations. It can be a career-long intellectual 'high'.

It also requires an intensity of focus and commitment to client service that generate an adrenaline-like 'rush' not found in many other intellectual activities. Partners may have developed work habits that they find difficult to switch off. They miss the intellectual stimulation that comes from solving complex problems and operating at high levels of power and prestige. Work behaviours that they may feel contributed to their success are no longer, if they ever were, expected or even desired.

Remaining mentally active can produce important emotional insights during this period in a lawyer's life, too. It is only in their 50s and 60s that some people become more aware of how the heart and the head are balanced. Lawyers are no exception. Many of them describe greater insight as they enter their 50s and 60s. They find they are more emotionally expressive; more accepting of others' limitations and differences; better able to negotiate interpersonal issues with confidence; and less likely to take personal offence from others.

This mental and emotional balance enhances relationships with clients and colleagues, as well as learning opportunities and new experiences. This may be one reason why so many mature lawyers pursue career options in practice areas such as mediation and negotiation.

In short, a senior lawyer's mind might not just be better able to handle continued intellectual challenges and emotional growth; it might demand them. It may also be just at this time that a partner comes face to face with the reality of imminent retirement.

6.8 Still having fun

The desire for continued mental activity and growth produces a heightened sense in many lawyers that they still have goals to achieve and unexplored opportunities for intellectual enjoyment and professional satisfaction. Senior lawyers realise that professional maturity also brings an opportunity to reinvent themselves. They resist being 'thrown over' when there is still so much that they want to do.

6.9 Difficulty coping with change and a sense of loss

A crucial factor in succeeding as a lawyer is a healthy and active mind. This is also a crucial factor in letting go.

The risk of becoming mentally and emotionally rigid is very real, even as lawyers profess to want to remain mentally active through continued service to the firm and clients.

Lawyers can become so self-absorbed about their past glories or bitter about disappointments and missed opportunities that they turn inwards, retreating into self-defeating behaviours. They can hang on to their 'right' views of how things should be done while depleting their own intellectual energy, as well as the goodwill of the next generation of leaders and partners in their firms, who have differing expectations and priorities. In essence, they stop listening.

People react differently to change in their lives.

Senior lawyers sometimes turn their personal energy inwards and 'retire in place' instead of committing to new directions in their careers and in their firms. They might become obstructionists, resisting new procedures: "If it ain't broke, why fix it?" They also might personalise proposed changes: "The old way was good enough for us."

The economic, professional and social disruptions caused by the COVID-19 pandemic of 2020–2022 forced many lawyers – for whom things previously were 'not broken' and were 'good enough'– to examine the paradigms of what constitutes a successful, rewarding career. This frequently happened in difficult financial circumstances and when reason was often hampered by professional loss and personal grief. Some of the effects have been long lasting and may result in permanent changes to the professional cultures of law firms and the personal aspirations and values of their members.

Some law firm cultures are more comfortable with outward expressions of sadness, anxiety, frustration and grief. However, even today, after the shared experiences of a devastating pandemic, a partner's display of emotions is perceived in many law firms as a lack of self-control at best. This encourages partners to conceal and internalise their feelings of sadness or distress relating to their retirement. They do not want to appear weak or, worse yet, incompetent.

Sometimes it is more difficult to let go when a retiring partner has unresolved feelings of regret or shame, particularly in relationship to other partners or even to clients. These feelings linger, making it hard to refocus on a new beginning beyond the life of the firm.

Some lawyers at this transition point become acutely aware of their own physical decline. They may have suffered their first major illness or have a chronic condition that makes them confront their own mortality. They may also have recently lost a parent or a spouse. Coping with these personal losses can make it more difficult to accept and proactively deal with the conclusion of a longstanding professional career.

Retirement may become an emotional lightning rod for all of the painful feelings associated with prior losses and unrealised aspirations, expectations and potential. The net effect can be mentally and emotionally paralysing and physically exhausting, even for the most competent and intelligent partner.

6.10 Inertia

In many law firms, there is an institutional inertia that forces complex decisions about transition and retirement of partners into a case-by-case mode. This is more accurately described as 'making it up as we go along'.

Not seeing any clear policy, precedent or practices in their firms, many partners are reluctant to initiate a discussion about their transition out of the firm or to a new role in the firm. It seems too risky. They might wonder, "Will I be letting my clients and colleagues down? Will my inquiry force decisions that I might not like? Will I become a 'lame duck' or irrelevant too soon?"

At least the *status quo* has some degree of certainty for senior lawyers and their firms – even if that certainty is: "We'll cross that bridge when we come to it." The problem is that any progress towards the bridge takes place only when suddenly changed circumstances force movement on the parties. When forced change is necessary, the effectiveness of the responses usually suffers. Decisions must often be made with limited or inaccurate information and with an overemphasis on short-term action and results. Even a reasonable sense of urgency can become exaggerated, sometimes bordering on panic. People tend to seize on erroneous 'causes' of the problem and line up in support of overly simplistic 'solutions'.

But until they find themselves 'at the bridge', most law firm partnerships feel more comfortable doing almost nothing. In the case of the retirement of a partner, this inertia can be further encouraged by the fact that gradual retirement can be very difficult to manage. The preference for inertia is reinforced by the work ethic that most senior lawyers display – especially founding partners of the firm – and by partner compensation systems that can create strong disincentives to letting go.

Some law firms – particularly multi-generational family firms – also struggle with role reversals. The senior partners sometimes retain their nominal positions of authority in the firm, but their practice is effectively managed by the younger generation of partners, which may include protégés, sons and daughters, and former associates. This reversal of longstanding roles, tied to respect for and authority of the 'elders', causes the younger generation of partners – sometimes who are even in their 50s – to avoid stepping into needed leadership roles and making certain decisions. They may have legitimate fears about damaging lifelong personal relationships by implementing change.

In some firms, inertia is part of a broader cultural discomfort about talking frankly about performance or wellness concerns. Lacking the confidence and skills to address situations or behaviours that worry them, partners often allow this reluctance to spill over into retirement considerations, making it difficult to be proactive about succession and retirement, both for the partner involved and for the partnership collectively. In some firms this reluctance manifests in self-reassurances: "I trust my colleagues to do the right thing when the time comes." This is almost always a cop-out and is unfair to everyone involved, including clients.

Perhaps each law firm needs to develop its own special rite of passage into senior lawyer status. Like many such rites in other aspects of human life and experience, this could provide guidance about intense personal and far-reaching business issues such as the following:

- When is the right time for a senior partner to begin a transition?
- How will the relationships between the partner and the firm change after the rite of passage?
- What existing rights, benefits, roles and privileges will be put away?
- What new roles, responsibilities and opportunities will be available?

As in traditional cultures, law firms benefit when they define these issues and, to some extent, ritualise the transition from equity partnership to retirement or a continued post-equity role in the firm. Rather than remaining the great unknown factor looming darkly at the end of a partner's career, the transition ideally becomes a celebratory part of one's career in the firm – a natural next step in the partner's life that is planned, ordered and anticipated with an energising sense of new opportunities for both the partner and the firm.

7. When does letting go become a problem in a law firm?

There are several signs that reliably indicate that a law firm could soon find itself in a serious business crisis arising from the failure to transition its older partners. The risks of inaction not only affect the internal operation and financial management of the firm, but could also involve serious ethical issues and possible liability to third parties.[11] These signs are as follows:

- Senior lawyers are underperforming relative to other partners, as well as compared to their own previous performance. This can be especially dangerous for law firms in which the senior partners remain the best-paid beneficiaries of a seniority-driven lockstep compensation system or those in which the senior partners, due to the firm's partnership structure, enjoy disproportionate power in decision making.[12]
- Senior lawyers contribute a disproportionate amount of revenue. The sudden departure of a senior lawyer could result in a dire business crisis for a law firm that manages transitions and retirements on an *ad hoc*, case-by-case basis.
- Senior lawyers are hoarding work. This is frequently a sign that they are hoarding client relationships, which will be at risk when they leave the firm.
- Younger partners are expressing frustration with their lack of opportunities for meaningful involvement with major clients and for meaningful responsibilities in the leadership and management of the firm. These are frequently cited as reasons for young partners to move to another law firm.
- The firm does not provide for a reasonable financial exit from the partnership or from the firm.
- The partners do not want to talk openly about retirement. The reasons for this usually include:
    - the lack of a financial structure that makes retirement feasible;
    - the absence of any serious succession planning to manage the transition of responsibilities to younger partners;

---

11 Ted A Waggoner, "Ethical Issues as You Age or Plan for Retirement", *Experience*, ABA (July/August 2022) pp18–21. In the United States, lawyers have a responsibility to protect the public and maintain the integrity of the profession. In some situations, there might be an ethical duty to report an attorney who appears to be suffering from an age-related cognitive decline. See ABA Formal Opinion 03-429, "Obligations with Respect to Mentally Impaired Lawyer in the Firm" (11 June 2003), www.americanbar.org/content/dam/aba/administrative/professional_responsibility/aba_formal_opinion_03_429.pdf.

12 This problem is especially risky for first-generation law firms, which are firms in which one or more of the founding partners are still active equity partners. Some law firms create a special partnership class for founding partners and give them special voting rights, such as the right to override a majority vote of other partners on certain issues (eg, admission of new equity partners, expulsion of partners, merger with another law firm, dissolution). This is not to suggest that such special rights and privileges are inappropriate; however, they must be defined with care and should not be permitted to allow one partner to function as the *de facto* dictator of the firm.

- a reluctance by founding partners to let go of the firm in which they have invested so much of their professional lives and energy; or
- a combination of these factors.

In addition, unresolved tensions among partners might affect their willingness to have candid discussions, even with adequate structures in place. Previous experience might lead them to question motives, commitment and even loyalty. These conditions will create uncertainty and anxiety for clients and for the entire firm, not just among partners.[13]

8. How can a law firm encourage senior lawyers or lawyers who have 'retired in place' to begin to let go?

Law firm managers should remember that a senior partner is unlikely to make changes if there is no intellectual and financial context in which to make a well-informed decision. The best thing that a law firm can do to help a partner make the best decision for all parties concerned is to provide information, guidance and support.

Law firms that manage succession and retirement well usually have eight components built into their governance systems, as discussed below.

8.1 A partnership agreement that addresses rights and responsibilities

A partnership agreement or similar document that addresses the mutual rights and responsibilities of the firm and the partner who is considering a transition avoids sloppy, stressful, *ad hoc* decision making.

The following provisions might be included, among others:

- A stated presumptive retirement age: This is the age at which an equity partner is normally required to retire, unless the partnership authorises him or her to continue as an equity partner or in some other status, such as a non-equity senior partner, lawyer of counsel or legal consultant. Worldwide, the most common presumptive retirement age is 65.
- Terms and conditions for continued partnership after the stated presumptive retirement age: For example, upon reaching the presumptive retirement age, an equity partner may request to continue as an equity partner for a stated period. Sometimes the partnership might condition this continuation on the transfer of part of the continued partner's equity back to the firm over the period of the continuation. Many firms permit the partner to request an extension to the continuation, usually in increments of an additional two or three years. However, whether a partner may continue as an equity partner

---

13 See Lisa M Walker Johnson, *Stress and Burnout in Law Firms: Leadership Challenges and Choices*, (Globe Law and Business, 2022), p149.

after the stated presumption date, and the length, terms and conditions of such a continuation, should be decisions for the partnership.

- Mandatory retirement age: Most firms with a presumptive retirement age also provide for a mandatory retirement age, at which a continued equity partner must withdraw completely from the equity partnership. The trend in recent years has been towards older mandatory retirement ages of 70 or 75, although some law firms have abolished mandatory retirement ages in favour of sequenced confirmation of continued partnership status, most often in 24-month intervals, after a partner reaches a presumptive retirement age.
- A governance structure within which to plan transitional and post-retirement career options: Some law firms include in their partnership agreements or bylaws a structure and process to implement:
  - the 'early' retirement of an equity partner;
  - continuation as a non-equity partner or consultant; or
  - the creation and management of a new practice group, or similar special initiatives.

8.2 Financial and other incentives

Law firms that manage succession and retirement well provide financial and other incentives for non-billable roles for senior lawyers in the firm and with clients. In firms that use a presumptive retirement age, partners who continue beyond the presumptive age are often assigned new duties in management, professional development and client relations. These non-billable roles can be strategically and financially valuable activities for former partners who remain active in the firm as legal consultants or as lawyers of counsel. In either option, the key feature is that a retiring lawyer is permitted to perform these non-billable activities without worrying about the reduction in personal fee production that is likely to result.

8.3 Institutionalising the transition

A third component in a well-managed retirement policy is the institutionalisation of the transition at the working level of the firm, especially in the reassignment of supervision and management responsibilities to others. Some law firms require all partners who are within two or three years of the expected retirement date to develop a specific written plan, with actions and milestones, to manage this transition. This can remove the uncertainties that frequently make retiring partners reluctant to go through a transition to a new role in the firm, and that also make the other partners anxious about whether they will be prepared when their colleague departs.

8.4 Peer mentoring and assistance

Offering assistance from external specialists and peer mentors can address the senior lawyer's individual adjustment and career concerns in a confidential and supportive relationship. After devoting so many years of investment and hard work to the firm, partners should not have to deal with these challenges on their own. Personal assistance and mentoring can sometimes be the single most important factor in the successful transition to retirement, both for the partner and for the law firm.

Even otherwise brilliant and successful partners are not immune from substance use, cognitive decline and mental health issues that may compromise their effectiveness and pose real risks to the firm and its clients. Problems can occur at any point in their careers.

All partners owe it to each other to stay alert. Even subtle indicators, such as changes in a colleague's behaviour or performance, can be signs that a partner needs help. Knowing when and how to intervene or provide assistance takes sensitivity and an awareness of options.

When partners talk about and agree to their shared leadership responsibilities – in advance of problems – they are much more likely to take timely action to make inquiries and respond to potential needs. Thinking about sensitive behavioural issues and their potential consequences helps all partners to put performance into more of a business and professional context. This also makes them easier to address should the time come to do so.

These actions are key to managing performance in any law firm. They have special significance when it comes to valuing and honouring colleagues' evolving careers, contributions and longstanding professional relationships:

- Check in with each other regularly to keep information and feedback current and relevant: Use respectful and non-judgemental discussions to describe your concerns in behavioural terms. Share why the behaviours concern you and how this makes you feel. Ask questions to try to understand the breadth and depth of a potential problem.
- Plan to communicate: Otherwise, time passes and these important discussions may never happen.
- Don't wait for a crisis: The results are almost always worse. Urgent situations leave fewer options with less time to respond the way you would want to, adversely impacting everyone involved. Reputations are hard to rebuild, for the partner as well as the firm. Legal risks may become realities that cannot be ignored.
- Develop a plan together: Collaborative actions can be decisive and effective without scapegoating or isolating a vulnerable and valued partner. An agreed plan should address the needs of the partner, the firm and the firm's clients, especially those that the partner serves personally. It should manage the potential risks and prevent – or at least reduce the risk of – serious possible consequences.

8.5 Time to communicate

Successful law firms take into account these considerations about communication:

- They anticipate how prevailing practices and partner dynamics have affected candour and transparency in the past.
- They take steps to rebuild trust and increase engagement with partners well in advance of actions and decisions. In this way, partners can approach discussions about career options and retirement, as well as decision making, from a foundation of mutual trust.
- They talk candidly with the retiring partner about the firm's expectations. Senior partners are often relieved to know what their peers are thinking and expect of them. Not knowing creates far more stress and anxiety.

Sometimes lawyers need the chance to vent with a trusted colleague. Without this, frustration and anger build up, creating mental blockages and potentially spilling over into resistance to change and other behaviours with a negative impact. It is not so much what the firm's partners say; it is the fact that one's peers take the time to listen and to care that makes the difference.

This is not always easy. For example, it might be difficult for some partners to talk about their financial needs and post-retirement concerns. If they resist retirement and do not disclose their concerns, misunderstandings and distrust can arise as others in the firm might assume bad faith or evasiveness from the partner's silence. Each side in the conversation has a responsibility to communicate candidly and to draw out all potential concerns so that they can be managed. When they feel unable or unwilling to do so, a qualified third party may add great value by facilitating sensitive discussions with partners, using approaches and communication tools that the partners might not have tried.

Law firms that communicate effectively about a partner's transition to retirement also focus on a partner's individual situation and aspirations. For example, the partners can:

- explain or explore options together to help the retiring partner work out a strategy (eg, a senior lawyer might be unsure about how to communicate a new role to others in the firm or to clients); and
- draw out any doubts or concerns that the retiring partner has so that both the firm and the partner confront reality by defining the problems accurately and finding workable solutions to implement together and separately.

Communication also involves communication with the clients that the partner serves. They should be informed of the planned transition well in advance, not as a partner is about to go out the door. This is not only good client relations, but also good marketing, because it communicates the depth of the firm's commitment to continuation to meeting the client's needs and expectations with the same high degree of responsiveness and expertise.

Positive ownership of the changes that are required for any transition is much more likely if the partner is involved in internal discussions, as well as in communications and planning with clients. If senior lawyers are active participants in anticipating and resolving transition issues, rather than passive bystanders – being talked about behind closed doors by other partners – they are much more likely to assist with the transition efforts, which helps to produce the best long-term results for the firm and its clients.

8.6 More than just accommodating

Sometimes senior partners want to do something innovative, which they might not have had the opportunity to do previously. For example, a partner might want to develop a mediation service as an adjunct to the firm's employment law practice.

If the idea makes good business sense, the partners may want to support it. If not, they should state why and resolve their concerns directly. Without this discussion, younger partners might feel that the firm is merely finding something for the senior lawyer to do and might resent the investment. A partner whose interests are merely accommodated, rather than endorsed, soon discovers that his or her efforts are not considered to be meaningful, but instead are viewed as 'busywork' or worse.

8.7 Rituals

Implement rituals to commemorate retirements and transitions to new post-partnership roles.

These should involve more than presentation of the traditional gold watch. Celebrate the retiring partner's contributions and career in a way that is meaningful and memorable to him or her, as well as to the partner's colleagues. If a partner is not leaving the firm but transitioning to a post-partnership position, this is a good opportunity for him or her to make a presentation about the new role and the opportunities it will provide to the firm.

8.8 Creating bridges

Create bridges back to the law firm and its practice for partners who are retiring and leaving the firm.

This can help to reduce the emotional pain of loss and dislocation that the retiring lawyer may feel in cutting ties to the firm as an institution, his or her colleagues and the client relationships.

Some firms provide on-request office space and limited clerical support to retired partners. Many firms continue to include retired partners in partner meetings, retreats and firm social events. These gestures cost relatively little, and they can produce a large return on investment from new clients and new business referred by the retired partner from among his or her contacts in the community.

9. How can each lawyer prepare for retirement or a post-partnership role in the firm?

This chapter has outlined how policies and preparations for succession planning and retirement should be an integral part of good governance in law firms. There is much that each lawyer can also do to prepare:

- Take a gradual approach to transitioning clients and management responsibilities by involving and developing others.
- Be confident enough to hire and develop talent even better than yourself.
- Don't seal yourself off from the new generation of lawyers and their ways of seeing the world. 'Withdrawing' from the partnership is only a legal term. Stay involved until the last day in the office and even beyond.
- Find value in other types of contributions to the law firm, such as mentoring, teaching, *pro bono* work and other service-oriented pursuits, and serving as an 'ambassador' of the law firm to the business community. There is no reason why these activities cannot begin before the effective date of retirement.
- Find ways to give back to the profession or the community in some meaningful way. This is sometimes known as 'generativity': receiving something from the past, putting your unique contribution into it and passing it on to the future. Meaningful involvement with schools, communities, the extended family and other groups and organisations contributes to psychological wellbeing. It can be a strong factor in a successful transition to a post-partnership professional life or to retirement.
- Expect to feel a sense of loss. This is a natural and entirely normal phenomenon. Sometimes it helps to ask for input from an older lawyer who has already gone through the transition. Benefit from the wisdom and experiences of others in dealing with your own personal challenges. Reading, mentoring others and developing post-retirement goals and plans can all help a retiring partner to look at the bigger picture and encourage a sense of purpose that helps one to deal with the sense of loss.
- Take care of yourself throughout your career by investing in relationships, good physical and mental health, and financial planning.
- Think early and often about what you want to leave behind in the firm

as your legacy and act accordingly. The strongest legacy consists of the values that you make a part of the lasting culture of your firm. What values do you want to promote and model?

According to psychotherapist Irving Zyalom, there is a danger that those who have lived through their productive years immersed in a materialistic culture will enter late middle age with a deep sense of existential emptiness. They might realise for the first time that they have not used their time on earth to discover who they really are or to ponder life's deepest mysteries. Instead, they have squandered their years in a mindless and frequently frustrating attempt to adapt to the superficialities in the world around them.[14]

- Develop interests outside the law firm and the practice of law in order to build a bridge to the future. One of the most reliable predictors of whether an older partner will have a satisfying transition to his or her future, or will experience a crisis, is the extent to which he or she has already developed relationships and passionate interests in areas other than the law.

10. Thinking differently about the role of governance

Lawyers and law firms are thinking differently about issues of post-partnership roles in the law firm, transition, and retirement. Many of the old rules, such as 'up and out', are no longer relevant to the needs of law firms and their clients or to the capabilities of older lawyers. Progressive law firms – many of which are experiencing unprecedented levels of partner turnover due to recent and imminent retirements – realise that good governance in the context of succession planning involves more than just updating the partnership agreement. It also requires two-way communication and interactive planning to protect the best interests of the retiring partner and of the firm.

Although succession planning and transition management are highly firm-specific issues, a strategy that is most likely to produce the best results for law firms and their lawyers over the next 20 to 30 years will involve:

- better definition of roles, responsibilities and options to govern the relationships between law firms and their transitioning partners;
- retention of the talents and capabilities of lawyers who want to continue to contribute to their firms for decades beyond the traditional retirement ages that prevailed in most law firms as recently as 20 years ago and that still prevail in some firms today;
- structured but flexible solutions that meet the needs, aspirations and expectations of all parties involved; and
- promotion and support of the development of skills, interests and

14 Thomas Armstrong, *The Human Odyssey: Navigating the Twelve Stages of Life* (Sterling, 2007), p188.

capabilities that encourage professionally satisfying and enjoyable careers, so that lawyers have options upon retirement – either by staying active in the law firm or by exploring new opportunities outside it.

Retirement and career transitions in law firms will continue to be complex and often emotionally intense issues. There is no universal best practice that applies. However, the professional relationships, flexibility and intellectual discipline that have made lawyers and their law firms so successful in their practices can also promote new and better ways to understand and approach these important governance issues.

Governance for lawyers in a new era – 'alternative' law firms

Stephen Revell
Making Change Happen

1. Introduction

In the early part of the twenty-first century, Australia and the United Kingdom have allowed legal services to be provided by alternative law firms: organisations owned and/or controlled, in whole or in part, by non-lawyers. These changes were and have remained controversial – many believe that alternative firms with external owners present significant new risks to clients and to the profession. A number of questions were raised at the time. How would such risks be managed? What governance and regulatory structures are needed to adequately protect clients? Would the profession fall into disrepute and/or lose its status? Policy makers, bar councils and lawyers around the world have watched Australia and the United Kingdom to see what has happened as a result of these changes. Some jurisdictions are opening up, while others have firmly rejected the idea. In North America alone, we see a significant divide. The American Bar Association (ABA) president stated categorically that the ABA was "years away" from allowing any non-lawyer ownership or fee sharing. Taking a different position, the Canadian Bar Association recognised that "the status quo is not an option" and launched the Legal Futures Initiative to promote a debate on what it saw as an inevitable transition.

Building on the insights elsewhere in this book about the strategic role of governance and executive decision making in modern law firms, section 2 of this chapter seeks to put the discussion on governance in alternative law firms in context by looking at how and why the changes in Australia and the United Kingdom came about, the arguments for and against allowing alternative law firms, and the different structures that are emerging in the United Kingdom and Australia. Alternative firms are not 'one size fits all', but rather consist of anything from a traditional firm with one non-lawyer partner to estate agents with in-house conveyancing teams, multi-disciplinary partnerships, firms owned by private equity or employees and even, as is the case in Australia (and the United Kingdom), publicly listed law firms – one of which is on a global acquisition trail, recently acquiring law firms in the United Kingdom.

Section 3 of this chapter looks at the global trends and innovation in the legal services sector that emerged in the late 1990s and 2000s and continue to evolve. In the United Kingdom, Canada and the United States, firms are changing the way they charge clients and offer legal services in response to customer demands. Companies are providing legal information and documents online. In response, traditional and alternative firms are finding new and distinctive ways to brand and distinguish themselves. The scope and the creativity are extensive and more change will come, driven by the need to meet the changing needs of consumers of legal services.

In section 4 we examine the governance issues and risks that alternative law firms are thought to present, and the validity of the concerns surrounding alternative law firms. The chapter concludes that many of the risks attributed to alternative law firms are already present in traditional law firms today. It considers the safeguards that were put in place by an improved regulatory regime to address these new risks. It is arguable, given those safeguards, that sometimes clients might be safer seeking advice from an alternative firm rather than a traditional one.

While it has taken some time to test the effectiveness of the new regulatory regimes, a remaining challenge has been balancing the need for regulatory certainty with the flexibility required to meet the variety of different structures being developed. With innovation a key driver for enabling alternative law firms in the United Kingdom, regulators face the ongoing struggle of protecting the public and maintaining the reputation of the profession while providing the scope for the creativity required to meet the policy goals of competition and improved access to justice.

Thus far, regulation appears to have sought to address the most relevant risks, and as a result has arguably raised the governance bar for all law firms, traditional or otherwise. The approach of the Solicitors Regulation Authority (SRA) of imposing licensing conditions on those seeking to operate an alternative firm seems a sensible way to address the bespoke risks of each new form of legal services provider.

2. Structures for the alternative law firm

2.1 Traditionally a closed shop

One particular feature of law firm governance is that lawyers traditionally have been kept separate from non-lawyers. As a result, there is an almost complete reliance on the 'ethics on the profession' (whatever they might be) to address governance – from both an internal perspective and an external perspective. Most countries have had long-standing laws or regulations that prevent non-lawyers owning or joining together with lawyers in a fee-sharing arrangement. Many countries maintain that position today.[1]

1 Rule 5.4 of the American Bar Association Model Rules, under which a lawyer or law firm is prohibited from sharing legal fees with a non-lawyer.

The traditional structure for the provision of legal services has generally been either a sole practitioner or a partnership in which all partners are lawyers. The former attorney general of the Australian state of New South Wales[2] is among many who have claimed that a partnership structure provides better governance, since it:

> *ensured that partners maintained a direct interest in the affairs of the partnership and in the conduct of its solicitors. For these reasons, partnerships have been seen as the best business structure to ensure that the ethical and professional responsibilities of the legal profession are observed.*[3]

Things have started to change; many countries have allowed firms to incorporate, although ownership and control of the incorporated firm have largely been restricted to lawyers.[4] This helps to illustrate that it is the ownership and control, and the governance that flows from them – and not the legal structure as such – that is the real issue in this debate. Those countries that have permitted law firms to incorporate have done so, in effect, at the request of the lawyers; they have sought to use incorporation – particularly in the form of limited liability partnerships – to, as the name suggests, limit their liability towards the clients. Clearly, the insurance industry has supported such moves. Incorporation in turn opens up a wide range of possibilities for external investors, but this has not come about in most of the countries that have permitted lawyers to incorporate.

In Australia and England and Wales, non-lawyers can own up to 100% of a law firm or enterprise that practises law. Other jurisdictions have allowed non-lawyer ownership to a lesser degree,[5] and some have allowed multi-disciplinary practices (MDPs) (practices with other professionals such as accountants) in some form or another, but not necessarily ownership by other (non-professional) non-lawyers.[6]

Since Australia and England and Wales were the first to allow complete non-lawyer ownership, the rest of the world continues to watch their experience closely. Hence, this chapter closely considers this experience and the accompanying governance and regulatory challenges.

---

2 New South Wales was the first jurisdiction to permit non-lawyer ownership.

3 Stephen Mark and Georgina Cowdroy, "Incorporated Legal Practices – A New Era in the Provision of Legal Services in the State of New South Wales", 22:4 *Penn State Law Review*, 2005, 671–693 at 677, referencing The Hon Jeff Shaw QC MLC, "Incorporation of Legal Practices under the Corporations Law", 68 *Law Society Journal (NSW)* 1999, 67–70.

4 For example, in New Zealand, although firms can incorporate under the Lawyers and Conveyancers Act 2006, voting rights and directorships in the company are limited to lawyers actively involved in the business and only their immediate relatives can acquire non-voting rights (www.lawsociety.org.nz/for-lawyers/legal-practice/incorporated-law-firms).

5 Scotland (up to 49% by the end of 2013), Italy (up to 33%), and Austria (family members and spouses only).

6 For example, some provinces in Canada, Washington DC, the Netherlands, Italy, Germany and some cantons in Switzerland.

2.2 Changes to law firm structures and regulation

The Australian state of New South Wales was among the first jurisdictions to enable change. Despite allowing MDPs and 'solicitor corporations' in the 1990s, the restrictions on these structures meant that concerns about the lack of competition in the sector remained. In 1998, the National Competition Policy Review of the Legal Profession found that the Legal Profession Act of 1987 remained anti-competitive, for three main reasons:[7]

- Partnerships' horizontal management structure created cumbersome decision-making processes that were outdated for modern businesses.
- Partnerships had limited ability to raise capital, restricting firm growth and competitive abilities.
- Partnerships were lacking in transparency, since they were not subject to the same degree of public scrutiny as corporations.

While these reasons appear to relate more to partnership governance, the report focused on the consequential, in its view, negative impact on competition. This report was the impetus behind legislative change in New South Wales with the introduction of the Legal Profession (Incorporated Legal Practices) Act 2000 (LPA) and the Legal Profession (Incorporated Legal Practices) Regulation 2001[8] allowing incorporated legal practices (ILPs).

With equivalent provisions having been rolled out in other states and territories across Australia,[9] over 1,000 firms are incorporated[10] (with the potential for outside investors). Three of these are now publicly listed companies: Slater and Gordon, Shine Lawyers and Integrated Legal Holdings.[11] The motivations for the other 997 firms are likely to be mixed, but since Australian firms do not have the option of becoming a limited liability partnership, a desire to limit liability rather than a need to raise capital externally or bring in non-lawyers may be behind many of these incorporations.

The UK story is slightly different. The Office of Fair Trading (OFT) had conducted an investigation into restricted practices in the legal profession and recommended a number of changes. In addition to competition, a key driver for change was an increase in complaints against lawyers and inefficient handling

7 Mark and Cowdroy, note 3.

8 *Ibid.* The provisions of the act and regulations are now found in the Legal Profession Act 2004 New South Wales (NSW) and the Legal Profession Regulation 2005 NSW, which generally cover the conduct of lawyers in NSW.

9 Each state and territory in Australia adopts its own version of the LPA, but provisions regarding ILPs are largely similar. This chapter refers to provisions in the Legal Profession Act 2004 NSW (LPA).

10 Sam Glover, "Is it Time for Non-lawyer Ownership?" *Lawyerist*, 24 September 2013 (http://lawyerist.com/time-for-non-lawyer-ownership/).

11 Neil Rose, "Listed Australian Firm Considering United Kingdom Opportunities", *Legal Futures*, 15 August 2013 (www.legalfutures.co.uk/latest-news/listed-australian-law-firm-considering-uk-opportunities).

of these complaints by the then regulators (the Law Society and Bar Council).[12] Complaints ranged from delays to failure to meet deadlines, being misled as to costs and lawyers improperly accessing client funds. These problems, as well as the OFT finding that lawyers were surrounded by a "regulatory maze" of 22 different regulators,[13] pre-empted the complete regulatory overhaul recommended by the Clementi Review,[14] examining the regulation and structures of the legal profession.

In addition to regulatory change, the Clementi Review recommended that lawyers[15] have greater freedom to choose how to organise themselves, as this would promote innovation and competition. Governance safeguards were recommended to maintain standards. The groundbreaking and controversial Clementi Review formed the basis of a government white paper, which, following lively debate, in turn formed the basis of the Legal Services Act of 2007 (LSA).

As the above would suggest, the LSA provided not only a new regulatory regime for lawyers,[16] but also the ability to adopt new structures in which lawyers could work. It provided for the introduction of the alternative business structure (ABS) in 2012, along with some transitional forms of non-lawyer ownership permitted in the interim, such as legal disciplinary partnerships (partnerships of lawyers with different professional backgrounds such as barristers and solicitors).[17] Although not defined in the LSA, except as a licensable body, the ABS is a business that conducts reserved legal activities[18] with some form of non-lawyer ownership and/or management.[19]

The Legal Services Board, set up to oversee legal services regulation under the LSA, stated that "a liberalised market can improve access to justice; protect and promote the interests of consumers; promote competition; and encourage an independent, strong, diverse and effective legal profession".[20]

---

12 John Flood, "Future Directions in the United Kingdom Legal Profession: Life after the Legal Services Act 2007", presentation for Future of the Global Law Firm Symposium, Georgetown University Law Centre, Centre for the Study of the Legal Profession. 17–18 April 2008 (www.slideshare.net/tomwinfrey/how-the-clementi-review-came-about).

13 *Ibid*, at 6.

14 David Clementi, "Review of the Regulatory Framework for Legal Services in England & Wales", December 2004 (www.jambar.org/clement_report.pdf).

15 In England and Wales the term 'lawyer' covers the eight branches of the legal profession: solicitor, barrister, chartered legal executive, licensed conveyancer, patent agent, trademark attorney, costs lawyer and notary.

16 For solicitors, the regulatory and representational functions of the Law Society were split, such that the Law Society retained its role to represent solicitors and the Solicitors Regulatory Authority was formed to regulate and discipline solicitors.

17 Legal Services Board, "Wider Access, Better Value, Strong Protection: Discussion Paper in Developing a Regulatory Regime for Alternative Business Structures" (www.legalservicesboard.org.uk/what_we_do/consultations/2009/pdf/140509.pdf).

18 Reserved legal activities are those that can only lawfully be provided in the United Kingdom by a lawyer. They include conveyancing, probate, advocacy, litigation, administration of oaths and notarial activities. There is ongoing debate as to whether this is adequate and whether all legal advice should be regulated.

19 See Section 72 (Part 5) of the LSA which describes licensable bodies – a licensable body is an ABS.

20 Legal Services Board, note 17 at p17.

2.3 Outcomes of change – forms of alternative law firms

This chapter refers to 'alternative law firms' to describe all forms of ABS as enabled by the United Kingdom's LSA, incorporated firms as allowed in Australian jurisdictions and other similar structures. When considered together, the Australian and United Kingdom experiences have seen the development of a range of different firms and structures. These are discussed below. Alternative law firms can generally be grouped into two categories: those that retain the partnership structure, but allow some level of non-lawyer ownership and involvement; and those that involve a corporate structure with external 'non-lawyer' capital (which can amount to 100% ownership).

(a) Non-lawyer partnerships

The first group, partnerships with non-lawyer partners, generally has two forms. The first is MDPs – partnerships that provide both legal services (reserved legal activities in the United Kingdom)[21] and non-legal services such as accountancy.

The second subgroup is comprised of partnerships providing legal services where at least one partner is not a lawyer. The latter is the most common form of ABS that was initially licensed in the United Kingdom. Usually it brings into the partnership a long-term manager of a firm, or the spouse of a partner who is not a lawyer.[22] The motivations for this type of alternative firm are relatively simple – firms wish to reward and recognise a spouse or a finance manager who has been actively involved in the business for some time and/or add non-lawyer expertise, for example in financial management so as to improve governance.

Since these arrangements generally do not challenge the control of the firm, this type of alternative law firm tends to be less controversial. Tony Williams[23] ably summarised the point when interviewed by the *Law Society Gazette* back in 2009:

> *Why shouldn't non-lawyers have equity? ... They have been doing that for years through quasi-equity arrangements where they have remuneration or bonuses linked to the profits and so, to some extent, it is only regularising what firms have done for years anyway.*[24]

On the other hand, MDPs have had a somewhat chequered history. The most internationally accepted form of alternative law firm, MDPs began to be allowed in the United Kingdom, Australia, some provinces in Canada and some cantons in Switzerland, Washington DC, the Netherlands, Germany and Italy. The motivation for MDPs is clear – to provide a one-stop shop where clients can

---

21 See note 18.

22 Since the definition of 'lawyer' in the United Kingdom is limited to those eight forms of legal professionals (note 16), all of whom need to be qualified in England and Wales, a partner of a traditional firm who is a foreign lawyer is considered to be a non-lawyer partner and thus such a firm must apply for a licence as an ABS.

23 Tony Williams is founder of the management consultancy Jomati, and former Clifford Chance managing partner.

24 As quoted in Jon Robbins, "Why Legal Disciplinary Practices are off to a Slow Start", *The Law Society Gazette*, 9 April 2009 (www.lawgazette.co.uk/50223.article).

get legal, accounting and other professional advice. It is plain to see that this might be attractive to clients from a cost, convenience and choice perspective. However, the commercial benefits behind MDPs suffered a blow after the Enron scandal, which highlighted the need for independence of the audit function. As the International Bar Association (IBA) notes: "In the aftermath of Enron, many MDPs, in particular those between accountants and lawyers, were dissolved, and MDPs became, if possible, even more controversial."[25]

These concerns, and the restrictions on offering legal advice to audit clients, however, did not prevent PricewaterhouseCoopers (PwC) Australia from becoming an MDP in 2008. PwC claimed to be Australia's largest MDP and uses this structure to differentiate itself to clients.[26] Its website claimed that "the MDP structure provides our clients with seamless access to specialist legal and non-legal expertise across a broad spectrum of commercial disciplines".[27]

While MDPs were slow to take off in the United Kingdom a few have surfaced. Unlike PwC in Australia, where the legal services division provides general commercial advice and works much like a separate law firm, UK MDPs were formed by existing businesses acquiring specialist legal expertise. An example was Systech, a global project management consultancy that manages large infrastructure and energy projects. It acquired SLS Solicitors, a specialist construction law firm. Similarly, accountancy firm Price Bailey bought a specialist employment law firm to assist with employment issues that surfaced from its payroll solutions work.[28]

The UK experience may be indicative of a broader trend in MDPs. Although the benefits of being able to provide general corporate legal advice within an MDP might be offset by independence and conflicts concerns, it seems that some businesses are seeing value in joining forces with specialist law firms and providing a 'one-stop' specialised service.

(b) Corporate legal services providers – with 'non-lawyer' capital

The second group of alternative law firms includes incorporated practices in Australia, including those listed on the stock exchange, as well as – in both Australia and the United Kingdom – private companies owned or invested in by private equity, venture capitalists or employees.[29] Law firms that have merged with or been acquired by other businesses, such as estate agents and insurance companies in the United Kingdom, also come within this broad grouping.

Many of these firms have chosen to become alternative firms in order to

25 International Multi-Disciplinary Committee Overview (www.ibanet.org/PPID/Constituent/Multi-displry_Pract/Overview.aspx).

26 "What is old is new: PwC opts for MDP", *Lawyers Weekly*, 12 February 2008 (www.lawyersweekly.com.au/news/what-is-old-is-new-pwc-opts-for-mdp).

27 www.pwc.com.au/legal/.

28 Baker Tilly, "Legal Innovation 2013 – New Developments in an Old Profession", June 2013 (www.bakertilly.co.uk).

29 Edinburgh firm Fox and Partners became the first UK firm to be wholly owned by its employees. The firm specialises in claimant employment law and equality matters.

access external capital. This is unsurprising, since traditional partnerships seeking capital are generally limited to debt and partners' own funds. The desires of partners, of various ages and with differing financial commitments, may conflict regarding the amount of capital to be put into or kept in the firm. Furthermore, the retirement of an ageing population of equity partners can be draining on a firm's funds and inhibit growth and investment.

Additionally, at least in the United Kingdom, the financial crisis restricted funds available via bank debt and changed the way that banks lent. This, combined with the need for investment in technology, made the ability to access external capital very attractive. The results of a 2012 survey of United Kingdom firms by Fox Williams show:

> *nearly eight out of ten respondents (77%) identified access to finance (not available from partners or traditional bank borrowing) as either being important or very important when considering an alternative business structure and seven out of ten (70%) identified improving the firm's cash flow.*[30]

As mentioned earlier, three out of the 1,000 incorporated Australian firms are listed on the stock exchange. Slater and Gordon, the first firm to be publicly listed, gave "funding for growth" as the reason behind the decision.[31]

Australian firms have been able to incorporate for some years, but UK firms have had the ability to access external capital only since 2012. The Fox Williams survey results indicated that UK firms were interested in exploring this type of structure and in seeking investment from private equity and other external investors.[32] The report also indicated that private equity investors were interested in the legal sector, particularly in the "volume end of the market",[33] where legal services can be commoditised and systemised. This interest is indicative of greater trends in the legal services market. Arguably, these trends are driving competition to the advantage of the consumer as envisaged by the OFT – more choice, fixed pricing and competitive pricing, albeit at the expense of personalised service and a form-based approach.

In his book *The End of Lawyers?*, Richard Susskind reflects back to 2006, when he attended debates regarding the Legal Services Bill in the United Kingdom where business people were "talking about call centres, outsourcing to India, online legal services, the automatic generation of documents and more".[34] Those ideas still seem to be driving external investor interest today, but arguably at a slower rate and with less impact than originally envisaged.

---

30 Fox Williams, "ABSolutely Fabulous? A Study of Alternative Business Structures and their Role in the Legal Services Market", June 2012 (www.foxwilliams.com/ABS).

31 "Incorporation: Why are Law Firms Reluctant to Move Away from the Partnership Model?" *Lawyers Weekly*, 18 August 2011 (www.lawyersweekly.com.au/news/incorporation-why-are-law-firms-reluctant-to-move-).

32 Fox Williams, note 30.

33 See quote by Sovereign Capital's Nick Miller at p14 of the Fox Williams report – note 30.

34 Richard Susskind, *The End of Lawyers? – Re-thinking the Nature of Legal Services*, Oxford University Press, 2008, p11.

Such developments have been particularly popular in the high-volume section of legal services. We have seen the merger or acquisition of personal injury firms by insurance companies, conveyancing and property law firms by estate agents, and probate and will lawyers with will-writing and estate management professionals. The focus is to provide end-to-end business services. For example, having acquired Manchester firm Lewis Hymanson Small, legal expenses insurer Abbey Protection Plc scaled up its call centre to provide commercial litigation services beyond that of insurance.[35] Conveyancing Direct, a volume-based conveyancing and property law business, became part of an estate agency group owned by Skipton Building Society.

Another point Susskind recalls from 2006 is being told that seven out of 10 adults, as surveyed by *Which?* (a consumer magazine) thought it a good idea to purchase legal services from a high-street brand. While fears of 'Tesco law' were rampant post the Clementi Review, it did not eventuate as expected. The Co-op Group was one of the biggest household names to enter legal services since the liberalisation of the legal sector. As one might expect, the Co-op Group, of which Co-op Legal Services forms part, is a co-operative, owned by its members (individuals and other independent co-operative societies). According to its website, the group raises finance by issuing debt securities listed on the stock exchange.[36] Having access to funds enables Co-op Legal Services to conduct research and development around a consumer-focused retail model. Despite its initial success, the group reported a loss of £3.4 million for the first half of 2013. The company attributes this loss to the 'start-up' nature of the business.[37]

Although 'Nike law' did not enter the market as predicted either, Stobart Barristers did. Building on the brand recognition of Stobart Logistics, Stobart Barristers "links members of the public and businesses direct to a barrister without needing to employ a solicitor".[38] An innovative pricing model was also used – fixed-fees through a 'pay-as-you-go' model during the litigation process.

Both Co-op Legal Services and Stobart Barristers are examples of alternative firms that are externally funded, but provide a ring-fenced legal brand that leverages off the greater group for brand recognition and marketing. QualitySolicitors, discussed below, has also sought to leverage brand recognition through bringing together mostly traditional firms in a franchise-like arrangement.

2.4 Why not the big firms?

Contrary to Susskind's predictions, the legal services market in the United Kingdom has not yet seen the largest firms seeking to adopt alternative firm

35 Baker Tilly, note 28.
36 www.co-operative.coop/corporate/Investors/.
37 Neil Rose, "Co-op undeterred by £3.4M loss by Legal Services Business", *Legal Futures*, 29 August 2013 (www.legalfutures.co.uk/latest-news/co-op-undeterred-despite-3-4m-loss-legal-services-business).
38 See press release on the Stobart Group website (www.stobartgroup.co.uk/news/general/stobart-group-drives-into-legal-services-market/).

structures. Some innovative exceptions to this, however, have focused on creating separate businesses using the firm's name, connections and expertise which do not all involve the provision of legal advice. Berwin Leighton Paisner, for example, created Lawyers on Demand, a separate company which provided freelance lawyers on a contract basis to practices and for companies' in-house legal teams. Irwin Mitchell became the first firm to be awarded multiple ABS licences. The group's five licences covered Irwin Mitchell LLP – the law firm with non-lawyer partners – and a range of companies: Ascent Collections Ltd, Coris United Kingdom Ltd, Irwin Mitchell Trustees Ltd and Irwin Mitchell Trust Corporation Ltd.

There are a few possible reasons behind the reluctance of large law firms to become an 'alternative firm'. Since non-lawyer ownership is prohibited in most other jurisdictions, firms with an international presence would be severely constrained in the structure they could adopt. In 2012, the New York Bar went as far as to ban New York-qualified lawyers from working for foreign alternative law firms.[39] A possible second reason is that the structure is unpopular with individual lawyers. Non-partnership structures require all lawyers to be, and remain, employed solicitors. This has two clear implications for lawyers. First, lawyers will never achieve the title of partner (although that title could in fact be used in a corporate structure), which has traditionally carried significant status within the legal fraternity, especially within large corporate firms. Secondly, these lawyers will most likely never be involved in the governance of the firm. It is interesting to note that Slater and Gordon's board contained just three lawyers (two are executive directors – one of whom is the managing director and the company secretary).

Another reason for the continuing traditional approach in the profession may lie in the fact that although capital is needed to set up legal firms with high systemisation, traditional law firm models do not actually require a great deal of external funding. Premises are typically leased and, other than covering cash flow and working capital, the asset base of law firms is traditionally very small – desks and computers – and therefore overall funding needs are not that extensive. Similarly, although pricing pressure from clients continues and increases, incorporation with external capital and external investors does not, in the main, provide any solutions from the law firm perspective. The experience in Australia is not dissimilar. The larger corporate firms have not adopted alternative law firm structures (other than to create, in some cases, limited liability protection). The rest of the world is watching to see whether the Australian and United Kingdom legal professions fall into disrepute now that they are open to ownership by non-lawyers. If this does not happen, other

39 "New York Lawyers Told They Cannot Run the Big Apple Operation of an ABS with External Investors", *Legal Futures*, 22 March 2012 (www.legalfutures.co.uk/latest-news/new-york-lawyers-told-they-cannot-run-the-big-apple-operation-of-an-abs-with-external-investors).

jurisdictions may be more likely to relax their laws, which in turn might increase the appeal for large international firms to take alternative forms.

2.5 The nay-saying traditionalists

With all this innovation brought about by enabling alternative law firms and the arguable benefits of competition, consumer choice, reduced costs and access to justice, why were Australia and the United Kingdom the first two jurisdictions to fully allow non-lawyer ownership?

The rationale for retaining the traditional model and keeping non-lawyers out is fairly similar across all jurisdictions. A lawyer has a duty to the courts, as well as a duty to act in the best interest of his or her clients. Since only lawyers have these obligations, some consider that only they can really be the guardians of them, and that the involvement of non-lawyers without these obligations erodes the position of lawyers. In a traditional practice where all decision makers are lawyers, it is expected that these duties will be observed. Simply put, alternative firms are seen as undermining certain fundamental values of the legal profession: independence, avoidance of conflicts of interest and maintenance of legal professional privilege.[40]

Traditionalists consider that where non-lawyers are involved in decision making or, worse still, have effective control of a firm, the independence of a lawyer is, in the views of some, more susceptible to being compromised. Similarly, traditionalists also hold that in order for lawyers to properly fulfil their duties to the client and the court, they must be free from other influences or conflicts of interest. Pressures to raise or generate profits, or meet targets, create conflicts of interest. Where alternative law firms adopt corporate structures, the first two concerns are more pronounced: a general profit motivation creates potential conflicts of interest for the lawyers between their duties to the company and shareholders and the professional ethical obligations they have. This concern was clearly voiced by the Council of Bars and Law Societies of Europe (CCBE), which noted that:

> *due to their professional status lawyers ... are presumed to operate their law firm not with a purely economic objective, but also from a professional perspective. Their private interest connected with the making of a profit is thus tempered by their training, by their professional experience, and by the responsibility which they owe, given the fact that any breach of the legal rules of professional conduct undermines not only the value of their investment but also their own professional existence.*[41]

---

40 These perceived challenges to values are clearly enunciated by the opinion of the Council of Bars and Law Societies of Europe in its views on MDPs, "CCBE Position on Multi-disciplinary Partnerships (MDPs)", June 2005 (www.ccbe.eu/fileadmin/user_upload/NTCdocument/ccbe_position_on_mdp1_1182254536.pdf).

41 "CCBE Response to the Solicitors Regulation Authority's Consultation on New Forms of Practice and Regulations for Alternative Business Structures", 4 September 2009, p5 (www.ccbe.eu/fileadmin/user_upload/NTCdocument/EN_CCBE_Response_to_1_1253696350.pdf).

As is discussed in more detail below, this distinction may be difficult to maintain in modern practices, which are run as profitable businesses for the benefit of lawyers – indeed, has it ever been otherwise? It is argued that this conflict does not arise under the traditional model, where regulators monitor and enforce professional standards on individual lawyers. Thus the presumption appears to be that non-lawyers will focus purely on economic interests, ensuring a satisfactory return on their investments, whereas lawyers will easily balance their desire for profit and their professional obligations.

These conflicts are clearly possible, especially if one were to consider solely the short-term economic interests of the alternative firm – this could translate to a pursuit of profit through lower costs and/or higher charges. Lowering costs may take the form of reducing the amount of effort spent on a case and producing work of a lower quality, while higher charges might be achieved through unnecessary billing of the client. Clearly, both are contrary to the lawyer's duty to act in the best interest of his or her clients. If, however, investors were to consider the longer term, then ethical and sustainable business practices in which lawyers fulfil their duties and meet the expectations of clients are clearly a better business proposition.

Another objection lies in the fact that privilege, the cornerstone of legal practice, is generally not extended to other professions.[42] Although the protections provided by legal professional privilege differ across jurisdictions, especially between common and civil law systems, lawyers in most jurisdictions have special duties regarding client information. Since the concept of privilege seeks to enable clients to place unrestricted confidence in their lawyers and encourages complete disclosure by removing the concern that the client may be prejudiced in the future by any of the information disclosed, there is at least the concern that confidentiality may be compromised and the principle of legal privilege undermined by bringing non-lawyers into a law firm. Since disclosure of privileged information can amount to a waiver of privilege, severely impacting a client's rights, the duty to maintain privilege of client information applies to all lawyers in many common law jurisdiction law firms. Extending that to non-lawyers, who do not have this duty and may not understand its seriousness, is considered dangerous by traditionalists.

In addition to non-lawyers not being subject to the same duties as lawyers, they are generally not subject to the same regulation or sanction as lawyers. Hence, they are (supposedly) more prone to acting in some ethically reproachable manner or contrary to client interests. As such, another argument often raised is that the introduction of alternative law firms will undermine the

42 In *R (on the application of Prudential plc and another) v Special Commissioner of Income Tax and another* [2013] 1 United Kingdom SC 1, the UK Supreme Court decided that legal privilege did not extend to legal advice given by non-lawyers. This position was subsequently confirmed by the Ministry of Justice.

lawyer-client relationship and, therefore, erode the professionalism of the legal sector. Some traditionalists have also pointed out that having non-lawyers working together with lawyers may confuse clients about whether qualified and regulated lawyers are advising them and handling their case. It is argued that this may undermine the trust a client has in a lawyer, thus further undermining the standing of the profession more generally.

This four-pronged argument clearly seeks to protect the client. However, given one of the strong reasons behind allowing alternative law firms has been to increase competition, client choice and access to justice (United Kingdom) and enhance governance (Australia), the second part of this chapter considers whether this argument is as strong as it first appears.

A further question that is raised by many is whether the traditionalist view is rather a misguided attempt to protect the profession. Professor Susskind said:

> *I want to challenge whether this is about protecting clients or protecting lawyers. I distinguish between professions that behave as jealous guards and those that act like benevolent custodians. From this side of the Atlantic, I fear that many professional legal bodies and some lawyers in the U.S. are veering worryingly toward the first category. We should survive as lawyers because we have the knowledge and experience to bring value in legal affairs that others cannot, and not because we regulate so that competitors are not allowed in the arena.*[43]

2.6 The 'traditionalists' prevail – the US rejection of ABS

Following the enactment of the LSA in the United Kingdom in 2007, many looked to the United States to see whether it would adopt a similar change, and amend the Model Rule that prohibits fee sharing between lawyers and non-lawyers.[44] In December 2011, the ABA Commission on Ethics 20/20 issued a discussion paper proposing to amend the Model Rule 5.4, and permit a highly restricted form of non-lawyer ownership in law firms. The commission rejected publicly listed law firms, passive non-lawyer investments and MDPs, but suggested allowing non-lawyer owners who are active in the firm providing services that support the delivery of legal services by the lawyers. The non-lawyer ownership would be subject to a percentage cap, so as to ensure that lawyers retain control of the firm.[45] This discussion paper was met with strong opposition from a group of nine general counsel of large corporations such as IBM, GE and Intel, who argued that the change would erode legal

---

43 Neil Rose, "Susskind ABSs will have international ripple effect and break down protectionism", *Legal Futures*, 5 July 2013 (www.legalfutures.co.uk/latest-news/susskind-abss-will-international-ripple-effect-break-down-protectionism).

44 See note 1.

45 "Alternative Law Practice Structures Report", ABA Commission on Ethics 20/20 Discussion Draft for Comments, 2 December 2011(www.americanbar.org/content/dam/aba/administrative/ethics_2020/20111202-ethics2020-discussion_draft-alps.authcheckdam.pdf).

professionalism.[46] On April 16 2012, the ABA released a statement that rejected any change to the existing Model Rule 5.4.

In September 2013, ABA President James Silkenat stated that the United States was "years away" from enabling non-lawyer ownership of law firms, but that he thought:

> *It's worth considering if, after we've seen the experience in the United Kingdom and Australia, we find that the protections that are at least described in the laws are effective – and [he thinks] US lawyers are not yet convinced of that – and that the ethical considerations don't arise, and that there are good business reasons to do it, we might take another look at it again.*[47]

Ethical and governance considerations appear to be at the heart of the US rejection of non-lawyer ownership. The adequacy of safeguards to address this appears to be the key to change.

Although the traditional ring-fencing continues to exist in the majority of the world, it is by no means uncontested – even in the United States. In 2011, Jacoby & Meyers, a US consumer law firm known for its use of extensive advertising, filed lawsuits in New York, Connecticut and New Jersey to challenge the rules which prohibit non-lawyer ownership in law firms. The firm complained that the rules restricted its ability to raise capital for technology and infrastructure improvements, office expansions and hiring.

Jacoby & Meyers claimed that the rules in question are unconstitutional, and set out eight grounds of claim, including that they violate a firm's right to equal protection of the law, in that other professions do not have restrictions to capital investment even though they face similar issues of confidentiality and conflicts of interest. Thus, it is argued, a firm is denied the opportunity to access outside capital that has enabled other professions, such as investment banks, to expand and grow. This, in turn, constitutes a violation of the right to equal protection of laws under New York State Constitution, Article 1, Section 11. The firm also claimed that the rules violate the rights to freedom of association of lawyers and interested investors by prohibiting them from freely coming together to pursue a mutual benefit. More indirectly, the firm claimed that the prohibition of outside investment raises the cost of legal services to consumers, restricting the public's access to the civil justice system, which in turn violates their rights to freedom of speech.[48]

Despite the New York District Court initially dismissing the claims, the case

46 "Comments of Nine General Counsel on the ABA Commission on Ethics 20/20's Discussion Paper on Alternative Law Practice Structures", 29 February 2012 (www.americanbar.org/content/dam/aba/administrative/ethics_2020/ethics_20_20_comments/ninegeneralcounselcomments_alpschoiceoflawinitialdraftproposal.authcheckdam.pdf).

47 Farrar's Building, "US Has no Appetite for ABSs, Says New ABA President", *Solicitors' Journal*, 30 September 2013 (www.solicitorsjournal.com/news/legal-profession/legal-services/us-has-no-appetite-abss-says-new-aba-president).

48 *Jacoby & Meyers LLP v Presiding Justices of the Appellate Division*, Complaint for Declaratory and Injunctive Relief, 18 May 2011.

was resurrected by the US Court of Appeal and remanded back to the district court for Jacoby & Meyers to amend its claim. At the time of writing this chapter [in the first edition], the cases in all three states were awaiting judgment. If Jacoby & Meyers are successful, it might well bring profound changes to the legal landscape in the United States and may potentially mark the introduction of alternative firms.

Interestingly, in Canada there appears to be recognition that the traditional 'ring fencing' cannot last:

> *A wave of unprecedented change is affecting every aspect of the legal profession – competition, the price of services, how services are delivered, law firm structures, legal education and training, and regulation.*
>
> *Given the complexities of the changing legal marketplace, and the impacts of this change on current legal practice, lawyers themselves must take responsibility for shaping the future of legal services in Canada. If not, others will.*
>
> *The status quo is not an option, nor is a piecemeal approach where issues are addressed in isolation. What is required is a comprehensive, knowledge-based, client-focused, lawyer-driven initiative which involves a broad cross-section of the legal profession and its stakeholders, and develops strategic initiatives, guidance and practical tools to help lawyers transition. That's what the CBA Legal Futures Initiative is about.*[49]

3. Innovation and future trends for traditional and alternative firms

Both traditional and alternative firms across the globe are developing innovative ways to provide services to clients. Such innovation also relates to the means through which legal advice is delivered, including the development of virtual firms, which have no office and provide advice from lawyers who work from home. Examples include Keystone and Everyman Legal in the United Kingdom, Axiom in the United States and Cognition LLP and Conduit Law in Canada. Similar examples have different business models. North London sole practitioner Emil Hussein founded the site iSolicitor.co.uk, which offers legal advice face to face or via Skype and document checks provided by a team of freelance lawyers for a small fixed fee. Legal expenses insurer, DAS, created Instant Law Line, which offers unlimited telephone legal advice for a small monthly retainer.

Other innovations relate to how legal services are packaged and paid for. Lawyers from both traditional and alternative firms from a range of jurisdictions have for some time now offered fixed fees, as opposed to hourly billing. This trend has extended to offering unbundled services that enable a pay-as-you-go facility. In the United Kingdom, both Stobart Barristers and Brilliant Law, a firm set up by non-lawyers, offer fixed-fee, pay-as-you-go legal services to businesses

49 www.cbafutures.org/About-the-Initiative/Change,-the-Legal-Profession,-and-You.

and consumers. Brilliant Law is particularly targeting clients that are start-up companies or small-to-medium-sized enterprises.

Innovation in legal services has not been limited to the United Kingdom despite an alternative structure, that of non-lawyer ownership, being initially available only in the United Kingdom and Australia. Lawpal, founded by Paypal founder Peter Thiel and others, is based in California and is also aimed at start-up clients. After clients log in online, they are given access to a choice of qualified local lawyers. Upon selection, clients enter a secure, online deal room in which they can converse with their lawyer, store documents and manage the progress of their transaction, which is conducted on a fixed-fee basis.

Yet another way in which alternative firms have been innovative is in the actual advice that they provide. Alternative firm Everything Legal, which is owned by legal expenses insurer DAS, runs the website Law on the Web. Visited by over one million people each year, Law on the Web provided free legal guidance and free information on a range of legal issues. Legal documents such as will templates and popular agreements are free to download. US companies are also offering online legal information and documents – these include branded networks LegalZoom and RocketLawyer. RocketLawyer also owns LawPivot, in which qualified attorneys provide confidential answers to legal questions asked online. The upsurge in this type of legal service recognises yet another trend: self-help. In an age where consumers are accustomed to doing things for themselves – booking flights online, for example, as opposed to going through a travel agent – consumers are looking to do some of the legal work themselves.

New forms of traditional legal services are also developing. One proactive model developed in response to the changing UK legal market was that of QualitySolicitors. QualitySolicitors is an affiliation of small and medium firms (traditional and ABS) which share costs, adhere to core customer services promises and leverage off a communal distinctive branding and advertising designed by Saatchi & Saatchi. The aim is to have a QualitySolicitor firm in each town and city across the United Kingdom, and thus to 'keep solicitors local'. The company, in which it seems firms take a share, was majority-owned by private equity investor Paloman Capital Partners and has made a distinctive impact on the UK legal services market.

In some ways the QualitySolicitors model can be seen as a microcosm of the Swiss *Verein* structure used by large international firms, such as Norton Rose Fulbright and Baker McKenzie. Under a *Verein* structure strategy, branding, information technology and other core functions are shared, but profit pools, tax, accounting and partner compensation remain ring-fenced at a regional level. Importantly, liability – with regard to other partnerships in the association and to regulators – is also ring-fenced and veil-piercing attempts have largely been unsuccessful.

With innovation taking place quickly in the legal services sector, many jurisdictions are seeking to ensure they can embrace and enable change while keeping up with it from a regulatory perspective. In August 2012, the Canadian Bar Association (CBA) launched an Inquiry into the Future of Legal Practice. The focus is the legal profession as a whole and how the CBA can assist its members in adapting to a changing legal environment. Accepting that the "*status quo* is not an option", the inquiry focuses on four main areas: client expectations and experience; business structures and innovation; ethics and regulation; and education and training. One of 20 consultation questions asks: "What are the implications of non-lawyers owning or managing a law firm?"[50]

Even if one is convinced that the governance challenges for traditional firms and alternative law firms are not that different, it is apparent that totally new governance structures will be required to cover the gamut of innovation that appears to be taking place. How does governance work in a virtual law firm where partners and lawyers working together never meet? Can lawyers be effectively supervised by more senior lawyers solely through electronic means? How are standards maintained? A traditionally regulated law firm can already operate virtually under the rules of many jurisdictions (because there are no rules to prevent it) – even those that are adamantly opposed to alternative law firms involving non-lawyers. Regulators need to focus not only on how these innovative approaches to the provision of legal advice are appropriately regulated, but also on how these firms are encouraged (or even mandated) to have in place appropriate governance mechanisms to ensure that clients' interests are fully safeguarded and that the internal governance procedures of the firm are adequate to ensure a healthy firm that can well serve its clients.

4. Governance and regulation for a new era

As we have seen through other chapters of this book, governance is about structures for and approaches to 'good governance', with a focus on how decisions are made and consensus built. These structures are easy to identify within the traditional law firm – a partnership structure, where all partners are lawyers and decisions are made collectively by all partners. The same issues remain at the heart of governance for alternative firms: what should the governance structure be, who makes the decisions and how is consensus built? However, current wisdom has it that where non-lawyers are involved in a law firm, safeguards need to be built into the governance process to protect the client – indeed in many jurisdictions non-lawyers cannot formally be involved in a law firm, or at least cannot share profits.

We must take care that we do not look through rose-coloured spectacles when examining governance in traditional law firms – and this is not just a

50 www.cbafutures.org/CBA/media/mediafiles/PDF/Consultation/JoinTheConversation.pdf.

large versus small issue. We are all aware of firms, small and large, that are dominated by one or two partners, in terms of control, but also economics. It is hard to describe such firms as having 'good governance' even if they are well managed. The so-called partners of those strong, controlling individuals are much more like employed solicitors notwithstanding the title they have. Similarly, in many large corporate firms the sheer number of partners has led to a somewhat 'corporatised' approach to governance. Many larger firms will have an executive committee or management board of partners that functions very much like a board of directors in a corporation. Good governance in these types of firms will often involve ensuring that management boards are fully representative of partners, on a geographical, practice group or even age basis. Partnership meetings may very rarely take place and even then will be somewhat formulaic, with the consensus for the decision already built through the management board structure.

Ongoing consensus building and communication are central themes in the new, expanded concept of good governance presented in this book. This requires more than just formal discussions at partnership meetings. A traditional law firm structure does not give rise to good governance *per se*; nor does it necessarily preclude it. Good governance needs to be built and worked at in both traditional law firms and alternative law firms – indeed, the differences may not be as great as they first appear and the 'safeguards' in alternative law firms should be considered by traditional law firms.

4.1 Internal and external governance

For law firms, there are essentially two sides to governance: that which directly affects the client, and that which is internal to the running of the business. Governance that directly affects the client includes the decisions and structures relating to conflicts, legal professional privilege/confidentiality and the quality of the legal advice (and hence the supervision of lawyers). This has been the traditional focus of lawyer regulation – professional bodies require lawyers to observe their various duties to their client in order to practise. Regulatory bodies have traditionally 'monitored' this observance by responding to client complaints against a lawyer and then, if necessary, taking disciplinary action. As such, this form of regulation has focused on the behaviour of the individual lawyer, based on "minimum standards – at the point at which conduct becomes 'unsatisfactory professional conduct' or worse".[51] It is also somewhat selective – lawyers with more of a consumer client base (as opposed to those with large corporate clients) are more likely to have a complaint lodged against

51 John Briton and Scott McLean, "Incorporated Legal Practices: Dragging the Regulation of the Legal Profession into the Modern Era", Third International Ethics Conference, Gold Coast Australia, 13–16 July 2008, at p5.

them. This form of regulation is generally reactive in nature – to complaints. One exception is the requirement that lawyers meet continuous education requirements to ensure the standard of their advice, but even this is largely self-policed.

This traditional, complaints-based approach, focused on individual lawyers and their personal and professional ethics, has ignored the internal side of governance and the basic fact that most legal services are provided by lawyers working in firms or chambers, which are run as profit-making businesses. The inclusion of non-lawyer owned firms has precipitated a change of thinking and approach in this area, which is arguably for the benefit of the client and the profession. This shift was well summarised back in 2008 in a speech by an Australian regulator on the country's new regulatory approach:

> *The regulatory arrangements in relation to incorporated practices … recognises what ought to be obvious – that the law is not only a profession but a business; that legal services are delivered by individual lawyers to be sure, but by individuals who sell their services for profit within commercial enterprises; and that law firms like other commercial enterprises have the organizational and workplace cultures that shape the ethical conduct of the people who work for them, for better or worse.*[52]

There was a similar shift in the United Kingdom. The UK SRA has taken a principle-based approach to regulation that focuses more on firms and less on individuals. Two out of the 10 SRA principles relate to the way a firm should run its business: "run your business or carry out your role in the business effectively and in accordance with proper governance and sound financial and risk management principles" and "run your business or carry out your role in the business in a way that encourages equality of opportunity and respect for diversity".[53]

That the internal governance of a firm – how it runs its business – affects the client can be seen by what can and does go wrong in traditional firms. The problem was recognised and summarised by Sir David Clementi in 2004:

> *Research shows that complaints arise as much from poor business services as from poor legal advice. If certain lawyers continue to reject the notion that they are in business, such complaints will continue until they are indeed out of business.*[54]

An SRA report at the time,[55] analysing problems in firms, attributes some aspects of poor financial management to there being one dominant decision maker in the firm (a partner or CEO) who is wilfully blind to the seriousness of

52 *Ibid.*

53 The principles can be found on the SRA website at www.sra.org.uk/consumers/sra-regulate/sra-regulate.page#principles.

54 Clementi, note 14.

55 Solicitors Regulatory Authority, "Financial Stability Project: Legal Policy Issues Report to the Regulatory Risk Committee", 23 September 2013 (http://governance.lawsociety.org.uk/secure/meeting/204468/23_09_13_RRC_PUBLIC_Item_10_Financial_Stability_project_legal_policy_issues.pdf).

the firm's problems. In other words, the root cause is a decision-making and governance problem, not one defined by the structure of the law firm. Discussing the need for better governance in all firms, lawyer Ian Vicary states:

> *Whichever area of the market they operate in, law firms must understand that financial health, regulatory compliance and efficient processes are the cornerstone not only of attracting investment, but also of survival ... The need to run an efficient, financially robust and compliant business has never been more important to ensure survival. Whilst these fundamental hallmarks will not guarantee success, without them there will be a bleak and short-lived future.*[56]

There are also plenty of examples of traditional law firms that have inadequately dealt with the client side of governance. Statistics for 2012–13 from the Office of the Legal Ombudsman for the United Kingdom, 94.25% of which refer to solicitors, indicated complaints related mostly to failure to advise clients (18.19%), failure to follow instructions (16.21%), delay (8.76%), failure to keep the client advised (8.39%), provision of deficient information regarding costs (8.39%), excessive costs (8.27%) and failure to progress a matter (8.03%).[57] While these statistics do not distinguish between traditional firms and ABS firms, since only a small minority of firms currently have ABS licences (approximately 200 out of 10,000 firms), the bulk of these complaints must relate to traditional firms.

The problems that traditional firms have had and continue to have show a range of weaknesses, particularly around an absence of systems and failure to manage risks. This begs the question: to what extent are traditional firms adapting their behaviours and systems according to the risks identified by those in the know – professional indemnity insurers? Although the risk management of traditional firms is beyond the scope of this chapter, it is interesting to note that David Cable, head of professional indemnity at Allianz Global Corporate & Specialty, does not distinguish risk management on the basis of traditional or alternative law firm structures. He states: "irrespective of whether the law firm is an ABS or not, they need to ensure they are satisfied the law firm is well managed and has good internal risk management procedures."[58]

When considering the problems faced by traditional firms, alternative firms may not be as risky an option for prospective clients as they have been seen to be (at least by comparison). Corporations, which are subject to corporation laws and corporate governance standards, should be more transparent and should have clear decision-making structures. While examples of poorly run companies abound, corporations are in part premised on an approach, supported by

---

56 Ian Vicary, "ABS or Back to Basics? Lessons from the First ABS Demise", *Legal Futures*, 21 October 2013 (www.legalfutures.co.uk/blog/abs-back-basics-lessons-first-abs-demise). Vicary is a corporate partner in Weightmans LLP.

57 See the Office of the Legal Ombudsman's website: www.legalombudsman.org.uk/research-decisions/Complaints%20data/2012-13-pdf-versions/What_were_the_complaints_about.pdf.

58 Fox Williams, note 30 at p16.

regulatory requirements, aimed at encouraging sound financial management. What corporations do not have is a history of, or structure for, providing client-side governance. This is understandable since corporations are not considered to have a duty to their customers, but rather to their shareholders and possibly, in some jurisdictions, to their employees. Of course, alternative law firms that are corporations will have duties to their clients as well as to their shareholders, and consideration of the governance risks that alternative firms present requires an examination of the interplay of those duties. This is explored further below.

4.2 The governance divide

One possible difference in the approach of traditional law firms and that of corporations is the 'governance divide' between internal governance and external governance. In traditional firms, partners make decisions about practice and the business. Even if most partnership meetings are more about the business of the firm than legal issues affecting clients, partners come to these decisions with an inherent understanding and commitment to the firm's legal practice and professional obligations. Non-lawyers cannot easily bring this insight to the decision-making table. As is evident in the first part of this chapter, alternative law firms are not 'one size fits all'. Decision making cannot simply be equated to ownership, even though clearly there is potential, if not actual scope, for significant influence. So the relevance of the 'governance divide', like other governance issues discussed in this chapter, will depend on the level of control that non-lawyers have in the alternative firm, as well as the mix of services that the firm is offering and the way in which good client-focused governance is maintained.

While some traditional firms restrict decision making to lawyers, many in recent decades have moved to include finance and human resources professionals on management committees and/or appointed a non-lawyer CEO to manage the day-to-day operations of a firm. This recognises that non-legal expertise is crucial for good internal governance. Ultimately, lawyers are specialists in giving legal advice and there are sound reasons to leave the other aspects of running a successful business (eg, risk, human resource and financial management) to experts in those fields.

4.3 Governance risks presented by alternative law firms

The governance risks of a firm arguably depend not on whether it has a traditional or alternative structure, varied as that is, but rather on how decisions are made and consensus built within those structures, and how these elements affect the ability to manage the business and observe the lawyers' duties to their clients.

This section identifies the governance risks posed by alternative firms and considers the validity of arguments that these risks are unique to alternative firms. As identified in the first part of this chapter, there are two main groupings of alternative firms – those in a partnership structure with some non-lawyer partners and those with external capital, generally in a corporate structure.

(a) Non-lawyer partnerships

Alternative firms with non-lawyer partners who collectively do not have a controlling stake in the firm are considered by many to be reasonably non-controversial, despite such a proposal being rejected by the US legal profession (see section 1.6 above). Hence, some jurisdictions allow a limited ratio of non-lawyer partners to lawyers. Certainly, when non-lawyers are a minority within a partnership, few governance concerns are raised. Arguably these types of alternative law firms can result in improved governance – non-lawyers can bring internal governance expertise to improve the running of the business and lawyers can bring insight from practice and ensure professional obligations are observed. This should be a win-win situation for both the client and the law firm.

As lawyers get more remote from the decision-making process and non-lawyers have a greater "relevant degree of control over the affairs of the organization",[59] concerns as to independence and the creation of conflicts of interest grow. Again, this is largely based on the traditionalist premise that because non-lawyers are not subject to the same duties as lawyers, they will be motivated in ways which might conflict with such duties. The validity of this premise is considered at the end of this section, although clearly it is a risk.

MDPs – partnerships with non-lawyer partners that carry on non-legal activities – face this 'lawyer dilution' risk as well as other specific governance risks. There are two types of risk relating to conflict of interest. The first, as discussed above, is that non-lawyers will have interests, including a profit motive, which conflict with a lawyer's duties. This is discussed in the next section on alternative firms with external capital. The second is that the non-legal side of the business has a client which is on the opposite side of a transaction or legal case of a client on the legal side. This conflict, however, is no different from that which two lawyers in one firm might have, and conflicts systems developed in traditional law firms can be easily be used to deal with situations of this type. This second form of conflict of interest is also a governance concern that is equally faced by traditional law firms and there are plenty of examples of firms being reprimanded for poor management of conflicts of interest. In any event, there is a basic business driver to avoid conflicts. A client which is being advised in any capacity – for example, being sued on another matter by the same enterprise – is unlikely to be happy with

59 This is the language used by the CCBE in its report on non-lawyer-owned firms (www.ccbe.eu/fileadmin/user_upload/NTCdocument/ccbe_position_on_non1_1182254612.pdf).

that enterprise. This may be borne out of a fear of confidential information moving from one side of the enterprise to the other to the detriment of the client, but is more likely to be founded in a more basic reaction – you are either my adviser or the adviser to my enemies. Basic good business and a sensible approach to the appropriate development of clients should completely support an ethical approach (as a lawyer would see it) to conflicts of interest.

More serious concerns regarding privilege, however, are apparent when different professions enter the mix. Only through lawyers can clients attain legal professional privilege, and sharing client information with non-lawyers would normally amount to a waiver of that privilege. This is difficult for MDPs to manage, since one of the main advantages of the MDP structure is to offer seamless services to clients and this is difficult to do if information cannot be shared. Safeguards that are now in place to manage this are discussed in the next section.

Another governance risk for MDPs that have a legal and an audit function is one that the Enron scandal highlighted: the desire for there to be independence in the audit and legal functions so that each can act as a check on the other. As noted earlier, PwC Australia, an MDP with both functions, places restrictions on the legal advice that can be given to audit clients of the firm. It may be that these types of restrictions have reduced the popularity of MDPs for firms offering both functions.

The particular risks that MDPs present are recognised by professional indemnity insurers. David Cable of Allianz Global Corporate & Specialty states: "having different professions operating under one roof poses possible conflicts of interest, possible coercion and cross discipline exposures."[60] Similarly Bhavik Desai from another insurer, Chartis, notes:

> *where you have an accountant, a lawyer, a surveyor and an estate agent, this is where traditionally you had the fraud rings. We are worried that one side of the business might put pressure on the other side of the business.*[61]

In addition to these concerns, MDPs remain a partnership, with the consequential lack of transparency and public scrutiny with regard to their work. This combination leads some to the conclusion that MDPs are likely to be the most risky of all forms of alternative law firm. Whether there are sufficient 'safeguards' in place to ensure that adequate governance in MDPs is explored below in section 4.5.

(b) Legal services providers – with 'non-lawyer' capital

Next to consider are alternative law firms with external capital, which operate within a corporate structure. Here, the primary concern is that a profit-

60 Fox Williams, note 30 at p16.
61 *Ibid.*

motivated corporate strategy and culture based on the 'demands' of shareholders will lead to conflicting duties and a lack of independence for lawyers, with an alleged consequence being that clients' interests are not best served. With respect, this argument is too simplistic and somewhat fallacious. Most traditional law firms carry on business to make a profit and junior lawyers have long been complaining about pressure to meet billable hour targets. If profit motive creates a conflict for lawyers in an alternative law firm, then it does so for lawyers working in traditional firms also – hourly billing itself, the usual way that traditional firms charge for services, presents a conflict between the clients' interest and that of the firm, regardless of ownership.

As pointed out by one commentator:

The incorporation and listing of law firms accentuate and bring into focus certain ethical issues, but it is not incorporation and listing as such that are the main thing we should worry about. Law is already a business as well as a profession and has been so for a very long time. The ethical issues that come with incorporation and listing are already with us at least among the largest firms and those that aspire to them.[62]

Some may say this concern is more pronounced in alternative firms since lawyers, who are now employed solicitors with limited or no say in the governance and management of the firm, may have effectively lost their independence – this argument is also weak. Concerns could be just as valid for a firm run by a dominant managing partner who has promoted a profit-focused culture because, for example, he is due to retire in five years and needs to remove significant capital from the partnership. In short, there should be no issues with requiring a governance approach that seeks to protect the client and ensure that the business is well run (and, in being well run, is profitable), and this need should not be driven by structure.

The extent to which the profit motivation is a concern depends significantly on the type of firm, the level of investment, the degree of control of the investors, management and decision-making structures and, importantly, culture. In other words: its governance. Since venture capitalist and private equity investors are known for their desire to make a quick but profitable exit, it is no wonder that their involvement and control of law firms are most feared by traditionalists. However, concerns may be different for a lawyer-run corporation with a silent non-lawyer investor, a law firm listed on the stock exchange and a law firm owned by a parent company, largely left to run itself. The devil, as they say, is in the detail for each firm. Non-lawyers invest in, and own, firms because they want them to succeed and that requires the company's

---

62 Christine Parker, "Peering over the Ethical Precipice: Incorporation, Listing, and the Ethical Responsibilities of Law Firms", 24 April 2008 at 29 (www.law.georgetown.edu/academics/centers-institutes/legal-profession/documents/upload/Future-Law-Firm-Symposium-ParkerWebsiteArticle.pdf).

lawyers to perform their jobs properly – including adhering to their professional obligations. The governance divide is relevant here. The insight lawyers have about the practice of law is relevant to business decisions, but as long as lawyers remain involved in the decision making of the business, this insight can be accessed. Non-lawyers interested in owning and even managing a law firm would ignore the advice of lawyers as to the practice of law at their peril. Lawyers may need to discover better ways to explain how their professional obligations need to be incorporated into business decisions, so that non-lawyer owners and managers can understand that – but it should not be seen as an unbridgeable divide.

Incorporated law firms face another conflict – that between the duties of a lawyer and those of a company director. Many legal systems, including the relevant legislation in the United Kingdom and Australia, impose fiduciary duties on directors and officers of a corporation. For example, under the Australian Corporations Law[63] a director has a duty to act in good faith and in the interest of the corporation rather than his or her personal interest. Directors' duties must therefore be discharged in accordance with the context of the business. If the company's only business is the provision of legal services, these duties should not be in conflict, since acting in the best interests of the company will require the professional obligations of legal staff to be observed. The next section on safeguards discusses how publicly listed firms in Australia have sought to disclose the requirement to meet both sets of duties. A greater conflict may be perceived when the legal services provision is only a small part of the business. However, the risk of regulatory punishment, lawsuits and reputational damage that come when a lawyer breaches his or her obligations to the courts and the client should support a decision that observing these duties remains in the best interests of the company.

A corporate structure does, of course, bring governance benefits. Improved governance, and the governance deficiencies identified in partnerships (see section 1.2 above), was one of the reasons why Australia moved to allow alternative firms. When the bill proposing those changes was first introduced in the New South Wales Parliament, it was expected that:

> *within a corporate structure, the accountability of individuals for the management of the practice will be enhanced, and this is likely to lead to better delineation of responsibilities within firms and to more efficient service provision.*[64]

To summarise, there are risks posed by alternative law firms. The greatest risks, however, are not posed by the profit motivation of incorporated firms, as these exist already within law firms, but possibly where there is a mix of professions or where the legal services business is a smaller part of a larger

63 See generally Sections 180–183 of the Corporations Law.

64 Mark and Cowdroy, note 3 at 675–676.

whole. The answer to minimising these risks lies in the governance systems and, from a consumer protection perspective, the regulations that support good governance. Corporations have clear laws, governance requirements, regulatory safeguards and transparency. MDPs, on the other hand, lack transparency and have a patchwork of regulation dependent on the professions involved. In both the United Kingdom and Australia, legal regulators have put in place regulations and systems across the board for alternative firms, and in the case of the United Kingdom, some regulation has also had an impact on traditional firms. The remainder of this chapter considers the systems and safeguards used to regulate alternative firms in these jurisdictions to see what lessons can be learned for the good governance of all law firms.

4.4 Regulatory regimes to cover alternative firms

As noted in section 2 of this chapter, the move to allow alternative firms was accompanied, in Australia and the United Kingdom, by a shift in regulatory focus, and in the case of the United Kingdom, regulatory structure. Instead of the traditional focus on individual lawyers, regulation is now focused on the firm as a whole, while at the same time still maintaining the codes of conduct imposed on individual lawyers. Under the new approach, the firm is expected to achieve certain outcomes and will be held to account when it falls short of these expectations. On the other hand, there is less regulation of specific acts and procedures.

The Legal Services Commission in Queensland, Australia describes its approach as "firm about outcomes, flexible about means", with "increasing emphasis on broadly stated, high level principles" and less on "detailed prescriptive rules which describe exactly how lawyers should conduct themselves".[65] Similarly, in the United Kingdom, the Legal Services Board states that regulation of the ABS is to be "based primarily on clear outcomes supplemented by guidance".[66] These outcomes generally reflect the ethical principles that underlie the standards of conduct expected of lawyers, such as promoting access to justice and acting with independence and integrity.

Due to the general "firm about outcomes, flexible about means" approach adopted by the various regulatory authorities of the legal profession in Australia, there is no specific prescription as to how an ILP should be governed and managed. Despite also being principles based, the position in the United Kingdom is different due to an ABS being licensable under the LSA. Overseen by

65 Legal Services Commission of Queensland, "Regulatory Guides – An Overview", 16 September 2013, p2 (www.lsc.qld.gov.au/__data/assets/pdf_file/0005/108572/Regulatory-Guides-an-Overview-v4-September-2013.pdf).

66 Legal Services Board, "Alternative Business Structures: Approaches to Licensing. Guidance to Licensing Authorities on the Content of Licensing Rules" (www.legalservicesboard.org.uk/what_we_do/consultations/closed/pdf/abs_guidance_on_licensing_rules_guidance.pdf).

the Legal Services Board, licensing authorities such as the SRA[67] impose conditions on firms obtaining an ABS licence. Such conditions should, according to Legal Services Board guidance, "not seek to restrict commercial activity unless there is evidence of consumer detriment that requires regulation". Rather, conditions should ensure that lawyer and non-lawyer employees, among other things, "respect the professional principles" and "act with independence and in the best interests of their clients ensuring confidentiality and client money are protected".[68]

4.5 Safeguards

The fact that the United Kingdom and Australian legal professions have not collapsed or fallen into further disrepute following the implementation of rules to allow alternative firms suggests that at least some of the worries about alternative law firms may be unwarranted if appropriate governance and other safeguards are put in place. As noted above, the authorities in the United Kingdom and Australia have recognised the potential concerns and have put in place regulatory measures to prevent, or at least mitigate, the risks. Contrary to what some scholars, experts and commentators predicted, alternative firms have not caused widespread problems. The traditionalists would add "Yet!" Further, traditional law firms in many jurisdictions continue to have problems resulting from poor governance, which regularly affect the client.

(a) Individuals responsible for adherence to professional and regulatory requirements in alternative firms in the United Kingdom and Australia

Both the LPA[69] in Australia and the LSA in the United Kingdom[70] have specific provisions with regard to alternative firm governance. Both countries require that a person be responsible for ensuring the compliance of the corporation with the relevant regulatory requirements, and that a lawyer be put in charge of the legal services division.

In Australia, an ILP must have at least one director who is an Australian legal practitioner holding an unrestricted practising certificate (the legal practitioner director). This director must observe the general directors' duties under the Corporations Act 2001 and duties specific to an ILP under the LPA. The legal practitioner director is responsible for the management of the legal services provided by the ILP, and ensures that "appropriate management systems" are in place to enable the provision of legal service to accord with the professional obligations of lawyers, which are unaffected by the non-lawyers. The legal

---

67 Each of the eight different legal professions has their own regulator, some of which can authorise an ABS. For a full list see www.legalservicesboard.org.uk/can_we_help/approved_regulators/.

68 Legal Services Board, note 67.

69 See generally Part 2.6 of the LPA.

70 See generally Part 5 of the LSA.

practitioner director is also obliged to take all reasonable action to ensure that no breach of professional obligations occurs and to take remedial actions should this happen.

A breach of these obligations by the legal practitioner director is capable of being professional misconduct with the related penalties. Given the legal practitioner director is not a specific role in the governance structure, any Australian lawyer who is on the board of directors of an ILP is a legal practitioner director, and thus under these obligations. Similar provisions apply in regard to MDPs. Each lawyer who is a partner in the MDP has the same obligations as the legal practitioner director in an ILP (save in relation to stopping a breach and taking remedial action), and can be disciplined if he or she fails to meet these obligations.

In the United Kingdom, the compliance role is split into the head of legal practice, who must be an English-qualified solicitor or registered European lawyer, and the head of finance and administration (who need not be a lawyer), who is in charge of compliance with accounting regulations. The SRA has re-termed these roles as compliance officer of legal practice (COLP) and compliance officer of finance and administration (COFA) respectively.

One very significant difference between Australia and the United Kingdom is that while the former requires a legal practitioner director or equivalent only for ILPs and MDPs, the latter requires a COLP and a COFA in all legal practices, including traditional law firms.[71] Unlike the legal practitioner director in Australia, COLP and COFA are positions to which individuals must be specifically appointed. The nominations for these posts must be approved by the SRA, which has stipulated that the individuals must be of sufficient seniority and in a position of sufficient responsibility to fulfil the role.

The obligations of the COLP are essentially the same as those of the legal practitioner director in Australia. The COLP is obliged to take all reasonable steps to ensure the compliance of the ABS to the relevant professional obligations, as well as the relevant terms and conditions of its ABS licence.

(b) Regulation of non-lawyers

One difference between the role of the COLP and the legal practitioner director is that the personal liability of the COLP is likely to be of a more restricted scope. In 2012, the SRA made the statement:

> *although the COLP and COFA are formal focus points for compliance, they are not the sacrificial lamb so that others within the firm, particularly the senior managers, can absolve themselves of their responsibilities.*[72]

---

71 The Law Society of England and Wales, "Compliance Officers", Practice Note, para. 1.1 (www.lawsociety.org.uk/advice/practice-notes/compliance-officers/#co11).

72 *Ibid.*

This difference is arguably unsurprising, given the difference in the position occupied by the roles of the COLP and COFA in the governance structure as compared to that of the legal practitioner director. Thus, notwithstanding the provisions for the COLP and the COFA, the directors and management professionals in an ABS in the United Kingdom need to ensure compliance with regulatory requirements as well.

Under the SRA's authorisation rules,[73] it is the responsibility of managers to ensure that suitable arrangements are in place to ensure compliance and to enable the COLP and COFA to fulfil their obligations. Managers must also be approved and subject themselves to the disciplinary jurisdiction of the SRA. Since a manager includes partners, directors or members of a governing body of an ABS, this again emphasises that the focus of regulators, and hence their perception of where the risks lie, is not in the ownership structure, but rather in the degree of control of non-lawyers.

Managers do not need to be approved under the LPA in Australia (directors will need to meet the requirements under general corporation law). However, the Supreme Court can, upon application by a relevant regulator, make an order preventing lawyers from going into partnership with someone who is not considered suitable to be partner of an MDP that provides legal services. Similarly, the court can also ban ILPs and disqualify someone from managing an ILP.

(c) ***Specific provisions on independence, conflicts and privilege***

The creation of the roles of legal practitioner director and COLP are clearly to 'protect' the client by 'protecting' the lawyers from the influence of non-lawyers so that independence is maintained and conflicts of duties avoided. In Australia, to protect lawyer independence even further, it is an offence for any employee of an ILP (or MDP) to cause or induce a lawyer to contravene the LPA or their professional obligations. The Australian legislation retains responsibility for avoiding conflicts of interest and maintaining professional privilege on individual lawyers working in ILPs and MDPs. For conflicts, the interests of any partner in the MDP are taken into account.

In Germany, members of professions with whom a lawyer can work in an MDP must comply with the rules of conduct for lawyers – such rules are not dissimilar to the professional conduct rules for accountants and tax advisers, and hence a number of MDPs between these professions exist.[74] The Canadian safeguards are significantly more onerous for non-lawyers.[75] Non-lawyer partners must be of good character and are limited to those who practise "a

---

73 See generally www.sra.org.uk/solicitors/handbook/authorisationrules/content.page.

74 Stephen McGarry, *Multidisciplinary Practices & Partnerships: Lawyers, Consultants and Clients*, Law Journal Press, New York, 2002.

75 See generally Part 3 of By-law 7 of the Law Society of Upper Canada at www.lsuc.on.ca/WorkArea/DownloadAsset.aspx?id=214748580 and for a summary of the Canadian approach to MDPs see www.cba.org/cba/epiigram/pdf/multi.pdf.

profession, trade or occupation, that supports or supplements the practice of law". Not only do non-lawyer partners have to agree to abide by lawyers' professional rules, non-lawyers must agree in writing to give lawyers effective control of the MDP.

The United Kingdom has sought to put safeguards in place to reduce this governance risk through Section 190 of the LSA, which extends privilege to the entire ABS where the communication is made "through and under the supervision" of a lawyer. While this means that privilege will not be broken when privileged information is shared and stored on communal platforms, non-legally trained staff will need to be trained on the importance of confidentiality relating to privileged information. This is quite a significant extension of privilege, although clearly in a traditional law firm many non-lawyers, such as secretaries, can access privileged information. Since the Ministry of Justice has stated that legal privilege does not extend to legal advice given by non-lawyers,[76] systems may need to be in place to distinguish privileged from non-privileged information.

To avoid client confusion over who will be doing their legal work in an MDP or ILP in Australia, lawyers must also ensure there is full disclosure to the client as to whether all legal services will be provided by a qualified legal practitioner and, if not, the name and qualifications of the person who will be providing those services.

(d) Firm-wide compliance requirements

Along with the principles-based approach, regulation has also shifted to put greater responsibility on the firm to consider risk management and governance, and to demonstrate this to regulatory authorities. The SRA's approach to ABS authorisation specifically addresses many of the risks associated with ABSs. It asks three key questions:

- Do the firm's proposals pose any particular risks to clients?
- Who will own and run the firm?
- How will the firm be managed?

These questions and the sub questions that feature under each question appear to act as a checklist for firms prior to submitting an application for an ABS licence.

The United Kingdom's inclusion of a COFA also addresses internal governance and improves the internal financial management of law firms for the benefit of clients and the law firm. That the United Kingdom has seen fit to extend the requirements of a COLP and a COFA to traditional firms implies that

76 *R (on the application of Prudential plc and another) v Special Commissioner of Income Tax and another* [2013], note 42.

they can see the benefit in having specific individuals responsible for compliance. In the case of the COLP, one lawyer is responsible for ensuring the the firm culture is in line with professional obligations and ethics, rather than leaving it up to all the lawyers. This is especially important for traditional law firms, which – even though operating in a partnership structure – may well have been 'corporatised'. A key question here is how these compliance mechanisms translate to better risk management and to better governance.

Similarly, in Australia, the regulator has the power to conduct compliance audits to review a firm's ethical performance. This takes two forms: an external audit and a self-assessment. The self-assessment is conducted by the legal practitioner director, focusing on the practice's management systems and supervisory arrangements in relation to compliance with the 10 objectives of a sound legal practice.[77]

(e) *Bespoke regulation for a UK ABS*

The general provisions of the SRA authorisation rules have been discussed above. However, the SRA is also at liberty to impose specific, bespoke conditions on particular ABS licensees. This is both useful and sensible in the United Kingdom, since a range of diverse and innovative firms are applying to be licensed. In one example, the SRA required Abbey Protection Group to restructure so that its non-legal divisions were transferred to a new subsidiary[78] – presumably to prevent breaches of privilege, avoid conflicts of interest and ensure lawyer independence. The SRA has also imposed conditions relating to the ratio of the number of lawyers to non-lawyers and to firms outsourcing work overseas, requiring that SRA approval be sought before changes are made to the nature of such outsourced work.[79] As more firms apply for ABS status, it is expected that the SRA will begin to categorise risks and develop a more standardised set of licensing conditions dependent on the perceived risks.

(f) *Self-imposed safeguards*

Unsurprisingly, given that appropriate governance safeguards are generally good for business, some firms have adopted self-imposed safeguards. One example relates to the publicly listed law firms in Australia. The Slater and Gordon prospectus clearly address the issue of conflict of interest, identifying it as an area of possible risk. In both the "Investment Overview"[80] and "Corporate Governance"[81] sections of the prospectus, the firm clearly states that "lawyers

---

77 Briton and McLean, note 51. While these comments were made with reference to regulation in the Australian state of Queensland, the relevant provisions are based on the provisions of New South Wales, to which other regulations in Australia also refer.

78 Baker Tilly, note 28 at 9.

79 *Ibid.*

80 Prospectus, Slater and Gordon, para 1.3.

81 *Ibid*, para 4.3.

have a primary duty to the courts and a secondary duty to their clients". It warns that:

> *there could be circumstances in which the lawyers of Slater and Gordon are required to act in accordance with these duties and contrary to other corporate responsibilities and against the interest of Shareholders or the short-term profitability of the Company.*

Similar declarations were made by the other two publicly listed law firms in Australia.

(g) Assessing these safeguards

In the United Kingdom, the jury arguably is still out on whether the regulatory safeguards on the ABS are working to avoid the risks predicted by traditionalists. Many ABS applications are still being approved; the slow application process, according to the SRA, is due to focus on engagement and risk assessment on each and every application. Whether this approach will work to proactively avoid misconduct and ensure that the standards of the profession are met, only time will tell. In September 2013, the first ABS, Hackington Ashton, collapsed and entered liquidation.[82] However, there is no reason to suggest that the ABS structure was relevant *per se* to the collapse since during the same month the SRA identified 1,200 firms at risk due to financial instability.[83] Although the SRA did not distinguish between ABS and traditional firm, since just 200 ABSs were then licensed, the large majority of these at-risk firms must be traditional firms.

In Australia, anecdotal evidence suggests that ILPs generated 65% fewer ethical complaints than traditional firms.[84] If true, this begs the question: why? Is it that the safeguards are working or is it that, having been through the process of ILP application and with the increased transparency of being a corporation, lawyers are behaving better or have better systems in place? Are alternative law firms better run and managed? A full analysis of the complaints received by UK and Australian regulators against alternative firms compared to traditional firms would be useful here, but is well beyond the scope of this chapter.

Some Australian firms have found that the shift has enhanced governance. Managing director of Slater and Gordon Andrew Grech argued that the "governance structures, disciplines and processes required of a public company ... gave assurance to banks that we are a credit worthy organisation".[85] Peter

---

82 Joanna Craig, "Solicitors Announce their Imminent Closure", *Uttoxeter Advertiser*, 27 September 2013 (www.uttoxeter-news.co.uk/News/Solicitors-announce-their-imminent-closure-20130927120000.htm).

83 Simon Goldhill, "Closures, Insolvencies and Forced Mergers: Troubled Waters in the Legal Market", Lexis Nexis, The Future of Law, 7 October 2013 (http://lexislegalintelligence.co.uk/intelligence/blawg/2013/10/closures-insolvencies-and-forced-mergers-troubled-waters-in-the-legal-market/).

84 Sam Glover, "Is it Time for Non-lawyer Ownership?" *The Lawyerist*, 24 September 2013 (http://lawyerist.com/time-for-non-lawyer-ownership/).

85 "Why are Lawyers Reluctant to Move Away from the Partnership Model?" *Lawyers Weekly*, 18 August 2011 (www.lawyersweekly.com.au/features/incorporation-why-are-law-firms-reluctant-to-move-).

Bobbin – managing principal of Argyle Lawyers, part of the ILH group, another publicly listed Australian firm – said:

> *The legal ethics and professional standards, duty of confidentiality, duty of utmost discretion, is in fact enhanced ... It is part of the auditing process to ensure we are adhering to professional standards.*[86]

Accordingly, it is arguable that the safeguards put in place in Australia have raised the bar for all firms in terms of governance. It is difficult to argue that the same has not happened in the United Kingdom, since the United Kingdom requires all firms, not just ABS, to have a COLP and COFA. In addition, the SRA, by imposing licence conditions on ABS, is for the first time sitting down with firms to assess risk and find appropriate governance solutions. This should raise awareness generally that governance must be heightened and practices improved. As a result, the governance benefits flowing from alternative firm safeguards should be reviewed carefully by traditional firms and adopted where applicable.

5. Conclusion

It is clear that good governance is not really a matter of structure. Alternative firms come in many forms and the risks emerge from the firms' decision-making process, the degree of non-lawyer control and the type of business in operation. Regulations are required to protect the client and the broader society (and indeed the profession itself) from the involvement of non-lawyers and the involvement of capital from investors expecting a return. In the United Kingdom and Australia, where 100% non-lawyer ownership of law firms is allowed, such safeguards are in place.

Given that many of the underlying tensions in alternative law firms can easily exist in traditional law firms, the challenge for the profession globally is twofold. First, how does one allow traditional law firms to innovate and meet the changing needs of clients while maintaining the core values of the profession? This requires regulators which are alert to these changes with flexible regulatory practices and lawyers and firms which are willing to openly address these risks. Lawyers working with non-lawyers need to take responsibility for ensuring not just that they maintain their own professional standards, but also that they can communicate those obligations to decision makers in a way that resonates with business objectives.

The second challenge is one which is easily neglected: whether traditional firms can learn any governance lessons from the approach that has been taken in alternative law firms. If one can reasonably argue that a client is better protected by the improved governance of an alternative law firm in, say, Australia (as stated above, ILPs generated 65% fewer ethical complaints), surely

86 *Ibid.*

traditional law firms should be rethinking their approach to governance to provide the same protection to their clients.

In the round, the answer lies in appropriate governance that looks both internally and externally. Many lawyers from outside the United Kingdom baulk at the idea of the principles in England and Wales that require the business of the law firm to be appropriately run. They should not. Many of the problems that have arisen in poorly run law firms severely affect the client. At its most extreme, a poorly run law firm is more likely to dip into client funds than a well-managed law firm that is appropriately financed and rigorously observes the basic principles of separation of monies. Similarly, even if a client does not lose money, if the law firm that is advising it collapses in the middle of a big transaction or a large and complicated case, the client may well suffer, and is certainly not well served. As lawyers, we should not be embarrassed to ensure that our businesses are well run, well managed and provide a profit for those involved in the business. This is achieved through good governance irrespective of structure.

Thus far, alternative firms have not destroyed the legal profession and only time will tell whether professional standards and the core values of independence, privilege and avoidance of conflict of interest can be upheld in the light of overt profit motives and differing degrees of non-lawyer influence. While the world watches the UK and Australian 'experiment', two observations cannot be ignored. First, as intended, alternative firms are driving innovation in the sector and increasing competition in legal services markets. This is causing a positive response from traditional firms – in the United Kingdom, this has come through a focus on quality, customer service and competitive pricing. Second, regulatory responses (safeguards) to the introduction of alternative firms have – at least in the United Kingdom, where these have been rolled out to all firms – lifted the bar in terms of governance and particularly focused on improving internal governance. These two outcomes in themselves can only be a good thing.

With the exception of some minor revisions to reflect the passage of time, this chapter is published as it appeared in the previous edition and has not been updated.

Leading change

Lisa M Walker Johnson
Walker Clark LLC

1. What the Maasai can teach law firms about change

Law firm partners everywhere can learn about leading change from the experience of the Maasai people of East Africa. Their story raises many instructive points that law firms should consider.

Killing a lion was a traditional rite of passage for adolescent Maasai boys and the only true mark of a respected warrior. Without warrior status, the young man could not find anyone who would want to marry him. He would be unable to start a family of his own and would be disgraced in his tribal community.

The Maasai people selected young leaders based on their lion-hunting prowess. The more lions a warrior killed, the greater his prestige. Solo lion hunting was respected as the ultimate test of passion and was also evidence of advanced hunting skills and extreme confidence.

For the Maasai, the killing of lions was a rational part of their traditional culture. However, in a remarkable turnaround that integrates ancient traditions with innovations, some Maasai communities are now choosing conservation over killing lions.

Why the shift? The custom of hunting lions is more than a test of manliness or a source of pride. It also has an economic purpose for the community. Lions and other big game kill domestic livestock such as cows, goats, sheep and donkeys. In doing so, they endanger the economic stability of the community and sometimes the physical safety of tribal families. The traditional response to an attack on domestic livestock was to track the predator and kill it.

This not only satisfied important economic needs, but also supported traditional Maasai culture. Maasai hunters needed to remove lions that killed livestock and would likely kill again. The Maasai also wanted to prevent lions from becoming dependent on domestic animals for food, which would also pose a risk to the safety of the people who tended them.

However, between 2001 and 2011, the environmental and economic context changed in East Africa. Hunting, combined with habitat loss, caused the lion population in Africa to drop from half a million in 1950 to fewer than 30,000 by 2013. The human population in East Africa was growing and therefore demanding more land and resources, and lions had been forced into closer proximity to tribal communities with even more people and livestock. By 2012, hunting by the Maasai and an increase in killings of lions in retaliation for attacks on livestock were major factors in an annual loss of 40% of the lion population in Kenya each year.[1]

In some areas, lions were becoming completely extirpated. If their populations could not be brought up to sustainable levels, they would disappear completely. The integrity of ecosystems was at stake and with it, the influx of tourist-based income to the region.

A fundamental part of Maasai culture had to change. Today in southern Kenya and elsewhere in East Africa, the Maasai are partnering with land preservation trusts, organisations such as Lion Guardians[2] and others to respond to these challenges.

Warriors in the Maasai culture are just as important as they always have been. However, the role of the respected male warrior is being redefined in terms of providing for the family and creating economic stability for the tribe, and no longer in terms of killing lions. For some, the status of warrior is now achieved by going to school and eventually working with others to get a job and earn money, rather than by killing a lion in a solitary rite of passage.

Maasai warriors also earn prestige as lion protectors, using new technology for tracking and migration monitoring. Traditionally viewed as experts on lion behaviour, the new warriors now educate their communities on the importance of wildlife conservation and improving the construction of livestock corrals. Technology is not the only tool, however. The Maasai even employ what could be described as 'proactive conflict mitigation' by anticipating attacks and scaring lions away from the improved livestock corrals. Usually the most effective 'technology' is banging pots and pans. Even though they are ancient, these tools still work well.

There are a number of successful arrangements in place whereby the Maasai are compensated for lost or maimed livestock through a verification and payment process. These economic incentives have had the most impact where elders and other members of the Maasai community, along with ranch administrators and local officials, all participate in developing and

1 Andrew Dubbins, "The Kenyan Maasai Who Once Hunted Lions Are Now Their Saviors," *Daily Beast*, 5 January 2021, www.thedailybeast.com/the-kenyan-maasai-who-once-hunted-lions-are-now-their-saviors.

2 Lion Guardians is a conservation organisation dedicated to finding and enacting long-term solutions for people and lions to coexist. Founded in 2006, Lion Guardians began with five guardians in one small area within the Amboseli-Tsavo ecosystem in Kenya. Currently, there are Lion Guardians-based projects successfully running in several countries and in the core area of Amboseli, with total operations spanning over close to a million acres.

Lion Guardians' conservation model is adaptable to various cultures and wildlife species. Founded on local value systems, community participation and science, it is based on a decade of research and rigorous measures of success. This approach involves recruiting young, traditional Maasai and other pastoralist warriors to learn the skills needed to effectively mitigate conflicts between people and wildlife, monitor lion populations and help their own communities to live with lions. By actively engaging in a solutions-based conservation model, people who were once lion killers are transformed into lion protectors. See http://lionguardians.org for more information.

implementing the guidelines for verifying and paying claims. Some warriors are touring the world to explain their innovative programmes and to encourage tourism and investment from philanthropic funds.

On some ranches that participate in conservation programmes, the numbers of lions are increasing and have almost returned to sustainable levels. Wildlife tourism is returning, in part due to the conservation efforts, which have dramatically increased the probability of seeing a lion in the wild. It is now illegal to hunt lions in Kenya and although violations still occur – frequently under the attempted justification of protecting livestock – the 2,000-year-old lion-hunting culture of the Maasai people has been permanently changed to respond to the environmental and ecological realities of the 21st century.

1.1 Why the Maasai changes succeeded

How could such a significant shift in thinking, values and behaviour take place in less than a decade? There are several factors that stand out, all of which have relevance for law firms implementing change:

- Committed leadership within the Maasai culture is evident from the number of ranches that are participating in conservation programmes. For example, Fathers of the Warriors – a group of men designated to teach Maasai traditions to the younger generation – began shifting their rites of passage to reject the killing of wildlife and focus instead on other tests of skill, as well as promoting a wide range of conservation activities to protect all wildlife, not only lions.[3]
- The change process embraces a broader community. Beyond the Maasai people, many others provide leadership and expertise, such as:
  - lion researchers;
  - local, national and international conservation organisations; and
  - experts in fields as diverse as geography, biology, human-environment relations, management and law.
- Data and evidence are compiled and shared with Maasai landowners, local officials and the government. This information initially confirmed the perilous state of the lion population and the changing demographics, particularly in East Africa. It also clearly linked the protection of lions, the preservation of the ecosystem and tourism to the economic future of Maasai communities.
- The information creates a compelling business case for change that financially benefits the Maasai people, as well as local, regional, national and even international stakeholders in the conservation movement.

---

3 For a presentation of the full range of educational and conservation activities that have arisen from the lion protection efforts, see the *Maasai Wilderness Conservation Trust 2022 Impact Report* (Maasai Wilderness Conservation Trust, February 2023), http://maasaiwilderness.org/wp-content/uploads/2023/02/2022-MWCT-Impact-Report-compressed.pdf.

- An informed decision-making process is used to select the strategic priorities for action.

Leading a change of such magnitude requires ongoing attention by all stakeholders, not just by those with the most formal power. In one programme, after Maasai representation in ranch governance was diminished, the Maasai felt disenfranchised. Lion hunting increased in frequency and severity and was no longer discouraged by elders. As one elder explained: "We have no reason to follow the rules."[4]

Participatory conservation interventions that respect Maasai knowledge and promote full engagement with management processes have been far more successful in persuading the Maasai to change or moderate such behaviours themselves:[5]

- Participants realise that no single action is the perfect solution. Planned change is addressed at many levels through different solutions and actions. Each has its limitations. For example, the Maasai lion conservation programme included a variety of actions, none of which would have been sufficient by itself to achieve the desired change. Some ideas needed to be tested and evaluated for risk factors and long-term effectiveness. These included:
  - financial compensation for families who lost their livestock to big game predators such as hyenas, cheetahs and jackals, as well as lions;
  - education of young Maasai men and women, with the help of the Maasai elders, to reframe their traditional perceptions and attitudes about what it means to be a Maasai warrior;
  - peer pressure in a creative agreement between one group of Maasai landowners and a local conservation organisation, in the form of collective penalties for all Maasai herders if anyone violated the rules;[6] and
  - political processes, policies and laws that supported the strategic efforts of local and regional interventions, and helped build lasting cooperative relationships that, in the case of the Maasai conservation efforts, included Maasai landowners, trustees of conservation programmes and local authorities which verified the losses of livestock and dispensed compensation payments.
- There are measurable results. Some interventions have been more successful than others; but when ranches and areas that use conservation

---

4 See comments by Mara Goldman, Colorado University, Boulder, in "Conservation Efforts might Encourage some to Hunt Lions, Study Finds", *Phys.org*, 5 August 2013, http://phys.org/news/2013-08-efforts-lions.html.

5 *Ibid.*

6 Kate Barrett, "Kenya Tribe Chooses to Save its Threatened Predators", *Conservation International*, 21 June 2007, www.conservation.org/FMG/Articles/Pages/kenyan_tribe_threatened_preadators.aspx.

> programmes are compared to those that do not, the results are impressive. Since the creation of the Lion Guardian programme in 2007, no lions have been killed for retaliatory or traditional reasons where the Lion Guardians are present. The lion population in the area has recovered to more than 60 adults and 54 cubs. The Lion Guardians have found 86% of lost livestock and have reinforced more than 500 livestock corrals, 95% of which reported no more lion break-ins.[7]

Of course, there have been and continue to be many questions about the future:

- Will non-African participants in lion conservation projects invest time and effort to understand the complex relationship between the lion and the Maasai culture?
- Will solutions take into account the complex tribal and regional political climate?
- Will local administrators respond to verification requests in a timely way?
- Will young men cease killing lions as a rite of passage?
- Will the Maasai refrain from hunting predatory game that they believe are killing their livestock?
- Will financial arrangements prove to be an effective alternative to killing lions?
- Will lion populations continue to increase to a sustainable level throughout the region?

These questions are as important today as they were when the change effort began more than 20 years ago.

The trends are very encouraging; but in the beginning, no one knew whether the proposed solutions would work. Some results were almost immediate. Other measures are taking longer to implement and come to fruition. Improvements are not always straightforward. Still, the impact of this collage of conservation initiatives is making a positive difference for lion populations overall.

Long-held perceptions and cultural values are changing. Programmes are documenting that as Maasai families begin to understand the link between their economic survival and the preservation of wildlife, they are using parallel approaches to protect lions and care for their own livestock. Families and local authorities are working in a cooperative way to fulfil their commitments to the change process.

---

7 Jenny Peek, "Guarding the Predators: Former Maasai Warriors Work to Protect Lions in Africa", *In Common* (Nelson Institute for Environmental Studies, University of Wisconsin-Madison, Spring/Summer 2012), www.nelson.wisc.edu/news/in-common/spring-summer2012/story.php?s=1409.

The warrior culture is changing. Young Maasai women still stand in line to become girlfriends of attractive future partners. However, they now demonstrate approval for young men who are going to school and getting jobs, rather than killing lions, to prove their manhood.

Economic incentives have been crucial to the success of these conservation efforts, but they are not the only motivating factor for change. There are also incentives for new conservation skills and improved job opportunities.

The Maasai and their change partners continue to face complex and unprecedented challenges. However, all of the stakeholders realise that their improvements could collapse unless they can trust each other to meet their agreed commitments.

2. Law firms must also change

Law firm partners today are asking hard questions about leading change. Their firms continuously face challenges to some of the traditional values and customs of the practice of law in a law firm, but often from unexpected sources such as a pandemic. Managing partners and other senior leaders of small, medium and large firms worldwide consistently cite[8] the following questions as being among their top concerns for the future of their firms:

- "How do you develop young leaders who will succeed as visionaries?"
- "How can we ensure that the business of practising law will be successful?"
- "How can we maintain long-term sustainable business momentum, especially when many partners have 'tunnel vision' about making money now and going to the next short-term step?"
- "How do we align changing external needs with internal people who are content with the *status quo*?"
- "How can we get our lawyers to understand the global view?"
- "How do we build merger capabilities into our firm?"
- "How do we differentiate ourselves from other excellent law firms in an increasingly competitive legal market?"
- "How can we get our partners to learn how to calculate and manage new alternative fee structures on projects?"
- "How can we pass the responsibilities for the leadership of our client relationships to talented senior and junior lawyers?"
- "How can we hire and retain good people?"
- "How can we focus on doing the right work for the right clients anywhere in the world?"

---

8 For example, in symposia and roundtable conferences organised and facilitated by Walker Clark LLC since 2002, there has been remarkable consistency in the highest-priority long-range strategic, management and operational concerns voiced by law firm leaders. Although the 'triggers' for those concerns might vary over time, the issues that they raise have remained essentially the same.

Their questions recognise that these managing partners and other law firm leaders see their inescapable roles as leaders of change in their firms. Whether it is talent retention, client care, people management, getting through a financial crisis, growth of the firm, quality control or the firm's reinvention for the 21st century, they know that major changes are inevitable and necessary for business survival.

2.1 Planned or forced change?

If lawyers do not plan for change, even if it seems inevitable, they will undoubtedly be forced into it.

Forced change happens when lawyers are unable – or simply unwilling – to predict future trends accurately and develop appropriate responses to what are often foreseeable challenges. When this happens, law firms must act quickly, without adequate preparation and with limited options.

A 'crisis environment' creates distress for lawyers, staff and clients. It also distorts the lawyers' perspective of the firm's priorities by requiring urgent attention to an immediate crisis at the expense of other competing and equally important concerns.

Any firm, or any professional person, who has gone through a period of crisis or forced change can attest to its unpleasantness. In firms, there are often problems with information flow. Productivity and relationships suffer. Power struggles emerge between partners. Cash-flow challenges create stress. People blame each other for not having foreseen the problems. People doubt themselves. Uncertainty is high and morale is low.

Forced changes may actually result in long-needed improvements, such as a change in leadership, new policies, the loss of an unprofitable client or the departure of an unproductive partner. A crisis usually shakes people out of their complacency and creates a high sense of urgency for change, but at what cost?

Waiting for a crisis to occur before making improvements obviously has its risks. In addition to the internal problems, clients may lose confidence in the firm's ability to plan for or respond appropriately and quickly enough to their changing needs.

Unable or unwilling to speak candidly and objectively about a crisis, partners often bury their resentments and concerns without resolving them. Rather than raise these concerns, they push onward 'for the good of the firm'. Not learning from their past mistakes, they tend to repeat them again and again.

2.2 Implementing change: what should leaders expect and what should they prepare for?

Implementing planned change is undoubtedly a high-stakes business proposition for law firms, regardless of size, client base or region. More often than not, doing it well becomes a matter of survival.

What should law firm leaders expect and what should they prepare for? There are eight key points that managing partners need to know about the change process in law firms.

(a) *A significant investment*

Implementing planned change typically involves a significant investment of the partners' time and intellect. Without their leadership, critical thinking and analysis, and ongoing involvement, planned change in law firms is doomed. Partners' roles cannot be delegated to staff – principally because, unlike in other businesses, the partners are the decision makers, the business owners, the principal revenue producers, the firm's front-line salesforce and the primary contacts with clients.

(b) *Impact on productivity and teamwork*

It is natural during times of change to experience feelings of uncertainty, confusion, frustration and even anger. It is uncomfortable when partners are initially asked to work in a way they have not been trained for, such as conducting peer performance reviews with each other or building a new – albeit more profitable – practice area. Associates may have difficulties adjusting to increased performance expectations and moving the law firm from one location to another is always challenging. There is a natural transition that leaders can anticipate as people let go of the old and get used to the new.

Whether and how they do this is shaped by the fact that people adjust to change in different ways and at different rates. The level of stress caused by an anticipated or pending change can significantly affect people's individual reactions and their readiness to commit to actions. This in turn affects the speed and facility with which commitment can be expected to be built in a group.

There is much that leaders can do to build resilience and prepare their colleagues for change. These leadership actions include the following:

- Pay close attention to small indicators of stress in order to resolve and minimise fears and distractions;
- Stay engaged;
- Educate people about what to expect in a change process;
- Accept that power dynamics may create barriers to change;
- Assume that feedback from others will be necessary;
- Plan to communicate and involve others;
- Make the time to analyse and interpret data before jumping into solutions;
- Check in with each other regularly to get relevant information and show support;
- Remind yourselves that you are not always right;

- Set a good example; and
- Take pre-emptive action whenever possible.[9]

Partners usually expect a temporary downturn in productivity and teamwork, depending on the scale and scope of the change initiative. Some might use this as a reason not to change: "It's a nice idea, but we can't afford it right now." This is why it is important for the leaders of change to be able to point to plausible, tangible benefits that will result. Any loss of productivity and fee revenue during the change process can therefore be properly characterised as a short-term investment that should produce a positive long-term dividend.

When partners propose change, others in the firm want to know how it will affect them personally. They may have questions and objections. Keeping a climate of openness where people can ask questions and discuss objections will save time later. It takes time to explain changes so that others will understand and cooperate with firm management and each other.

Encouraging ideas from others on how to implement change in a way that will minimise any anticipated short-term negative impacts will aid the smooth and efficient implementation of needed actions. The more informed people are, the better equipped they will be to make informed decisions about how to contribute to the change process and make it go well.

At the same time, people can only make a fully informed and intelligent decision about whether something new is working when they commit to trying to make it work. Ask for their cooperation in deferring objections for a set period of time, so that they can focus better on present work requirements and give 100% to the change. Afterwards, each person will be in a better position to assess whether the change is working for him or her.

Give people time to adjust. Encourage them to modify unrealistic expectations. Any change – such as requirements for new skills, tools, technologies, management structures or policies – will require an investment of time and energy before people resume previous levels of productivity. If the change is managed well, people will soon have the capabilities to exceed previous levels of productivity. If a transition is managed well, teamwork is an observable by-product.

The experiences of successful change leaders in law firms suggest some clear and consistent guidelines:

- Do not overreact to dips in productivity and teamwork, or assume that they indicate deep resistance to change.
- During this time, help others to look at their own personal strengths and how these can be applied in new situations.

9 Lisa M Walker Johnson, *Stress and Burnout in Law Firms: Leadership Challenges and Choices* (Globe Law and Business, 2022), pp63–69.

- Ensure that fee earners can set and manage realistic deadlines during the transition, so that they are not creating more frustration for themselves and others.
- Maintain contact with all levels of the firm, so that you know how people are perceiving the changes and how stress is affecting their reactions to it.

(c) Involvement of others

The more that partners need commitment from other people in the firm, the more they should involve other fee earners, staff and sometimes even clients at points in the change process, as appropriate to the role of each.

Even when the partners make the decision about what strategic priorities the firm will undertake, if they expect buy-in, they should still involve others in planning how these strategies will be translated into action and within what timeframes.

Use one-to-one conversations and small group discussions to deal with specific concerns and generate ideas. This is usually much more effective in encouraging people to adapt to change than even the best-written email or the most inspiring speech.

Some leaders feel more comfortable building buy-in or needed cooperation one on one. However, if this is done to the exclusion of meeting with groups, implementation is at risk, because most changes require teamwork and group support to get the desired results.

(d) Leadership role in planning

The more involved leaders are, especially in certain aspects of planning, the smoother a change process will go. People will look to them to confirm priorities and provide resources including training, coaching and opportunities for practice and feedback.

Leaders have a unique level of authority in defining what success will look like and what the firm is striving to achieve. Their behaviour will be observed closely by others to send important signals about how seriously the firm takes a change initiative. Especially with organisation-wide changes, evidence that the partners are working together in a timely and thorough way on planning increases others' optimism that change will actually take place. It also strengthens their resolve to contribute productively.

Planning will help in bringing to the surface and addressing or deferring objections that some partners might have to the proposed changes. In many instances, what appears to be opposition from partners is really an expression of a desire for more information. They do not oppose all changes – only those which appear to be *ad hoc* improvisation.

Waiting for a crisis to occur before implementing change is an excellent way to minimise buy-in from the partnership and derail the type of planning that will ensure successful and sustainable outcomes for the firm and its clients. Using a structured approach to planning in the context of a three-step change process (ie, anticipate, plan and execute), described later in this chapter, partners can ensure that their planning is well informed, efficient and effective.

Planning is a skill. It can be learned. The types of planning methods and tools can range from simple to complex, from a six-step delegation model to in-depth business contingency planning. When leaders are less informed about the benefits of planning and the ways to go about it, they tend to procrastinate about planning itself and about the actions they want to take to address needs.

When lawyers have opportunities to gain experience with planning, it becomes second nature. With a wide range of planning methods that are supported and modelled by leaders in the workplace, everyone in the organisation is better prepared to contribute to change.

When lawyers have well-informed plans, and especially when those plans are documented, they have greater flexibility to prioritise their time. Even when urgent matters come up, people stay the course with longer-term goals because they understand the purpose behind the goal and what is at stake; and they know how to get back into it in a step-by-step fashion, modifying timelines and their actions as needed.

(e) Avoid procrastination

Seeing the need for change and actually acting on it with commitment and purpose are two different things. Just as leaders need plans to avoid procrastination, they also need to talk about their past experiences with procrastination so they can avoid similar problems in the future.

For example, a common phenomenon in law firms is partner procrastination about decisions to admit associates to the partnership. This occurs most often when the firm has no objective career development plan in place. Senior associates are often compelled to look outside their own firm to feel appreciated and valued. When senior associates hand in their resignations or threaten to leave, the partners jump into action, making long overdue promotion decisions to 'keep people happy'. Too often, lawyers are given junior partner status before they have the business development and management skills needed to contribute adequately to the firm's bottom line.

When partners are experiencing a 'crisis', they typically have fewer options. In this case, they may even resent the senior associate for pressuring them into a decision that they themselves know they should have anticipated and acted on, perhaps years before. It's evident that lawyers and their leaders can't stay productive if they are just reacting to one crisis after the next.

Assessing 'what went wrong' in the past is not meant to self-incriminate or blame oneself or others. The purpose is to identify behavioural tendencies or organisational limitations that contributed to disappointing results in order to plan how to improve in the future. The willingness to consider our past experiences and learn from them is likely to build confidence about working through future problems together. This strengthens professional relationships and optimism in stressful and difficult times that are often brought about by changes in our organisations.

(f) ***Addressing cultural obstacles honestly***

Without realising it, many partners want to keep the old culture with the same old rules, but with different results. They plan for change, but they do not introduce the thinking and behaviours that are required to support it.

In one law firm, the partners implemented a new career development plan. They hoped that clarity about how one progressed in the firm would automatically motivate the lawyers and improve productivity.

The partners defined career paths and promised to conduct annual performance reviews. However, they did nothing to respond to the associates' previously stated concerns about the absence of feedback throughout the year. Nor did they follow through on the associates' requests for greater predictability about compensation and bonuses.

The partners basically wanted to pacify the associates and achieve different results, but they were still clinging to their old 'sink-or-swim' culture of professional development. They did not want to change their own behaviour or pressure their peers to change either.

They attempted to rationalise their past actions by explaining that their *ad hoc* feedback about technical work should be sufficient performance feedback for associates. Although some partners were better at frequent feedback than others, they confessed that they didn't really have the skills or the time to have periodic performance and development discussions with associates.

Obviously even the most elegant and insightful career management plan is doomed from the start if the partners are not willing to look honestly at cultural values and current behaviours – in this example, the 'sink-or-swim' method of professional development – that need to be changed.

(g) ***Dynamics of the change process: conflict, confusion and inertia***

Partners operate at fairly high levels of stress and constructive conflict every day. Sometimes they have very little in reserve to adapt to change – particularly unexpected, forced change in which they experience what feels like, and perhaps is, a loss of control over their clients and their careers. Mergers and acquisitions result in a particularly complicated and challenging work environment.

Partners and staff alike need reassurance, information, patient explanations and clear expectations about the 'what' of the change, along with opportunities to give input and get involved in the 'how' of the implementation.

Firms minimise negative stress by anticipating what needs to change so that they can take steps to plan those changes in advance of a crisis. This approach increases their capacity to respond in a timely and effective way to further change requirements. Continuous improvements can be made without a lot of confusion, political posturing and upheaval, because the necessary foundations for change – including documented goals and plans – are already in place. Lawyers are more likely to follow through on their commitments and change does not stall during long periods of inaction.

To overcome inertia, the need for change must be so strong that it overrides the partners' natural tendencies to proceed with 'business as usual'. Having reliable information and credible, persuasive evidence of the need for change discourages complacency and instead promotes action. There needs to be a clear and compelling reason to do things differently, as well as ongoing incentives for the partners to follow through on their commitments, financial and otherwise. Even then, people often fail to perceive what is right in front of them, which should be obvious. Therefore, change leaders should always be aware of fixed mindsets and paradigms that might blur the relevance and importance of the data for some people[10] and understand how to address these tendencies.

(h) Changing partners' perceptions

Planned change that is actually implemented often requires a significant shift in partner perceptions about their roles in the change process.

There are two vital shifts in partner perceptions that aid a change process. The first is for every partner to accept the need to work on one's own knowledge, skills and leadership behaviours if he or she expects others to contribute their best efforts to the change process. Partners can only lead if they have earned the respect of their peers and professional colleagues in the firm. Structured feedback from one's peers, colleagues and even clients, along with leadership coaching, is an excellent way to understand where one's strengths and weaknesses are – as perceived by yourself and, even more importantly, those who depend on you to lead.

The second shift in perceptions about one's role is to let go of the urgent desire to fix or control everyone else. My colleagues and I often hear the complaint: "I understand the need to change; it's my partners who don't get it!" This usually translates as: "I have the right answer about what we need to do and it's my job to fix those who disagree with me." A mindset of "I'm right; you're wrong" is more likely to cause arguments and resistance than to stimulate the communication and collaboration needed to shift others' thinking.

10 See *ibid*, pp154–157, for a further discussion of the effect of fixed mindsets as obstacles in a change process.

At the group level, in many instances, influencing the partnership's perceptions about the strategic and business context of their shared future feels more difficult than implementing the changes in organisational structures, policies and procedures that respond to the emerging realities.

Shorter term, partners will want to work together in conditions that allow them to relate to each other differently. Partners will not get different results if they use the same approaches with the same set of assumptions, interpersonal dynamics and information. There are numerous effective ways to shift partner perceptions and explore what they are willing and able to accomplish together as a partnership depending on their purpose, urgency, available data and many other factors. Methods of engagement vary and could encompass anything from a simple senior-level structured group meeting on a particular topic to more complex strategic planning processes that promote decision making by involving multiple stakeholders in finding common ground.

Partners may use one-on-one conversations to improve the quality of their interactions, learning to share different views in a constructive way in order to make decisions and move forward. Using a communication structure such as a learning conversation provides an intellectual roadmap for lawyers to use in conversations that otherwise may be more difficult. Leaders learn over time that they exert more positive influence over others' perceptions and outcomes if they take a more consultative approach. In addition, they have many choices about how to encourage greater open-mindedness and collaboration, depending on factors such as the purpose of the interaction, the level of urgency, the willingness of their colleagues to participate in feedback and the types of desired change.[11]

A longer-term proposition, improving the partnership's effectiveness as a leadership team, can achieve concrete results in less than six months.

In many cases, the partnership as a group – as opposed to the individual partners – has not functioned effectively for years. Decision making in group meetings, for example, may have typically resulted in a lack of follow-through on commitments. Second guessing behind closed doors after a meeting may be standard operating procedure. In other cases, only certain partners may speak up, while others keep silent, not voicing what they want to say.

These conditions are not uncommon and are surmountable if a partnership wants to improve its effectiveness. At an interpersonal level, when partners really start listening to each other; when they are more willing to start saying

11 See *ibid*, pp36–38, on strategies that leaders can use to be more effective in influencing and building buy-in for needed change, such as engaging senior leadership; pp75–78, on quality interactions and conversations; pp84–95, on well-informed choices in dealing with disagreements; pp119–123, on having learning conversations; pp139–141, on the use of questions; pp129–135, on engagement with groups; pp165–168, on seeing through the 'eye of the beholder'; pp173–178, on working through disagreements and building consensus; and pp213–217, on continuous questioning of one's own mindset and a realistic balancing of optimism and pessimism.

what needs to be said; and when they make the time to ask questions, learn from and encourage each other, their capacity as a group to perform increases incrementally.

However, they also need the feedback and tools to realistically assess what the group needs to do to improve its performance as a team and which types of leadership behaviours will best support it. In this way, members of the partnership stop thinking in terms of how to change one another and start thinking in terms of what they can achieve by working together and how they will do it.

3. Building continuous change capacity and resilience: what do leaders need to do?

How do managing partners and other firm leaders build into their firms and their lawyers a continuous capacity to change? How do they ensure that their firms can adapt and respond rapidly and efficiently to the changing business environment?

The strategy is very straightforward, although not necessarily simple. Partners who are successful change leaders pay attention to the following six components every day, not just when a problem or crisis occurs. Together these components create a strong but flexible foundation of engagement to support continuous change and resilience in the organisation. By reducing the need for reactive improvisation and unfocused experimentation, these six components improve efficiency in the decision-making process and provide a higher probability of sustainable success.

As has been the case with the Maasai lion conservation initiative and the substantial economic, social and cultural changes it produced, each of these six components can be observed in law firms that lead change effectively.

3.1 Component 1: Committed leadership

Planned change involves more than learning new terminology or benchmarking best practices which, even as industry standards, may not be relevant or useful to a specific law firm.

Implementing planned change also requires visible and engaged leadership that does not get distracted from the firm's strategic priorities. Leadership can come in many shapes and sizes. It can be charismatic and noisy. It can be quietly effective, building upon credible relationships over time. Sometimes the firm needs a stronger touch, more direction and less consultation. Sometimes just the opposite is true. Effective leaders understand the needs of people in the firm for direction, information and skills. They choose specific leadership behaviours that meet existing needs and help others transition to greater ownership and interdependence over time. All the firm's members nonetheless have leadership responsibilities in a change process, commensurate with their respective roles and duties.

Formal leadership usually comes from inside the firm, from a managing partner, practice group head or other person with designated management responsibilities. Leadership can also come from outside the firm, from experts who bring important information and needed skills, and to whom the firm can outsource some of the time investment required for successful achievement of the strategic priorities of the firm.

Partners influence the thinking and behaviour of their peers and others in the firm. There are certain messages that only the partners can get others to take seriously. In most cases, partners are those who define what success is and what the firm is striving to achieve. Their credibility is based on the fact that they are the rainmakers, the business developers, the professionals whom lawyers in the firm look up to and in most cases greatly respect – for their longevity and connections, if nothing else. The partnership, as a group, can be a key leadership force in the firm with important collective responsibilities during a change process.

(a) Four key leadership messages

There are four areas of committed leadership that partners can demonstrate, individually and collectively, during a change process which will increase their chances of success. They may need to test periodically to ensure these messages are getting through to those involved in, and impacted by, change.

The four important messages from partners are as follows:

- The planned change will be reinforced and rewarded: Change is something that all partners take seriously. It is not a fad that will disappear in a few months. Most importantly, it is an expectation for which all relevant parties will be accountable, including the partners. When even a few senior partners are allowed to 'do their own thing' at the expense of a firm-wide change initiative, firm members stop believing that positive change is really possible.
- The planned change will improve the strength and profitability of the firm: It will achieve strategic priorities such as improved services to clients, internal growth, expanded market presence and the development of capabilities to assess and take advantage of sudden opportunities, such as merger overtures. If a clear and compelling purpose for the change is not communicated and understood by affected parties, such as firm members and even clients, commitment and support will waver. This is usually the first indication that the change initiative will probably fail.
- The planned change will make everyone's professional lives more satisfying and financially rewarding: Members of law firms are professional adults who have the right to make career choices that benefit themselves and their families. Aspirations, priorities, values and

development requirements will vary among individuals and over time. Partners sometimes take an approach that "If it was good enough for me, it's good enough for them", without realising how damaging this is to the future of the firm. Creating a motivating work environment is a continuous challenge, a work in progress; but there are none more motivated to help partners achieve it than those who live in the firm every day and who in many cases have dedicated their professional careers to its future success. Partners who convey realistic optimism about the future, backed by supportive actions, get high marks in leadership feedback.

- The planned change will be achieved only through collective firm-wide commitment and actions: Change needs participation from all. However, partners can be held to a higher standard. They are in a unique position to raise issues, organise resources, make decisions, provide direction, set goals, support and encourage, coach and mentor, and set expectations for professional behaviour and performance. If they do not do these things, who will?

3.2 Component 2: Data and evidence

Managing partners frequently comment that they need something that will shake their partners out of their complacency – something that will make them think and help them to understand the opportunities and risks they face.

A good way to do this is by collecting and facing the facts together.

When law firms decide to review their strategic priorities to identify areas that need to be changed, most of them assign the preparation phase of the project to a group of selected partners and lawyers. Firms that do this well try to put together a group of lawyers who represent different viewpoints and constituencies in the firm, and who also have the respect of their peers for being reasonable and objective. It may seem easier and more efficient to have a group of people who are likely to quickly agree with each other, but the results usually suffer. One of the strengths of diversity is that it usually produces stronger, more reliable analysis. It also builds broader base support in the firm and achieves better long-term results.

Data collection and feedback are critical at this point to facilitating well-informed communication and decisions about whether change is needed and, if so, what changes are necessary and how to implement them. Law firms that are successful at implementing change usually collect a broad range of types of information from diverse sources to integrate into their analysis of the options and priorities. The five most common examples are as follows:

- They collect forecasts about relevant external trends at several levels, including international, regional and local. Sometimes there are early signs of trends that have profound implications for an industry sector or practice area. These are easily overlooked but could be very important to the economic future of a practice area or of an entire law firm.

- They consider the firm's significant internal trends and their probable future directions. This is essential to ensure development and to test planning assumptions. For example, if the firm is having difficulty retaining associates beyond the second or third year, this could have profound implications for the long-term viability of the partnership. Unintentionally, partners may have an inflated opinion of their own leadership capabilities and, as a result, might be overly optimistic about what is going on in the firm. This is a common phenomenon with most leaders. Being aware of this tendency helps partners to avoid their 'blind spots'. Having this data can alert partners to risks of which they may not even be aware.
- They seek input from members of the firm on relevant issues related to their perceptions and day-to-day experiences. For example, if associate productivity appears to be a major factor in declining fee revenue, input from associates is obviously essential to any intelligent approach to the issue. (Yet a surprising number of partners still issue standards for associates' billable hours with no input whatsoever from the associates who are expected to comply with these decrees.) The firm's leaders should also collect information about other aspects, such as the accuracy and ease of use of the firm's time and billing system, as well as policies and actual procedures within practice groups. Individual interviews, focus groups and internal surveys can be efficient and helpful sources of information about stress levels and obstacles to productivity, problem solving and innovation.
- Client input is essential to any contemplated change that might affect the delivery of client services. Soliciting client comments, where relevant, is an excellent way to identify any potentially undesirable consequences of a proposed change that people inside the firm might not foresee. Client surveys and interviews of selected clients are excellent ways to collect data and check the firm's internal assumptions. They are also excellent marketing tools, because most clients appreciate it when their opinions are sought about issues in the firm. They are reassured to know that their legal advisers are anticipating both their current and future needs, and will have the capacity to respond with necessary changes.
- Like client input, information about the industry sectors that the firm serves is critical to planning change. This includes, for example, specific business objectives and concerns of the firm's best clients. This information helps to ensure that the changes will not only have internal benefits for the firm, but also – more importantly – have positive competitive consequences. Change management should always have a market

orientation. The question should not be just: "Will this make us a better law firm?" Successful firms also ask: "How will this help us to differentiate ourselves from all of the other excellent law firms with which we compete?" The true masters of change management in law firms go even further: "How will we communicate these differentiating improvements to our existing client base, as well as to potential clients in our market?"

3.3 Component 3: A compelling business case with financial markers

When a significant change is proposed, the first question that some law firm partners ask is: "What is the business case for this?" That is a very good question and one worthy of discussion among all the partners.

Changes are more likely to be adopted if the proponents present a compelling and reasonably well-documented rationale, which defines and quantifies the effects of the *status quo*, as well as the risks of continuing with business as usual. It should also include a reasonable estimate of the costs of implementation actions. These cost estimates should include two frequently overlooked but potentially expensive items:

- the value of partner time needed for implementation; and
- opportunity costs arising from a diversion of the firm's attention to managing the changes and away from other proposals, ideas or initiatives that are competing for management attention.

3.4 Component 4: A well-informed process

The best-led changes in law firms are the product of a well-informed process that maintains a steady reference to the firm's strategic priorities, even when the changes might require a major adjustment to the firm's strategy.

Law firms that manage change well and get the best results consider the implementation of change initiatives as a process – like the litigation of a court case – rather than a single event. They understand that results cannot be achieved at a partners' meeting or at a weekend retreat. Even when the strategic or business issues are urgent, one hears statements in these firms such as, "It is better to do this well than to do it in haste", in contrast to the panicked immobilisation that one often observes in law firm partnerships that try to rely on a crisis to force decisions and demand changes.

3.5 Component 5: Other actions and solutions that fit the unique characteristics of the firm

What happens when a change implementation goes wrong, producing none of the desired results – only disappointing ones or even counterproductive ones? Even if an obvious response could be, "Partners didn't follow through on their commitments", there is a reason for this. Failed implementation sometimes arises from a failure to fully anticipate the change. This involves considering multiple options in advance, taking into account the unique characteristics of the firm, such as areas of expertise, client base, the legal talents of its people and the workplace culture.

Four questions can be very effective tests of the thinking and commitment of a partnership when it considers an idea for change:

- "How does this change respond to our strategic priorities?"
- "How would it affect our ability to deliver our business plan?"
- "What are our realistic options – particularly in light of our knowledge about the market, our firm's culture and the capabilities and current stress levels of our lawyers?"
- "Is this the right time – are we ready, willing and able to lead this change?"

This does not require endless hours in interviews and group meetings looking backwards. However, these four questions help law firm partners to be sure that they have considered, honestly and realistically, their firm's current expectations and capabilities – in terms of both strengths and vulnerabilities – in the context of proposed change. This should be done before planning the change even begins.

The experience of one law firm offers a good case study in the realistic assessment of different actions and solutions. This firm had lost an entire generation of lawyers during a financial crisis. The partners met to develop a plan for recruiting and developing a new core group of junior and lateral hires. They identified priorities and started to assign responsibilities to each other.

As they talked about their shared history in the firm, their career aspirations and their current life priorities, one senior partner said: "I do not want to spend my time building this firm back up. The solutions are right, but do we really have the collective will to implement our plans?"

The room was silent. The group of partners, all in their 50s, looked at each other and said "No!"

At that point, the discussion shifted to how they could merge with or join other firms in the region so that they could continue to practise individually, but without the management responsibilities that the proposed change would incur. Without the thoughtful candour and enquiry of one senior partner, the group may have gone down a frustrating path that did not fit the individual priorities of the partners.

Since partners are so key to the success of any change in the firm, it is important for them to consider the extent to which their own dynamics affect the ability of the firm to select and implement certain solutions or actions.

Sometimes past disappointments and issues of control can be silent killers of candour and cooperation, let alone future success. It is important for the partners to acknowledge and challenge these dynamics so that they do not dictate the terms and conditions for moving forward. If the past is hijacking the future of your firm, it is a problem that the partners must discuss and resolve.

Skilled external specialists can be effective resources in addressing and dealing with sensitive partner dynamics. With assistance, these blockages in communication can be resolved so that partners avoid procrastination, abdication of responsibilities or worse. These discussions are sometimes difficult. However, if managed well, they are often not as difficult as the partners feared. New alliances will emerge and old wounds can disappear almost overnight when partners turn their energies to shared priorities and a common purpose.

Never underestimate the importance and the complexities of a firm's culture in evaluating options. For example, partners sometimes ask: "We know that we have a strong business case for the merger; but can our two firms get along and each implement the changes that will be needed for us to be successful together?"

Cultural due diligence is a useful and systematic way to assess the cultural, structural, group dynamics, management and leadership issues that are present in the firms considering a merger or a firm considering a major change initiative. These factors could be strengths or could create barriers to important synergies. In a merger, knowing in advance how best to leverage the unique qualities and characteristics of each firm improves the probability of success and can eliminate most of the risk of disappointing results. Those options, however, must be identified with reference to the culture, expectations and change readiness of each firm, and not by following a generic methodology for mergers.

Law firms that rely on a change implementation philosophy of "We'll cross that bridge when we come to it" seldom recover from failed change. That failure can then undermine goodwill, feed cynicism and dampen productivity. It becomes a further obstacle to future change: "Why should we bother? Look at what happened the last time."

3.6 Component 6: Shared measurable results

The strongest pieces of evidence of the success of the change management strategy in the Maasai lion conservation were in the numbers: growth of the lion population, retrieval of strayed livestock and fewer lion attacks due to reinforced corrals. Those numbers are monitored to measure the overall effectiveness of the programme and to identify and address points where it has not been working as well as planned.

Reasonable estimates of costs and benefits are important elements of a compelling business case for making the decision for change, as discussed in section 3.3 above with respect to the need for a compelling business case with financial markers.[12] These are possibly even more important during the implementation process, for two reasons:

12 See section 3.3 above concerning the need for a compelling business case with financial markers.

- Published progress measurements help to sustain support for change and to discourage those who want to return to the old way; and
- More importantly, they can be highly reliable indicators of implementation actions that are not delivering expected results. Failure to achieve the targets at a progress point would be an indicator that implementation is not proceeding as planned, and that a management review and possible adjustments are needed. Inquiry and intervention at the first sign of a problem can prevent an implementation issue from deteriorating over time into a crisis that could jeopardise the entire initiative.

Progress measurements are perhaps the most effective tool to avoid one of the most frequent causes of failed innovation: sunk cost bias. Sunk cost bias is what causes partners and managers to respond to a failing initiative by saying: "We have already invested so much in this project that we cannot afford to quit now."

Qualitative indicators of progress – ones that are not expressed as numbers – can also be important. For example, it is difficult to measure accurately changes in attitudes, such as 'teamwork' or 'dedication to clients'. It is relatively easy, however, to observe specific behaviours that are indicative of these attributes and that can be measured by factors such as frequency of occurrence before, during and after a change. Clients are more likely to provide qualitative indicators about changes in a law firm that serves them. Therefore, qualitative measurements can sometimes be even more compelling, in terms of their long-term strategic importance to the firm, than the literal numbers.

3.7 Assembling the six components

Partners who lead change successfully in law firms throughout the world incorporate these six leadership components into a practical three-step framework: anticipate, plan and execute.[13] In the following examples, change initiatives for improving partner performance use these three steps.[14]

---

13 For a detailed exposition of this 'assembly' process, its benefits and its requirements for the best possible results, see Walker Johnson (n 9), pp186–193. See also Lisa M Walker Johnson, "From Strategic Planning to Strategic Success: the '3x3' model", *Walker Clark World View Library* (8 April 2017), www.walkerclark.com/worldview-blog/previous-worldview-posts/269-from-strategic-planning-to-strategic-success.html; and the linked paper, Lisa M Walker Johnson, *Implementing Strategic Priorities in the Legal Profession* (Walker Clark LLC, 2017).

14 The "Good governance and partner performance" chapter examines in greater depth the cultural, social and interpersonal dynamics of partner performance. This example looks at improving partner performance in the context of a structured change process, with an emphasis on leadership actions that are most likely to get desired results. The three steps sometimes overlap and implementation is not always completely linear; however, actions at each step in the change process are equally important.

(a) *Step 1: Anticipate*

The author has observed consistently that when leaders take actions that help lawyers to anticipate change – as both necessary and achievable – organisations are more resilient.

Lawyers who anticipate well discuss opportunities, issues and problems first. As the need becomes clearer, they then identify multiple responses and solutions, considering the pros and cons of possible approaches. Next, they reach tentative conclusions about what needs to be done and why in order to address an opportunity or a problem.

In this step, lawyers also look to the future. They spot vital signs and symptoms that might represent future risks. They understand legal and regulatory, economic, political and social trends that are changing the businesses of their clients and competitors, as well as their own organisations. They consider the consequences of these evolving business forces on requirements for lawyer knowledge, skills, capacity and professional ethics, including changes in lawyer expectations for their own careers and how they work. Then they select priorities for action and plan accordingly, in advance of a crisis.

So, performance improvement initiatives should develop an understanding of the following issues before implementing changes to policy and performance expectations:

- "Why should we do this?" For example, consider how a group performance issue specifically links to and affects the ability of the firm to deliver the business plan or achieve a strategic priority.
- "Do we have all the relevant and persuasive data that we need?" Assess your confidence levels about its accuracy and reliability.
- "What are the potential costs?" Consider:
  - the value of the partner time that will be required to address the performance issue;
  - the impact of the requirement for ongoing management attention to partner performance; and
  - whether there is likely to be a return on that investment.
- "Do we understand the root cause(s) of the underperformance or performance concern?" The work climate and internal systems in a legal organisation motivate and inhibit certain behaviours through the policies, structures and even leadership behaviours that a lawyer interacts with on a daily basis. Lawyers can develop more effective responses to problems when they can analyse and understand why the conditions exist and what is influencing their choices. Often performance concerns are most effectively addressed in multiple ways with consultation between the two parties. Prescriptive edicts to 'change' by simply 'trying harder' are demeaning to an achievement-

oriented professional and rarely produce more than superficial results.[15]

- "What are our options?" For example, it is important to be open to and possibly explore reasonable options before and certainly during performance discussions with partners. Understanding the root causes of performance issues guides the selection of priority courses of action.
- "What and how could things go wrong?" Lawyers routinely ask these questions when advising clients, but often overlook them when discussing and making decisions about planning for and addressing performance problems. For example, "What if we invest in coaching for this partner and she leaves? Are we agreed that we want to do our best to keep her regardless?"
- "What will success look like?" Those who are addressing performance concerns with their partners should confirm, before committing to changes, that they all envision the same desired results, as well as the measurements that will be used to help to assess progress. For example, "What do we agree are the specific elements of a quality performance discussion with one of our peers?"

(b) *Step 2: Plan*

In the second step, lawyers plan the needed changes by creating and documenting their action plans and goals, based on the well-informed decisions in Step 1. Even less than 'perfect' planning is better than no planning at all. As an example, law firms that, even by their own admission, had poor business plans prior to the COVID-19 pandemic in 2020–2021 were more adept at doing course corrections than those lawyers who had none. They said that they at least had some internal structure in place that gave them a starting point to discuss and evaluate what they needed to change in terms of expectations, revision of goals and financial priorities.

The author has also observed that when lawyers and their leaders use planning to discuss and document actions that they will take to deal with unexpected events or obstacles to success, they feel more optimistic and in control.

Planning flows naturally if adequate attention has been paid to the priorities of Step 1. Nonetheless, goals do not guarantee success. Performance goals can actually undermine resilience when they:

- are fixated solely on numbers;
- are imposed from the top with no consultation;
- are 'fixed in concrete';

15 The root causes of performance problems and their negative influences on a workplace culture almost always lie deep in the systems and processes by which the organisation works. A systems approach, characterised by multi-level inquiry – "Ask *why* five times!" – is more effective than repeating the same old admonitions and threats. See Walker Johnson (n 9), pp200–212.

- are used to 'send a message';
- lack planned support (eg, feedback, development and resources); and
- lack adequate financial and non-financial incentives.

For example, for there to be sustainable improvement in a partner's performance, the improvement process itself – what people actually do differently or 'better' – must be specific. This requires answers to questions such as the following:

- "What actions will we take?" These must be defined in terms of concrete steps and observable behaviours, not vague improvements such as a 'better' attitude, 'more professional' conduct or better delegation practices.
- "Who will do them?" Improvement of a lawyer's performance involves more than just actions and behaviours by that lawyer. Performance problems almost always involve work processes in the firm, not just individual shortcomings, and solutions usually require the support of colleagues. Sometimes the most powerful supportive question to be asked by a leader in a performance recovery situation for a partner is: "What do you need from me?" These supporting roles should be assigned.
- "When should we expect results?" It is counterproductive to set unrealistic deadlines or deliver ultimatums. However, the improvement plan should set a realistic timeframe for observable improvements and possibly interim milestones at which progress can be assessed and adjustments made as necessary to achieve the partner's performance improvement objectives.

(c) Step 3: Execute

When specific, measurable, agreed, realistic and time-based goals are documented during planning, lawyers and their leaders can begin to execute with confidence. They have already negotiated and agreed to certain actions and responsibilities. The priorities, expectations and consequences of success or failure to meet goals would also have been discussed during planning.

What's left is just to do it! During this step, lawyers achieve their goals. They follow up on commitments; measure and discuss results; make 'course corrections'; and remain open to new opportunities and risks. They also stay alert, taking nothing for granted.

No matter how thoughtfully lawyers construct their plans, things happen that may affect how realistic their commitments really are. Obstacles, such as time and resources, are not an excuse to derail the goals, but they are very important for the lawyer who owns the improvement to flag changes and concerns for discussion in a timely way, so that both parties can address them together. This doesn't mean that the goals themselves actually change.

However, it's important for lawyers to stay flexible – for example, during the implementation of a performance improvement plan. This means staying open to new ideas and adapting to changing internal and external circumstances.

If progress is not being observed, it is important to understand why and make adjustments to improve the probability of success. If, as is frequently the case, progress is better than expected, it also is important to understand why, so that the positive factors can be incorporated into how the firm manages individual performance, especially at the partner level.

Whether performance improvement efforts are successful or disappointing, one point is clear: partners have a choice to act in accordance with their performance commitments. If they feel that the element of choice is seriously compromised by circumstances beyond their control, they have a responsibility to discuss their real or perceived inability to follow through as originally planned. The parties then need to come to an understanding about priorities and determine whether expectations will be adjusted by, for example, providing more time to complete a task, more opportunities for practice with feedback or a different financial target.

An inflexible plan can be as ineffective and frustrating as no plan when trying to achieve goals. However, a plan that has not been brought up to date to reflect current expectations and commitments during a period of execution becomes highly risky to the professional relationship and business outcomes.

During the execution of performance improvement plans, all the partners involved should remain alert to these issues:

- "Are we on track with our goal(s)?"
- "Are all the goals still relevant?"
- "To what extent do we need to revise the goals or our plans to achieve them?"
- "Are the priorities shifting?"
- "Should we reconsider the goals in light of changed circumstances?"

Even when individual performance is the issue, improved performance almost always involves a group effort.

3.8 Three conditions for success

Performance improvement is a change process; and as with any other significant change in a law firm, the ultimate success of the plan – no matter how brilliantly anticipated, carefully planned or flexibly executed – is heavily influenced by three conditions for success: documentation, collaboration and measuring and sharing results:

- Without documentation in each of the three steps of the change process, the resulting ambiguity causes stress and distraction, which only increases the longer that documentation remains unaddressed.

- Without collaboration in each of the three steps, the amount and reliability of information are greatly reduced, relationships suffer and trust deteriorates.
- Without measurement and sharing of results appropriate to the tasks in each of the three steps, there is no agreement about what success should be, could be or is. Motivation decreases, priorities become blurred and untested assumptions lead to misunderstandings and worse.[16]

4. Using the dynamics of conflict, chaos and inertia

Law firms today confront change almost every day – not just in terms of improving individual and collective performance, but also with challenges that were virtually unknown to most law firms only 50 years ago, such as:

- the integration of fast-developing information management, communications technologies and emerging artificial intelligence capabilities with traditional work processes;
- the internationalisation of the practice, even for law firms that used to think of themselves as local or 'high-street' firms; and
- the changing expectations of younger members of the firm – especially about how, when and where they work.

The six components discussed in the previous section, along with the three-step change process (anticipate, plan and execute), provide a strong yet flexible foundation for continuous change in law firms. However, they do not guarantee success – particularly if partners do not pay close attention to the quality of the ongoing dynamics of the change process.

Three process conditions – conflict, chaos and inertia – can derail any change effort very quickly, regardless of the partners' intent, preparation or sense of urgency. At the same time, they are also natural, unavoidable and important conditions for change. Conflict, chaos and inertia can actually be a tremendous force for good by improving focus and motivation, problem solving, decision making and the achievement of strategic priorities.

How can both be true? The impact of these three conditions depends on how they are managed by the leadership of the change initiative – the partners. Most partners would prefer to avoid even saying these three words, much less trying to deal with them.

Herein lies the problem, since each of these three conditions is a natural element of any planned change. If partners avoid or deny their existence and therefore do not manage them well, positive planned change will not occur.

16 For a more detailed description of the three-step change management process and the three conditions for success at each step, see *ibid*, pp186–193.

4.1 Managing conflict

The successful resolution of issues – an essential ingredient in the change process – requires some degree of conflict.

Unfortunately, the word 'conflict' has a negative connotation for most lawyers, in part because of unhappy past experiences. It may conjure up images of partners yelling at each other and fighting or endless acrimonious debate. Actually, conflict can be observed in a wide range of behaviours that are simply related to presenting diverse views, discussing what is important and deciding what to do about them.

Partners tend to hide behind false collegiality to avoid what they perceive as conflict. They also tend to silence underlying tensions, even for extended periods of time. They may verbally spar and disagree in meetings. However, what they are disagreeing about is often not representative of the real issues that are bothering them.

Why don't lawyers talk about their real concerns in a more timely and open way?

They often say they do not have the time; or they are waiting for the right moment, but it never comes. They may even realise that unresolved tensions and unexpressed views only distract from performance and goodwill.

Encouraging someone to explain his or her view without an immediate rebuttal, such as "Yes, but ...", or asking questions to show interest and a willingness to work together, is likely to lead to much quicker decisions and effective follow-through on commitments. Avoiding unresolved tensions usually only makes them worse over time. Breakdowns in communication are deadly during change when timely and candid information is of the utmost importance.

Lawyers often wrongly assume that conflict will hurt their relationships and undermine trust. In fact, working through disagreements in a respectful way actually strengthens trust. It is a natural part of the development of any successful group of partners. Suppressed conflict damages relationships.

Some partners will say: "We don't have conflict in this firm. We never shout or argue. We operate on a consensus basis, never proceeding without full support from all of the partners."

There are several problems inherent in this perspective. An absence of shouting and arguing is not evidence of an absence of conflict. Conflict can be loudest during silence, when one or more partners are not expressing their true thoughts and feelings – a crucial misstep during change.

For this reason, consensus can be misleading. Just because one or more of the partners have decided to go along with it does not mean that they have bought into it or that they have the necessary commitment to a planned change. Never assume that you know what people are thinking. Ask them. Partners might acquiesce simply because they fear the alternative.

There is always a power dynamic in every partnership. Lawyers are politically savvy. They choose their positions judiciously. Since senior partners are more likely to look at partnership dynamics with rose-tinted spectacles, they can be lulled into a false sense of collegiality. These partners are quite often surprised by the feedback they receive from their peers.

So, partners need to know how to work through problems and disagreements with each other, as well as with other members of the firm, to shape realistic solutions and implement change. Sometimes the skills of collaboration and compromise need to be learned or relearned.

On an individual level, lawyers need the kinds of interpersonal and relationship skills that will enable them to:

- not take conflict personally;
- exercise emotional self-control;
- keep personal baggage from obstructing the needs of their partners, clients and the firm;
- face conflict even though they feel uncomfortable about it;
- not over-control what others feel a need to say;
- not attack or blame others, even if they themselves feel blamed;
- provide feedback without damaging their relationships; and
- help others to remain objective and keep talking in a meaningful way with their partners about the issues that are creating tension.

Resilient leaders model effective behaviours and help others to cope with conflict and change. They don't minimise the experiences and feelings of others by simply saying, "Everything is fine; just stay focused on clients."

Especially during stressful times, partners must be able to rely on their own emotional competencies to lead. When partners are not confident in their own skills, they tend to avoid doing what is needed most. For example, during change people depend on their leaders to help them:

- find answers in their shared experiences, learning from and then letting go of past mistakes, disappointments and failures so that these don't sabotage confidence and future possibilities;
- 'connect' in supportive ways that build trust even as they work through disagreements and concerns;
- keep feedback and information flowing;
- prioritise and deal with the consequences of a change, so that they don't get discouraged or stuck and just give up, or start blaming each other; and
- redirect their attention and actions in new directions, including responding to changing levels of urgency, evolving business and practice priorities, risks and the use of new technology and other resources.

Leading in new ways during change initiatives means that at times, partners will be operating outside their comfort zones. This is not the time to retreat, however. It is the time to ask for help as needed, be willing to ask questions, and learn and practise new methods and skills along with everyone else going through the change process.

Change is often stressful. It can be draining to incorporate new leadership responsibilities into an already demanding professional life. Partners who take good care of themselves – physically, mentally and emotionally – are more resilient. It is virtually impossible for leaders to counter negativity, help others to cope with the challenges of change and involve people in positive actions when they themselves are sleep deprived and emotionally exhausted.

Withdrawing into client work as an escape from dealing with firm management and leadership issues – especially during an important planned change process – is risky. When leaders are not present, chronic anxiety can set in. People close information gaps and compensate for a lack of direction by making it up as they go along, often with misinformation and fatalistic thinking.

Resilient leaders are self-aware. They can mentally step back in order to become more conscious of the choices they have made, their consequences and the options going forward. When they can anticipate and understand how their actions affect the perceptions and motivations of others, they are more likely to take leadership actions that make a positive difference.

All partners have a choice about how they want to lead. The question is whether they will use skills and behaviours that are more likely to get a better result and constructive responses from others, depending on the situation and needs of an individual or group. Some partners are more flexible than others about being willing to question and change something that is not working; and some are more courageous than others about learning new ways of thinking and acting.

If a Maasai warrior can completely shift his thinking about what it means to be a man and a respected contributor in his society, perhaps partners in law firms can find the courage to talk to another partner about performance concerns or improve marketing skills. If the Maasai people can implement a major cultural shift in their communities by working together to increase lion populations rather than eliminate them, perhaps law firms can find ways to respond to required changes in their professional working environments that are more likely to develop and motivate their lawyers and staff than discourage and discount them.

When dealing with potential conflict, simple tools and methods create helpful structures in partner meetings. For example, make a group list in advance, with all of the participants, describing what constitutes respectful behaviour or what behaviours will help to accomplish the objectives in the meeting. When leaders make the time to get group norms agreed in advance, this gives everyone the chance to make better choices about their own contributions, especially during disagreements.

The very existence of the agreed rules of engagement creates a kind of emotional safety that encourages candour and more balanced participation. Tension in the group decreases because partners can anticipate what to expect from each other. If a partner violates a rule of engagement, another group member or the leader can address the behaviour rather than attacking the person. A gentle reminder usually gets the partner back on track. Not using smartphones during partner meetings is a behaviour that frequently pops up on these lists, along with such behaviour rules as "No speeches" and "Ask questions to understand."

As a leader, you might want to take a break from a heated debate to encourage your partners to think about the bigger picture – for example, by asking them to remember why they decided to all practise law together. Further questions could include the following:

- "What is our purpose?"
- "What are our shared values?"
- "Where do we agree?"
- "What kind of future do we want together?"

It can be energising and intellectually stimulating to respectfully debate issues when you can trust your partners not to retaliate, humiliate or demotivate.

4.2 Managing the chaos dynamic (or dealing with confusion)

When you implement a planned change in a law firm, it alters the existing relationships among lawyers and staff, how they work together and their thinking, feelings and perceptions. The natural tension that exists between the *status quo* and new ways of doing things is what creates a sense of imbalance or instability that can feel chaotic.

Just like conflict, the other dreaded dynamic, chaos need not be a destructive force. Although it sounds dangerous in the risk-averse environment of a law firm, a feeling of chaos is not unusual during planned change. It is simply a natural mental state where firm members are testing old assumptions and ways of doing things and looking for solutions based on new perspectives. Things may not always go according to plan.

A strategic priorities review and an assessment of the partners' readiness to lead a change initiative provide partners with new information. These steps intentionally stimulate an intellectual challenge to the *status quo*. It is totally natural that as partners look at the data and evidence, make choices and take actions, they will continually alternate between conflict, cooperation and consensus, sometimes feeling a bit off balance.

4.3 A chaos dynamic does not mean a lack of control

In a change process, the leadership of the firm quite necessarily still wants and needs to provide direction and certain performance expectations along with clear lines of authority. This is one way in which the partners stay engaged and continue to manage the work environment. When leaders continue to establish limits of accepted behaviour and performance, it creates stability so people know what is expected of them and what they can expect from the firm.

Without any controls, a law firm environment will not be stable enough to learn and implement ideas. On the other hand, if firm leaders try too hard to control the outcomes of all change and improvement issues or situations, they risk undermining the very skills and behaviours that partners and other team members need to learn and practise to develop solutions and achieve success. It is a delicate balance – one that requires a great deal of communication and active listening, for both partners and firm members.

There is no recipe for the best use of power and authority in every change situation. Leaders in each environment will need to use their best judgement, based on many factors, including:

- their own experience;
- the capabilities and maturity of the lawyers involved in the change;
- the desired results; and
- the culture of the firm.

When attempting to negotiate the chaos dynamic, it is wise to proceed step by step with caution and not to overreact. Sometimes it may be best to allow conflict to develop or even simmer until cooperation begins to emerge on its own in a partnership meeting. It may take more than one meeting to arrive at decisions on cooperative action. Usually, a group member will intervene to get a discussion back on track when a group strays from its own rules for respectful engagement. Stepping in too soon and taking control can adversely affect the confidence and performance of lawyers who need to develop as a team and who are likely to be responsible for actually implementing the change.

Leaders can contribute best, in many situations, by guiding the process rather than owning it. For example, they can help others to commit to norms about how they can best work together in advance of a meeting rather than trying to control the behaviour of others after a meeting starts. They can also help others to develop structured discussion agendas that invite the most productive outcomes, then step back and trust the people and the process to succeed.

Sometimes a partner may want or need to play a more direct role, influencing outcomes and giving suggestions. Whether it is by giving direction or providing alternative ideas, a partner is still in a position to influence and, if necessary, set certain expectations.

Sometimes it seems easier to withhold information during a change process. Partners often say that they are concerned about how to handle untimely questions, for which they do not yet have answers. To 'minimise chaos', they reason that it is better to announce the final result – when everything is ready – rather than educate people gradually about what is happening in the change process. They feel this will avoid confusion and thus keep everyone more productive. But actually, the opposite is usually true. When lawyers think the partners are keeping them in the dark or hiding information, this creates anxiety and stress, which in turn gets everyone talking and gossiping, decreasing productivity.

So, the temptation to withhold information needs to be thought through carefully. Often, the truth is still the best course of action – for example:

- "We are still looking at options";
- "This the first planned step in a process that will take some time to execute"; or
- "We are unsure what the budget will allow this year; however, we will let you know as soon as possible."

Of course, when change is introduced to a firm, it raises expectations. Whatever the focus of the change is, firm members might start asking: "When will we be able to start other projects?" For example, when a firm introduces a career development programme, the lawyers may ask: "When are you going to start doing regular performance reviews?"

It is natural that people will start to bring up other areas of needed improvement in the firm when they begin to see opportunities for improvement and change. It is a healthy sign when lawyers and firm members can identify areas of concern. Information, direction setting and assurances from partners during periods of change will help people to understand priorities and keep focused on immediate goals.

Most firms find that it is helpful to start a planned change in a determined, yet cautious manner. They have learned – sometimes through false starts in the past – that even the smallest change can have an unexpected ripple effect across the whole firm, with a backlash that is equally unexpected. Most changes require different ways of working. They may also require skills and methods that many of the lawyers and firm members have not acquired or even bought into yet. Using the three-step change process (anticipate, plan and execute) reduces the likelihood of these false starts and misunderstandings about expected outcomes.

Firm leaders may want to explain that a change initiative is a first set of actions in a longer-term significant change that the firm is undertaking, and whether it is to improve how services are delivered to clients or how lawyers are developed and promoted in the firm. In other words, it is a first step.

Partners implementing a quality improvement programme explained it this way to their colleagues in their firm:

We refer to this initiative as a demonstration project, because it is the first application of quality assurance tools and methods, and not the only one. We would fully expect that after you complete the first demonstration project – and perhaps even before you complete it – there will probably be several other projects that you will be able to undertake simultaneously. By then, we will all be more confident in the process and in your ability to manage it to produce the best possible return on our firm's investment of time, intellect, and attention.

4.4 Overcoming procrastination and inertia

Partners are often very articulate in stating what they want to do, yet – even according to them – disappointingly ineffective in implementing and achieving their stated goals. They might say, "We want to do things differently", or "We want to maximise opportunities for growth"; and yet they struggle, stalled in a kind of inertia, doing very little for months or even years. Every law firm in the world has experienced the gap between optimistic resolutions made at a partner planning meeting and the actual execution of these well-intentioned plans.

It does not help to berate, blame, or criticise oneself or one's peers for past failures. A positive, planned change process – such as the three steps of anticipate, plan and execute – depends on leaders who can forgive themselves and each other. Self-reflection doesn't hurt if it is a way to identify potential obstacles to success and provides a means to learn from past mistakes. The important thing is to keep moving, with a focus on the future.

Every important change initiative involves learning and making adjustments along the way. Experienced leaders understand that implementation will never be perfect. Since perfectionism contributes to procrastination, it is an important message to get out. It is in the doing that we learn, and part of learning is identifying what we want to do differently next time.

Ongoing and frequent learning opportunities for lawyers and members of the firm keep them from becoming complacent. Education, as the Maasai have learned, is a perfect way to instil new values and ways of thinking while challenging aspects of the old culture that are no longer helpful or relevant.

A fear of losing a sense of identity and one's roots in the past can undermine even good intentions. When implementing change, partners ask their colleagues in the firm to assess their roles and responsibilities in a new strategic and cultural context. This means working in new ways. It is important to help people understand, though, that it does not necessarily mean giving up all the old values and professional traditions of the past. From ancient times, the Maasai had a tradition of conservation. What they decided to change were the roles and responsibilities associated with that tradition.

4.5 If it isn't broken, why fix it?

"If it isn't broken, why fix it?" is still proclaimed every day in partner meetings in law firms around the world. It can be a valid question. However, it is often pure inertia of rest: a desire to wait until a problem can no longer be ignored before paying attention to it. Fear of conflict, fear of chaos and fear of throwing out the old with the new are often the unspoken reasons why partners resist doing what they know they should and could be doing.

They may procrastinate because they dread the reaction from peers when they point out the need for change. They may be discouraged by a lack of cooperation and support from the firm in a previous change effort. They may resist the time, energy and effort that they feel they will have to invest to get their partners to take the next step. Whatever the reason, procrastination and inertia only increase risks and frustrations, reinforcing bad habits of leadership and inaction along the way.

Using the first step in the three-step change process – anticipate – partners can test their beliefs and assumptions against real data. Through such an informed analysis, they can overcome inertia and decide whether change is needed.

4.6 Identifying competing commitments and their underlying assumptions

It would be easy to assume that when partners do not do what they say they want to do, they are lacking in commitment to their agreed goals. However, that is not necessarily so. In fact, it is most probably not true.

It is far more likely that the partners, individually and collectively, have competing commitments that effectively cancel each other out. These competing commitments take enough of their time and mental energy that they virtually create an immunity to change. For example, a partner verbally commits to the need for cross-selling. However, she will not collaborate with her peers because she is equally committed to avoiding candid discussions about unprofitable practice areas. She assumes that these discussions will disrupt relationships and create tension in the partnership; so, she does nothing to further her commitment to cross-selling.

Without a structured change process to follow and help keep the initiative on track, partners become distracted and discouraged as they are pulled in many directions at once, sometimes unconsciously allowing untested or erroneous assumptions to paralyse them mentally. Questions to consider might include the following:

- Will efforts at cross-selling actually prompt sensitive discussions about profitability? If so, what can partners do to minimise tensions?
- Do discussions about profitability necessarily have to disrupt relationships? What is the evidence of such a risk?
- If concerns about such discussions create a significant obstacle to cross-selling, how can the partners address it?

Understanding the psychological dynamic of competing commitments and their underlying assumptions can help partners to get 'unstuck'.

When partners acknowledge and challenge the opposing assumptions that create inertia, they can then test whether those assumptions are even accurate. If they determine that their assumptions are fairly realistic, it becomes possible to identify ways to manage the risks effectively. If they learn that their fears and assumptions, once tested, are actually unfounded, this knowledge helps them to plan the next step.

4.7 Keeping on track

Some law firm partnerships appear to be staying on track because they are surviving. Yet survival by itself doesn't necessarily indicate resilience.

These partnerships exist for years, and every year takes a negative toll on their productivity, profitability and the collegiality of their relationships. They may be outwardly staying on track, but at risk and in a downward spiral.

Change leaders will need to overcome inertia over and over again during planned change. Keeping up the momentum and keeping the change on track is challenging but achievable when using a structured, well-thought-out three-step change process (eg, anticipate, plan and execute) with ongoing documentation, collaboration and measurements or markers of success.

The following three implementation tactics, already embedded in the three steps thus far, are worth emphasising because they so clearly differentiate resilient firms during times of change and become permanent fixtures of their evolving cultures. Law firms that do these things well and regularly find that their decisions are not only quicker, but also better informed. Commitment, follow-through and teamwork become the norm, not the exception.

(a) Asking questions

Resilient firms insist that inquiry form the basis for initiating changes in their firms and for transactions with clients and each other.

The biggest insulator against complacency – which brings change to a standstill – is to ensure that the law firm and its members are continually enquiring and learning.

Effective firms teach that it is better to ask questions first and form conclusions later when one wants to understand what happened and why it happened, or to explore another point of view. Firms that insist on inquiry expect tested information to shape their decision making, instead of snap judgements, personal agendas and hearsay.

One managing partner of a firm that was implementing a performance management system said, famously: "We are all learning together!" This message might not appear that profound on the surface. However, it was a novel idea to staff and junior lawyers. They were impressed that even their managing partner was willing to ask for feedback, learn new skills and practise new ways of interacting and solving problems with others. It was a motivating mantra, reinforced by his actions, that held throughout the entire change initiative. Sometimes a little humility goes a long way.

In this case, the managing partner did not have to drive the change process – a nebulous proposition at best. The members of the entire firm felt a sense of camaraderie and shared responsibility and clarity about how to 'do it together'.

The net effect of continuing to learn together is a collective wisdom that evolves in the firm. Stories emerge of successes and failures, the lessons learned and relearned, and the leaders and other heroes who pulled (not pushed!) everyone through. The shared experience of achieving a goal together builds confidence, skills and loyalty, which in turn makes inertia and procrastination less attractive.

Partners and others are much less likely to procrastinate – which is a form of resistance – when they are knowledgeable and informed, and feel a shared sense of commitment to learning. They know they have a stake in the future of the firm. They envision themselves developing and succeeding professionally for years to come.

Asking questions, analysing problems, testing different solutions and regularly circulating knowledge and information in the firm keep it from stagnating. Resilience depends on leaders being as transparent as possible. Partners do not keep information secret unless absolutely necessary. Clients notice when lawyers and staff are resourceful, show initiative and know the client's business. These attributes are a direct by-product of knowledgeable lawyers who are up to date and accustomed to using inquiry as a basis for working through challenging situations in an open and transparent way.

The comparison is stark between a firm that rewards inquiry and learning, and one in which professionals come to work every day with their heads down, keeping their real selves at home and their opinions to themselves.

In this 'heads-down' type of climate, firm members and clients alike are conditioned through their experiences to feel that asking a potentially provocative or sensitive question will provoke uncomfortable tension. At least some partners perceive associates who ask questions as troublemakers; and even a junior partner's loyalty is in jeopardy when he or she asks questions in a partner meeting.

This is more than just a morale problem. In surveys with these types of law firms, it is not unusual to have almost all of the associates and even some of the partners indicate that they are looking outside the firm for options.

When people stop asking questions, stop sharing knowledge with each other and stop learning together, procrastination and inertia thrive. Partners may 'drive' change by issuing edicts and forcing compliance; however, the real change is taking place in the plummeting levels of professional satisfaction and long-term commitment of lawyers and clients.

(b) *Rewarding feedback*

The author has observed that leaders are susceptible to falling into the bad habit of not seeking out or rejecting feedback that isn't comfortable, simply because they have the authority to do so.

However, if change leaders can depersonalise leadership feedback by objectively looking for common threads or patterns with relative strengths and areas for needed improvement, it is easier to look at information as clues – clues that flag up possible risks and opportunities for growth – rather than as personal affronts.

A constructive feedback culture is a real asset during a change process because it keeps information moving and people talking to each other. The greatest risk to a law firm during a change process comes not from poor service delivery or poor leadership skills, but from the failure to use effective feedback to confront reality. A lack of quality feedback – which includes input from diverse perspectives – leads to selective hearing, wishful thinking, distortions of fact, fears and unrealistic expectations of business potential.

Firms that are resilient and that successfully meet their change goals place a premium on inquiry and the learning and acquisition of information, knowledge and skills. How to give and receive feedback, both affirming and constructive, that gets results without damaging relationships is an important priority.

These firms put procedures in place that ensure an ongoing cycle of continuous feedback for the partners, internally and externally. They value both quantitative and qualitative input.

Partners do not keep information secret. They share business and performance measurements with each other to evaluate strategic priorities and develop business and professional goals.

When lawyers have continuous feedback from inside and outside the firm, based on trusting professional relationships and reliable data, they can anticipate problems and implement timely solutions, which keeps the change initiative on the right track.

Some firms implement confidential developmental feedback for lawyers that focuses on areas of emotional intelligence, in addition to technical competencies. These instruments often include a self-evaluation, as well as input from peers, colleagues and sometimes even clients.

Feedback instruments should always be tailored to the culture and needs of the firm. They give partners helpful information, usually from people they select. Trusted colleagues give partners feedback based on how effective they perceive the partners to be – through specific daily actions and behaviours – in areas such as:

- building and maintaining client relationships;
- developing high-performing teams;

- instilling a service orientation in others; and
- leading change.

Partners learn that their good intentions are not usually enough to get the desired results.

Partners then identify personal strengths and areas for development based on self-evaluation and feedback from others. All of this is in the context of what is currently happening in the firm. This is important, because the leadership requirements of a firm change and evolve with its strategic priorities and stages of development. Based on this feedback, the partner develops improvement goals in order to provide more effective leadership in the immediate future.

Resilient firms reward the ability to give and receive feedback as an important skill. Firms that reward feedback internally share the relevant data and comments from client surveys to receive additional input from staff and lawyers on how to improve. They are not afraid to probe gaps in perceptions between clients and partners. They also take care to share general themes from and actions taken at off-site partner retreats and certain partner meetings. They do not want to create an air of mystery about partnership meetings. They want all levels of the firm to have a sense of what the challenges, opportunities and priorities are. This way, everyone can take a more informed view of matters that affect their decision making and participation in the firm. Then they, in turn, can provide appropriate feedback to others. Thus, a policy of giving feedback can itself support feedback cycles throughout the firm.

At a planning retreat of one firm, a junior partner asked, "How do we know that we are 'the leading law firm', as our website proclaims?"

The senior partner stiffened, then emphatically replied, "We just know!" – implying that if the junior partner were smarter and more knowledgeable, he would know that, too.

When the junior partner still looked a bit dubious, the senior partner decided to strengthen her case by adding emphatically: "We certainly have never heard anything to the contrary!"

This example is not taken from a successful firm.

(c) Strategically building the capacity for continuous change

Partners understand that building resilience into a law firm's culture and its people is not a 'start-stop' event. They are always consciously preparing for incremental levels of change and transition. They plan and prepare their resilience.

They try to reduce as much uncertainty as possible, while encouraging people to find new solutions, set goals and be creative in adapting to new ways of thinking and working. These actions help people to feel less negative stress even as they take on greater ownership of challenging tasks and responsibilities during a change process.

Partners in these firms update partnership agreements and develop retirement options to accommodate a variety of needs. They create flexible governance structures to share leadership responsibilities. They document partner roles and responsibilities, procedures and policies so that the orientation of new members is efficient and consistent with firm expectations.

This is the type of firm that will keep looking for ways to improve competitiveness – not because the partners relish change, but because they are committed to the achievement of their strategic priorities. There are numerous characteristic behaviours of partners in these firms:

- They promote a sense of unity and purpose. As leaders, they understand that a strong sense of purpose is grounded in the beliefs that they and others have about their profession, the roles they have in the firm and the commitment they have to each other and clients. Yet beliefs without action are just beliefs. Mantras, marketing materials and partner aspirations are not enough to sustain a sense of purpose in law firms unless partners back them up with day-to-day decisions and interactions that are consistent with what they say is important. When a sense of purpose breaks down, resilience does too.

  What leaders believe has a tremendous impact on optimism, confidence and motivation to succeed during a change process. The following are belief statements developed by leaders with whom the author has worked:

  We are realistically optimistic about our economic future.
  We are committed to asking for and giving feedback in every aspect of our legal work together.
  Change is necessary and doable.
  We are stronger and more successful together.
  Our clients are happy with our services.
  We feel confident that we will be able to resolve our differences.
  We can achieve important goals.
  Our challenges have strengthened our leadership capabilities rather than weakened them.
  We each have responsibilities to help others develop professionally.
  We define our success as more than making money.

  They are examples of beliefs – when strongly shared – that can strengthen a firm's ability to stay on track. In other words, when leaders share a strong conviction and agreement with these particular belief statements, they show themselves to be better prepared to be resilient as a leadership group, which in turn impacts on every aspect of a change initiative and the people involved in it.

  Even if factually their shared beliefs are not 100% accurate, the extent to which they believe them to be important and true – as a group

– prompts them to work hard together to keep their unity and purpose intact. Their pride and confidence in these belief statements in turn become self-fulfilling.

- They show a willingness to go beyond aspirations and short-term fixes to assess honestly the evidence and get at the root of obstacles to success. This involves being open to others' experiences and perceptions.
- They consciously encourage regular, thoughtful and meaningful discussions, both internally and externally, in an effort to keep each other informed. For example, partners talk about positive planned change initiatives at retreats and partner meetings; but they also do so at weekly staff meetings, impromptu lunches and informal daily chats. This might look unplanned to some observers, but it is usually a conscious discipline. This is not to say that these partners share everything with everyone; nor do they spend hours chatting rather than performing client work. They simply understand that buy-in to change and the ability to stay focused on goals increase when people know that leaders are actively involved in planning and executing priorities, rather than just paying them lip service.
- They probe opportunities and consult with clients about strategic and performance issues.
- They know resilience is not accidental. They prepare their firms and their people for change by anticipating future requirements for knowledge, skills and resources. They then plan and execute well-thought-out solutions that emphasise using documentation, collaboration and measurements to stay alert, and flexibly make adjustments when needed.
- The partners create a professional working environment that is conducive to professional wellbeing and emotional perseverance. They promote continuous feedback and learning. Recognising that change is inevitable and ongoing, all lawyers have appropriate levels of awareness about what is going on in the firm. Partners make sure that everyone understands expectations about performance and delivery standards and receives what they need to meet them. Everyone knows what the priorities are, including client service values and how to negotiate ethical boundaries. Lawyers have support through training, coaching and mentoring opportunities that help them to grow professionally and cope with the natural stressors of their work. Lawyers also have the scope of authority to act confidently in their respective roles without fear of second guessing and blaming from others.

The opposite approach to leadership is to tell people that change is a single event – a point in time from which the firm will recover, as from a dreaded illness. During a situation that presented obvious changes at multiple levels to life in one firm, the author actually heard partners tell staff and lawyers alike: "We are not going to change as a result of these changes!"

Some partners will explain change as a temporary 'bump in the road', such as when the firm loses a profitable major client, a productive and highly visible practice group decamps to a competitor or a key rainmaker in the firm dies unexpectedly. The partners intend to send an optimistic message that all is well.

However, when partners explain the change away, rationalise its consequences on the firm and its members, and then go back to business as usual, discouraging others from discussing what happened, those actions only compound confusion and create distractions or worse. Also, in so doing, the partners abdicate their responsibility for helping firm members work through a difficult emotional period, such as a financial downturn, the retirement of a partner or the loss of an important client.

Denying that change will or has actually occurred is another way of denying the need to respond to change. It does not promote realistic optimism or offer opportunities to learn together. It discourages honest feedback. It certainly does not prepare the firm or its members to be resilient and ready to deal with the inevitability of future change.

(d) Rewarding a global view

The final practice observed in resilient firms that are effective at keeping their change initiatives on track and achieving their goals is ensuring that lawyers are rewarded for acquiring an informed, global view of their role, the legal profession and the firm's competitive challenges and opportunities. This in turn creates a highly stimulating and motivating working environment for achievement-oriented professionals.

Partners especially are expected to be critical, strategic thinkers with intuitive as well as technical skills. They know and accept that the futures of the firm and their firm's clients rest with the decisions and choices that they make today. Parochial thinking tied to personal agendas is not acceptable partner behaviour in these firms.

Partners attend conferences and share what they learn. Even junior lawyers are supported financially if they receive invitations to make a professional presentation or participate in a panel outside the local community. In fact, the firm celebrates this kind of recognition, especially when it happens to an associate.

All lawyers realise that their individual footprint in the market matters. The visibility and credibility that they earn as competent professionals help the firm too. The partners, in particular, assist developing lawyers in making international and national connections – politically, in the business community and with competitors. Partners also work hard – often with the assistance of marketing experts – to gain visibility in publications and achieve individual standing in reputable legal rankings.

The firm expects lawyers to participate in pro bono activities and to fulfil their commitments to social responsibility in the community.

5. Taking charge of planned change

There are no shortcuts for leaders in law firms. Leading change requires an investment of partner time and attention. An effective three-step change process – such as anticipate, plan and execute – relies on a compelling business case, backed up by data and evidence, that creates a shift in how people see themselves and their futures through inquiry and collaboration. This gives them a reason to think and act differently.

Planned change is not what leaders do when they make decisions about how to respond in a desperate, short-term attempt to save face or survive. Planned change is acting in advance of a crisis to select the strategic priorities of the firm. This is followed up by developing action plans in collaboration with others, which are supported by a realistic assessment of the unique characteristics of the firm and its market. Measurable results confirm the success and viability of the firm's progress and lay the groundwork for further decision making, course correction and ongoing implementation of priorities.

Continuous documentation, collaboration and measurement of goals propel a change process forward. Knowing what you are doing and why is far more important than rigidly executing a formulaic plan without reference to context and real progress. Change often feels a little messy. There is no such thing as a 'perfect' change process. Change itself requires an openness to testing and learning together, with a willingness to flex and adapt as circumstances and priorities evolve.

Successful change leaders keep in mind that anything that undermines their internal working relationships undermines resilience and preparedness for change. For when unexpected things happen – which they undoubtedly will, despite best efforts – it is those quality relationships that see lawyers through tough times, supporting the goals of the organisation and its people. Without others, it's impossible to keep learning and sharing information, feedback, feelings, values and ideas – essential elements in executing positive change.

Leaders quite naturally want to tamp down uncertainty, tensions and ambiguity during times of change. Even so, in professional relationships, a certain amount of stress is likely to occur. Even in cultures that place a priority on mutual respect, periods of anxiety and negative stress are not uncommon as people work through changes. But just because relationships seem upset and messier than before, it doesn't mean those relationships are broken.

Professionals working together in a planned and effective change process can keep goodwill alive along with their sense of shared purpose. Leaders don't need to be afraid of tensions, disagreements and expressions of negative stress – unless they ignore them. Trying just to 'keep the peace', coerce consensus and insist on superficial niceties will backfire. However, when self-aware leaders know how to invest in their relationships and address tensions in productive ways, they will develop self-confidence, productivity, trust and resilience, with both individuals and groups.

5.1 What is your firm doing to prepare and plan for change?

The Maasai lion conservation initiatives memorably illustrate the same observable strategies, priorities and behaviours that my colleagues and I observe in law firms that have led changes well. The changes for the Maasai livestock industry and its people involved complex cultural, historic, economic and scientific factors. No single 'expert' had the solution: not the Maasai elders; not the Maasai livestock ranchers; not outside conservation groups; not the government. Success depended in large part on the ability to communicate and collaborate about a compelling case for change, including substantial changes to traditional values and customs, and to demonstrate tangible economic success. There have been setbacks and obstacles in implementation, but close attention to performance measurements has helped to identify and respond to the problems in multiple ways at multiple levels, sometimes simultaneously.

Most significantly, as with the Maasai lion conservation programme, changes in law firms cannot be one-off events, but instead should be aimed at producing sustainable long-term results. A law firm's continuous capacity to implement needed changes with resilient leadership does not happen by chance. A well-informed process and timely decision making can ensure that future changes are identified and implemented with the best possible results.

The Maasai lions will be with us 30 years from now. Will your law firm?

About the authors

Martín Carrizosa
Lawyer
mcarrizosacalle@gmail.com

Martín Carrizosa is a lawyer from the *Universidad de los Andes* in Bogota, Colombia. He is a retired founding partner of Philippi, Prietocarrizosa, Ferrero DU & Uría – a leading regional law firm with offices in Bogota and Barranquilla, Colombia; Santiago de Chile, Chile; and Lima, Peru. Has served as chief of staff at the Organization of American States in Washington DC (1994–1996); foreign affairs adviser and economic secretary of the Presidency of Colombia during the Gaviria administration (1991–1994); and a member of the Colombia chapter and chairman of the Pacific Alliance Business Council (2015–2018).

Martín sits on the boards of Colombian bank Scotiabank Colpatria and Larrainvial Colombia, a broker-dealer; on the advisory board of Anglogold Ashanti Colombia; and on the board of not-for-profit institutions such as the *Universidad de los Andes*, the *Fundación Ideas para la Paz* and the *Fundación Crecer en Paz*. From 2018 to 2019 he was an academic visitor at St Antony's College, Oxford.

Norman K Clark
Managing principal, Walker Clark LLC
norman.clark@walkerclark.com

Norman K Clark is the managing principal of the international legal management consultancy Walker Clark LLC, which he helped to found in 2002. His consulting practice specialises in issues of strategic planning and implementation, law firm profitability, governance and quality management.

His 50-year career as a lawyer includes experience as a trial lawyer, trial judge, law professor and senior manager of legal services on a global scale. He has been a full-time business adviser to the legal profession for the past 29 years, having advised clients in law firms, as well as corporate and government law departments in more than 70 countries.

Norman holds a BSc, a JD and an LLM. He is a retired member of the Pennsylvania Bar; a past chairman of the International Bar Association (IBA) Law Firm Management Committee; and a past co-chair of the American Bar Association Cross-Border Practice Management Committee. He is also a member of the Commonwealth Lawyers Association.

Leopoldo Hernández Romano
Managing partner, KermaPartners
l.hernandez@kermapartners.com

Leopoldo Hernández Romano is the managing partner of KermaPartners. Leopoldo advises law firms on strategic planning, organisational structure transformation, compensation schemes, corporate governance issues and Ibero-American alliances in their strategies for positioning and retaining talent. Previously, Leopoldo was the chief operating officer for the Mexico office of one of the top New York law firms. He is a qualified attorney and holds an MBA.

Leopoldo has been a professor at the *Universidad Panamericana*. He is an active member of the Mexican Bar Association and the IBA, and a founding member of the Association of Legal Administrators, Mexico chapter. He is the chairman of the board of Appleseed Mexico. Additionally, Leopoldo is a founding partner of UNE Mexico; a member of the Promoter Group of the National Civic Front (FCN); and coordinator of the FCN's State of Mexico chapter.

Sarah Martin
Co-founder, Martin & Levin; associate fellow, University of Oxford, Saïd Business School; faculty member, Meyler Campbell
sarah@martinandlevin.com

Sarah Martin is a founder of leadership development and executive coaching consultancy Martin & Levin. She is a coach to professionals and executives in international business and works with senior leaders to design and direct development programmes. Her focus is on leadership and women in leadership. Her clients include professional services firms, private equity houses and C-suites.

Sarah originally trained as a lawyer, working in M&A with Allen & Overy, as general counsel to a FTSE 250 company and as senior counsel in the chairman's office of BP PLC. She has 25 years of business, legal and governance work at board level.

Sarah holds an MSc in leadership as a Sloan fellow at London Business School. She is a graduate and member of faculty of Meyler Campbell, teaching leadership coaches; and an associate fellow at University of Oxford, Saïd Business School.

Iryna Nikitina
Strategic adviser to law firm partnerships, IOCONS LLC
ion@iocons.com

Iryna Nikitina is a strategic adviser for law firm partnerships at IOCONS LLC, a consultancy she founded in 2013. With over 25 years of managerial experience, she has held top roles in commercial companies, educational institutions, non-governmental organisations and governmental bodies. Her consulting practice specialises in issues of firm strategy, partnership structure, organisational design and business processes.

As a chief operating officer, Iryna served at leading pan-CIS law firms (EPAM and Magisters) where she had firm-wide responsibility for business support operations, post-merger integration processes and the launch of new offices in the region. She has executed strategic reviews, mergers, market entries and complex change processes for top national law firms.

Iryna's expertise in the legal market and law firm management has made her a trusted adviser to clients in Europe, the Caucasus and Asia. She is also a skilled and empathic leader, helping to foster and nurture legal talents in multicultural environments. A seasoned professional navigating businesses through crises, achieving operational excellence and providing strategic guidance to law firms, her ability to match strategy with the best tactics, deploy innovations for business development and identify opportunities for organisational development has made her a valuable adviser to clients in various industries.

Stephen Revell
Founder, Making Change Happen
stephenrevell@makingchangehappen.com

Stephen Revell practised at Freshfields for over 41 years on three different continents and was a partner for 33 years. Following his retirement from Freshfields, Stephen established a law firm consultancy – Making Change Happen – through which he provides management advice to law firms and other professional service providers. He advises on a wide range of topics relevant to the management of law firms, from governance and remuneration to right-sizing business services and implementing new pricing strategies. He works for law firms all over the world and of many different sizes. As part of this work, he often speaks directly to law firm partners either in one-on-one mentoring sessions or at partner retreats.

He is the co-author of a variety of books and a regular speaker on law firm management topics. He has been very active in the IBA for many years and is presently co-chair of the Law Firm Management Committee.

Michael Roch
Managing director, MHPR Advisors
michael@mhpradvisors.com

Michael Roch is managing director of MHPR Advisors. For more than 20 years, he has been a trusted adviser to managing and senior partners, boards and remuneration committees of professional services firms worldwide. His clients include law firms, accounting firms, consulting firms, public relations and media firms, wealth managers, real estate advisers and other advisory firms in more than 40 countries. More than a dozen are market leaders in their respective jurisdictions. He co-authored *The Partner Remuneration Handbook: A Guide to Compensation in Law and Other Professional Service Firms* (Globe Law and Business, 2022), with Ray D'Cruz, chief executive officer of Performance Leader.

Beyond his consulting work, Michael is a technology entrepreneur and is currently chief commercial officer of allianceboard.com, a strategic alliance management SaaS platform. He served as Europe co-CEO of the Internal Consulting Group, an Australia-based global consulting ecosystem with more than 4,000 members worldwide; and was managing partner of KermaPartners, a consulting firm he co-founded that focused on the professional services sector. His early career involved stints at two Big Four accounting firms in the United States and Eastern Europe and a Global 10 law firm in London and Frankfurt.

Aku Sorainen
Founder and senior partner, SORAINEN
aku.sorainen@sorainen.com

Aku Sorainen is the founder and senior partner of SORAINEN, an international business law firm with offices in Estonia, Latvia, Lithuania and Belarus. Founded in 1995, the firm has grown organically to 44 partners and over 250 lawyers with integrated legal practice and sector groups, firm-wide leadership, quality management processes and business services. Aku is of Finnish origin but has worked as a lawyer in the Baltic states since 1993.

In 2015, Aku was honoured to receive the Knight's Cross, First Class, of the Order of the Lion of Finland from Finnish President Sauli Niinistö for two decades of work developing relations between Estonia and Finland; and in 2021, he was awarded the Service Cross of the Estonian Foreign

Ministry for promoting Estonia's national interest. Aku is also the honorary consul of Malta in Estonia. He is recognised as an eminent practitioner by international legal directories and is an active member of the IBA.

Rocío Vázquez Zavala
Senior associate, Modum
rvazquez@rocketmail.com

Rocío Vázquez Zavala is a senior associate at Modum, where she manages the compliance and administrative matters of the firm. She has over 20 years of experience in consulting, project management, strategic management, financial analysis and business process reengineering.

Before joining Modum she was a consultant with KermaPartners based in Mexico City where she specialised in business process reengineering, performance management and implementation of policies and procedures. She has a bachelor's degree in industrial engineering from *Universidad Iberoamericana*, as well as a master's degree in management from the University of Bath, in the UK. Rocío also holds a PMP certification from the Project Management Institute.

Lisa M Walker Johnson
Founding principal, Walker Clark LLC
lisa.walkerjohnson@walkerclark.com

Lisa Walker Johnson's professional background is as a counselling psychologist, with more than 30 years' experience in senior levels of business management and consulting to corporations and law firms worldwide. As a psychologist with deep experience in law firm management issues, Lisa assists law firms with sensitive and frequently difficult change management issues, such as the integration and retention of lateral partners; leadership transitions between generations of partners; cultural due diligence during mergers; and the implementation of strategic change in the disruptive business environments confronting the legal services industry. Lisa has published extensively in these areas and frequently speaks about them at major international conferences for legal professionals.

Tony Williams
Principal, Jomati Consultants LLP
tony.williams@jomati.com

Tony Williams is the principal of Jomati Consultants LLP, a leading UK-based international management consultancy specialising in the legal profession. Jomati's services are designed to support law firms, barristers' chambers and in-house legal departments on a range of strategic issues. Prior to establishing Jomati, Tony spent almost 20 years at Clifford Chance as a corporate lawyer; his last role was worldwide managing partner. In 2000, he become worldwide managing partner of Andersen Legal. He established Jomati Consultants in October 2002. In 2012 Jomati was awarded the Queen's Award for Enterprise in International Trade.

In 2013 Tony was named in the *National Law Journal*'s inaugural list of 50 Business of Law Trailblazers & Pioneers as one of two non-US-based people named on the list.

Tony is a visiting professor at the University of Law.

About Globe Law and Business

Globe Law and Business was established in 2005. From the very beginning, we set out to create law books that are sufficiently high level to be of real use to the experienced professional, yet still accessible and easy to navigate. Most of our authors are drawn from Magic Circle and other top commercial firms, both in the United Kingdom and internationally.

Our titles are carefully produced, with the utmost attention paid to editorial, design and production processes. We hope this results in high-quality publications that are easy to read and a pleasure to own. Our titles are also available as ebooks, which are compatible with most desktop, laptop and tablet devices. In 2018 we expanded our portfolio to include journals and Special Reports, available both digitally and in hard copy format, and produced to the same high standards as our books.

In 2021, we were very pleased to announce the start of a new chapter for Globe Law and Business following the acquisition of law books under the imprint Ark Publishing. Our law firm management list is now significantly expanded with many well known and loved Ark Publishing titles.

We are also pleased to announce the launch of our online content platform, Globe Law Online. This allows for easy search and networked access across firms. Key collections include the Law Firm Management Collection, Private Client and Energy and the Energy Transition. Email me at sian@globelawandbusiness.com for further details or to arrange a free trial for you or your firm.

Sian O'Neill
Managing director
Globe Law and Business
www.globelawandbusiness.com

www.ingramcontent.com/pod-product-compliance
Ingram Content Group UK Ltd.
Pitfield, Milton Keynes, MK11 3LW, UK
UKHW062251150926
8656IPUK00007B/44

9 781787 429345